W9-BMX-990

THE

OBAMAS

THE UNTOLD STORY

OF AN

AFRICAN FAMILY

THE

OBAMAS

PETER FIRSTBROOK

CROWN PUBLISHERS

NEW YORK

Library of Congress Cataloging-in-Publication Data
Firstbrook, P. L.
The Obamas : the untold story of an African family /
Peter Firstbrook.—1st ed.
      p.   cm.
Includes bibliographical references and index. 1. Obama family.
2. Obama, Barack—Family. 3. Kenya—Biography. 4. Luo (Kenyan
and Tanzanian people)—Biography. 5. Presidents—United States—
Family—Case studies. I. Title.
CT2227.5.O23F57   2011
973.932092'2—dc22
      [B]   2010032403

ISBN 978-0-307-59140-1
eISBN 978-0-307-59142-5

Printed in the United States of America

BOOK DESIGN BY BARBARA STURMAN
JACKET DESIGN BY JEAN TRAINA
JACKET PHOTOGRAPHY BY JO HARPLEY/FLICKR/GETTY IMAGES

2   4   6   8   10   9   7   5   3   1

First American Edition

FOR ROY SAMO

*May your dream of a better
Kenya one day be realized*

Contents

THE AFRICAN ANCESTRY OF BARACK OBAMA *(c. 1250 to the present)*

SIN-KURU aka **KUKU LUBANGA** (b. uncertain)

[12 WIVES]

LIOLEITUK DYANG
The Plains Nilotes
including the Maassai, Langi
Turkana, Samburu, and Teso

ODONGO POK BONI
The Highland Nilotes
including the Nandi, Kipsigis,
Pokot, Tugen, and Elgeyo

OPIYO PODHO KOMA
The River-Lake Nilotes
including the Shilluk, Dinka,
Nuer, Acholi, Alur, Padhola, and Luo

RINGRUOK (b. 1245?)
OWAT (b. 1274?)
TWAIFO (b. 1303?)
JOK I (b. 1332?)
. . . . . .
NAYO (b. 1361?)   OMOLO   OWINY
JOK II (b. 1390?)
RAMOGI I (b. 1419?)

PODHO II (b. 1450)

ARUWA (b. 1448?)

RAMOGI II (b. 1469?)   LANG'INI   OKOMBO   OMIA   DIDANG'

MUWIRU (b. 1479?)   OLAK (b. 1481?)

NYALUO (b. 1498?)   RAMOGI AJWANG' (b. 1500?)   MONGRA (b. 1502?)

NYANDGUOGI (b. 1508?)

OMOLO I (b. 1529?)   OCHIELO (b. 1531?)

ORIAMBWA (b. 1537?)

RAGAM (b. 1560?)   GEM (b. 1562?)   UGENYA (b. 1564?)

OWINY (b. 1566?)   GOMA   WIRI   ADHOLA

KISODHI (b. 1595?)   NYALA   ADHOLA

Naika   Jong'a

[2 WIVES]

OGELO (b. 1624?) NYABONG'O AGER WAMERAA OYO OMENYA ABURA OWINY SIGOMA

NYOGORO (b. 1653?)

OKWIRI (b. 1655?) NYAKWAR (b. 1657?)

OKOTH (b. 1684?)

ONYANGO MOBAM (b. 1713?; born with a curved back) NYANYODHI (b. 1715?)

OGOLA (b. 1742?)

OCHUO (b. 1771?) OTONDI (b. 1773?)

OGOLA (b. 1800?)

OBONG'O (b. 1802?)

OBAMA (b. 1831?)

OPIYO (b. 1833?, Kendu Bay) AGUK (b. 1835?)

OBILO (b. 1862?)

OBAMA (b. 1864?, Kendu Bay; d. 1935?, Kendu Bay) AGINGA (b. 1864?)

Nyaoke   Auma   Mwanda   Odero   Augo

[5 WIVES]

NDALO RABURU (b. 1893?, Kendu Bay) HUSSEIN ONYANGO OBAMA (b. 1895, Kendu Bay; d. 1975, K'ogelo) SALMON OGUTA (b. 1897?, Kendu Bay)

[5 WIVES] m. Unknown   m. Halima   m. Sophia Odera   m. Habiba Akumu (b. 1916?)   m. Sarah (b. 1922, Kendu Bay)
(b. ?)   (b. ?)   (Kendu Bay; d. Kendu Bay, 2006)

Sarah Nyaoke (b. 1934, Kendu Bay; d. ?, Nairobi)   BARACK OBAMA SR. (b. 1936, Kendu Bay; d. 1982, Nairobi)   Hawa Auma (b. 1942, Kendu Bay)

[4 WIVES] Kezia Nyandega, Kendu Bay m. 1957   Stanley Ann Dunham m. Feb. 2, 1961 (d. Nov. 29, 1995)   Ruth Nidesand, m. 1965, Nairobi   Jael, m. 1981, Nairobi

BARACK HUSSEIN OBAMA (b. Aug. 4, 1961, Honolulu)

[WIFE] Michelle LaVaughn Robinson (b. Jan. 17, 1964, Chicago) m. Oct. 3, 1992

Malia Ann (b. 1998, Chicago)   Natasha (b. 2001, Chicago)

Based on Weere, Melik Ogutta, *Mel Dhoudi moko mag Luo*, loosely translated as "Other Sub-Tribes of the Luo Community," second edition, Earstar, 2007, Ogot (1967 and 2009), Cohen (1968), original research, personal communication with Professor Ogutu, and oral history from Obama elders. For further details of methodology, see page 249.

WUOTHI EKA INE

To travel is to see plenty

THE

OBAMAS

PROLOGUE

WAT EN WAT

Kinship is kinship

WHEN THE American people elect a president, they choose, de facto, a new leader of the free world. U.S. presidential elections are interesting to foreign observers if only because the winner becomes the single most powerful person in the world, practically overnight. Yet the election of a young senator from Illinois in November 2008 caused even more of a stir around the world than usual. The primary reason was not his lack of experience in executive decision making but the fact that he was black—or, to be strictly correct, half black. Although Barack Obama was brought up in Hawaii and Indonesia by a single mother for most of his early years, his absent father was African, from a tribe called the Luo, who live around the shores of Lake Victoria in western Kenya. When President Obama's father came to Hawaii as a student in 1959, Kenya was still a British colony; after the country gained its independence in 1963, Obama senior—like many Kenyan students—returned home to find a job in the new government. President Obama recalls meeting him only once, during a brief visit that his father made to Hawaii just before Christmas 1971, when young Barack was just ten years old. The president never saw his father again, because

Barack Obama senior died eleven years later, when he crashed his car into a tree one night in Nairobi.

For anybody who has read his two books, *Dreams from My Father* and *The Audacity of Hope,* it is clear that President Obama is very conscious of his mixed heritage, and that as a young man he was unsure of his place in a multicultural world. In his self-deprecatory style, he referred to himself as a "mutt" in his first press conference after his election, when he spoke about getting a dog for his children: "Our preference is to get a shelter dog, but most shelter dogs are mutts like me."

In *Dreams,* he talks about his struggle as a young man to come to terms with his mixed racial heritage; later, he recalls his first visit to Kenya in 1987 to meet his father's family and to learn more about his African birthright. He felt welcomed in Kenya, and he came to understand the importance that Africans place on family. Obama was taken to see his stepgrandmother, Sarah Obama, who still lives in her husband's compound, which the family calls "Home Squared." Both the president's grandfather and father are buried adjacent to the house, and he wrote movingly about finding a connection with this little bit of Africa:

> I dropped to the ground and swept my hand across the smooth yellow tile. Oh, Father, I cried . . . When my tears were finally spent, I felt a calmness wash over me. I felt the circle finally close. I realized that who I was, what I cared about, was no longer just a matter of intellect or obligation, no longer a construct of words.[1]

The title of this first book hints at his regret of never really knowing his father: "I had been forced to look inside myself," he wrote in *Dreams from My Father,* "and had found only a great emptiness there."[2] When talking of his political beliefs in his second book, *The Audacity of Hope,* Barack Obama acknowledges that he is a prisoner of his own biography: "I can't help but view the American experience through the lens of a black man of mixed heritage, forever mindful of how generations of people who looked like me were subjugated and stigmatized, and the subtle and not so subtle ways that race and class continue to shape our lives."[3]

In perhaps the most telling part of Obama's prologue to *Audacity,* he makes a direct reference to his own father: "Someone once said that every man is trying to either live up to his father's expectations or make up for his father's mistakes, and I suppose that may explain my particular malady as well as anything else."[4]

Like many Americans, President Obama can trace the ancestral background on his mother's side to a broad mix of European blood: he is, apparently, about 37 percent English, with additional contributions from German, Irish, Scottish, Welsh, and Swiss forebears; many white Americans descended from European stock share a similarly rich mixture of Old World genes. On his father's side, however, the genetic makeup is much simpler: he is 50 percent African, descended from a long line of Luo tribal warriors who originally lived in the Sudan and over the centuries migrated south and east across more than 600 miles of desert, swamp, and jungle before eventually settling around the shores of Lake Victoria in Kenya.

I am a documentary filmmaker with a long-standing interest in Africa. Over the years I have visited Africa dozens of times, but I had not worked in Kenya since 1987. Within just a couple of weeks of Obama's election as the new president, I flew to Kenya with the intention of researching a film about the village where his family originated. I met many members of the Obama family; some had been in the media spotlight in the run-up to the election, but there were many more whose voices had never been heard. Even though I only scratched the surface of the history of the Obamas and the Luo people on this first visit, I realized that there was a fascinating story to be told. Putting the documentary on hold, I decided that the story of Obama's family—and the extraordinary history of the Luo people—could best be told in a different way.

This book, then, is the fruit of several more visits to the shores of Lake Victoria, to the part of western Kenya that is called Luoland. Barack Obama's upbringing and education in America and Indonesia have been well covered elsewhere, both by the president himself and by other writers. I hope, therefore, that this book will offer some insight into the little-known half of President Barack Obama—the half of him that is Luo and that comes from a long line of formidable African warriors. Of this rich family lineage, the president himself is only vaguely aware.

In 2006, President Obama made his third visit to Kenya, but this time it was in an official capacity, as a member of the U.S. Senate. He upset many senior Kenyan politicians on that trip because of his outspokenness against corruption, but the ordinary people loved him. His visit was brief and he had only a short time to visit the village where his father grew up. His relatives told me that he had less than forty-five minutes to meet his extended family, who lined up by the dozen in the hot equatorial sun outside Sarah Obama's hut, waiting for their brief few seconds with their most favored son. Barack Obama's aunt, his closest living Kenyan relative, showed me with obvious pride the set of drinking glasses she had been given on that visit; yet, sad to say, in the few seconds that she spent with her nephew, Hawa Auma did not have time to tell him about the extraordinary story of how his grandfather fell in love with his grandmother, nor the tragic circumstances of their separation; Charles Oluoch did not tell the senator his suspicions about how Barack Obama senior *really* died in 1982; nor have his father's friends ever had the chance to tell Barack Obama about the parties they had together at Harvard as students in the mid-sixties.

Despite his American upbringing, President Obama has attained the position of a near demigod in Kenya. Like all African tribes, the Luo have a rich anthology of proverbs and sayings, one of which strikes me as particularly poignant: *wat en wat,* "kinship is kinship," which, loosely translated, means "blood is thicker than water." The Luo will never consider Obama to be a white man. Regardless of where he was raised or what he might say or do, they will always see him as an African—a true Luo with an ancestry that can be traced back two dozen generations.

Without the patient support, help, and generosity of dozens of local people—eminent historians, members of the Obama family, and Luo elders alike—this book would not have been possible. These people unstintingly supplied me with all the elements of the story; all I have tried to do is to arrange them into a coherent picture of the past.

PETER FIRSTBROOK
Kisumu, Kenya

1

Two Elections, Two Presidents

BER TELO EN TELO

The benefit of power is power

T HE EVENING was drawing in, dark clouds rolled overhead, and ominous specks of rain were making themselves felt in the hot, sticky, tropical twilight. It was not the ideal start to the evening; five hundred relatives and friends had gathered in the Obama ancestral home to watch the inauguration of their most famous son as president of the United States. We were all sitting in the courtyard of the family compound in K'obama, a remote village in western Kenya, and the heavens looked as if they were about to open. Some of the people had walked several miles to get here, and many of them were related to the president-elect either through birth or by marriage. We had less than two hours to go before Barack Obama took his historic oath of office, but the inclement weather and encroaching darkness were not the worst of our problems. We still had no television, the only generator to be found had no fuel or oil, and there was no aerial set up to receive the broadcast.

Everything had seemed so simple and straightforward the previous day, when I sat down with the village committee—the Kenyans love their committees—to discuss their preparations for the celebrations. Yes, there would be three televisions for people to watch, and three generators to power them. The trees around the compound would be strung with 100-watt electric bulbs, so we would have plenty of light. They would slaughter a cow and several goats, and they welcomed my offer to bring a dozen crates of soft drinks, but definitely no beer, as they were all Seventh-Day Adventists.

The small village of K'obama lies just outside of Kendu Bay, itself a small township on the shores of Lake Victoria in the western province of Nyanza. K'obama is home to dozens of families, all of them related in one way or another to the recently elected president. Like many small villages in this part of Kenya, the ancestral name takes the prefix *K-* to denote the family homestead. Despite this clear indicator of the family's presence, K'obama had been largely ignored by the international press since the election of Barack Obama. Journalists and television crews had all headed to Nyang'oma K'ogelo (also called simply K'ogelo), a small village on the opposite side of Winam Gulf and home to Sarah Obama, known as Mama Sarah, stepgrandmother to the president-elect. And so here I was in K'obama on the eve of the presidential inauguration with not a journalist in sight, nor even another *mzungu* ("white man" in Swahili). I had my suspicions why K'ogelo had attracted all the attention of the world's press, but I did not get confirmation of the real reason until sometime later.

Meanwhile, although the party in K'obama was in full swing, there was still no sign of a television set. I had tracked down a couple of empty fuel cans and I sent our van off to buy some petrol for the generator, but that had not materialized either. Although Africa has always been one of my favorite places to visit, working here is not without its challenges. The Luo, Obama's African tribe, are known for being easygoing and generous, and I had received nothing but help and support from them. But they also had a reputation for, among other things, talking big and doing very little.

With little more than an hour to go before darkness fell over K'obama, my luck began to change: not one, but two televisions suddenly arrived. The first was one of the TVs promised by the organizers, and it made its entrance balanced precariously on a wheelbarrow. Then came the second television, which I had previously negotiated to hire for the evening from a neighbor. The van came back with fuel, and within minutes the little Honda generator spluttered into life and the televisions lit up into a grainy image. Perhaps we would be able to watch the historic inauguration after all.

Meanwhile, the Obama family members began to drag their cheap plastic garden chairs in front of the two screens. Darkness falls quickly in the tropics, and soon everybody was settling down for the evening, apparently oblivious to the gathering storm clouds. It was a wonderfully diverse mix of people, from six-year-old schoolchildren to great-grandmothers in their eighties. Dozens of people came and thanked me for helping to get the TVs working, some of them smelling as if they had been drinking more than fizzy soda. I had not actually seen any beer around, but illicit alcohol is commonly available in Kenya, and I suspect that some of the revelers were not conforming to the strict lifestyle expected of Seventh-Day Adventists.

Local brew has always been fermented in Kenya, but traditionally it was only as strong as beer. However, stronger and more potent brews have become more popular in recent years, encouraged no doubt by the high taxes imposed on alcohol by the government. The police often turn a blind eye to the brewing in return for a cut of the profits. Sometimes these drinks are "fortified" with methanol, a toxic wood alcohol, which can have disastrous consequences. Kenyans call the drink *chang'aa*, but it is also given other popular names such as "power drink" (which gives a hint to the strength of the industrial additive) and "kill-me-quick" (which, frankly, is a more honest description). People in illegal drinking dens have been known to complain that the lights had been switched off in the bar, when in practice the lethal concoction they were drinking had turned them blind in an instant. One of the most severe drinking accidents in Kenyan history happened in 2000, when an especially toxic batch of the brew resulted in the deaths of 130 people and the hospitalization of more than 400.

We managed to tune the televisions to gain a reasonable reception on the same channel, and the audience became transfixed by the events unfolding 7,500 miles away in Washington, D.C. Unknown to us at the time, some of the Obamas who had traveled to the United States had arrived at the White House only to be turned away because they could not take their seats in time before the president-elect arrived on stage. Apparently there had been a mix-up with the arrangements and they were picked up late from their hotel; despite producing their Kenyan passports and their official invitations, which showed the most famous surname in the world on that day, their pleas went unheeded, and they returned to their hotel where they watched the very same CNN coverage that we were watching in K'obama.

There was little interest in much of the early proceedings of the inauguration ceremony. As the commentators described the finer details of the president's new limousine, with its eight-inch armor plating and tear gas cannons, people chatted among themselves. After all, they lived in huts with corrugated iron roofs, with neither running water nor electricity; most of them did not even own a bicycle. They neither knew nor cared whether Obama's new Cadillac, which gets eight miles to the gallon, was a good thing or not. The long list of guests arriving on the podium meant nothing to the five-hundred-strong Obama family, either. As the assembled dignitaries shivered in the bitter Washington winter, where the air temperature had fallen to several degrees below freezing, the Kenyans were glancing nervously upward and wondering if the rainstorm was going to stay away.

One by one, past presidents assembled in front of the podium: Jimmy Carter, George H. W. Bush, Bill Clinton, and finally the outgoing president, George W. Bush. Then the president-elect appeared, and the imminent downpour over Kendu Bay was instantly forgotten as the crowd roared his name and stood up to applaud "their" man. As the proceedings moved at a glacial speed in Washington, the raindrops over Kendu Bay dried up in the tropical heat, only to be replaced by mosquitoes and flying ants.

Finally the big moment arrived. Supreme Court Justice John Roberts moved to the podium, where he was joined by the president-elect. (Cue more exuberant cheering from the Kenyans.) Obama was about to make history by becoming the first African American U.S. president. Before him, more than a million people were gathered on the National Mall, with the vast crowd stretching as far back as the Washington Monument in the distance. Justice Roberts led with the oath: "I, Barack Hussein Obama, do solemnly swear [pause] that I will execute the Office of the President faithfully." Like the majority of television viewers around the world, nobody in Kendu Bay was aware at the time that Justice Roberts had made an error in the order of the words. No doubt the two men had practiced this moment several times, and a faint smile seemed to cross Obama's face as he realized that Roberts, a fellow Harvard Law School graduate, had misplaced the word *faithfully* during the oath. Barack Obama continued, "And will, to the best of my ability, preserve, protect, and defend the Constitution of the United States."

With the president now secure in the most powerful office in the world, the Kendu Bay Obamas went wild, chanting, "Obama! Obama! Obama!" in an echo of the exuberant crowd in front of the White House. It was a night that united Kenya. At no other time since Nelson Mandela became president of South Africa has the continent been filled with such hope for the future, and, not surprisingly, it took several minutes before everybody in K'obama settled down to listen to Obama's inauguration speech.

Rarely has an American president taken office with so many profound challenges facing him, both at home and abroad. He began, "My fellow citizens: I stand here today humbled by the task before us, grateful for the trust you have bestowed, mindful of the sacrifices borne by our ancestors."

In Washington, as in Kendu Bay, the crowds were transfixed by both the mesmerizing rhythm of his elegant delivery and the content. Obama continued: "Yet every so often the oath is taken amidst gathering clouds and raging storms. . . . On this day, we gather because we have chosen hope over fear, unity of purpose over conflict and discord." He then laid out his priorities for the next four years: "We will build the roads and bridges, the electric grids and digital lines that feed our commerce and bind us together." As I looked around at the people watching his speech, their faces beaming with pride, it struck me that Kendu Bay could do with a few roads, bridges, and electric grids.

Obama continued with his manifesto for the world: "And so, to all other peoples and governments who are watching today, from the grandest capitals to the small village where my father was born . . ."

This was too much for the Obamas in Kendu Bay, who were sitting less than a couple of hundred yards from that very spot. The party dissolved into a riotous cheer, which surely must have been heard 7,500 miles away in Washington, D.C.

Three months earlier, Barack Obama walked out onto the stage in Grant Park, Chicago, on the evening of November 4, 2008, and made his acceptance speech to a devoted audience; many had been standing for over four hours in the chilly Illinois evening. "It's been a long time coming," announced the president-elect, "but tonight, because of what we did on this day, in this election, at this defining moment, change has come to America."

It had been a remarkable road for a nation to follow. When Barack Obama was born in August 1961, much of the American South remained segregated, and black and white American citizens were separated literally from cradle to grave. Black Americans were born in segregated hospitals, educated in segregated schools, and buried in segregated graveyards. In 1961, the year that Obama's father married Ann Dunham in Honolulu, a racially mixed marriage was not even legal in seventeen states of the Union. Forty-seven years on, their son stood in front of an international television audience measured in billions, to accept the mantle of leader of the free world.

As Barack Obama noted in his acceptance speech that evening: "The road ahead will be long. Our climb will be steep. We may not get there in one year or even one term, but America—I have never been more hopeful than I am tonight that we will get there. I promise you—we, as a people, will get there."

The president's rousing speech alluded to what is arguably the United States' greatest strength as a society—the ability over a period of three centuries to absorb many disparate groups of immigrants into a single nation, a people with a common purpose and a strong sense of national identity. As Obama himself said at the 2004 Democratic National Convention in Boston: "There is not a black America and white America and Latino America and Asian America—there's the United States of America."

The ability of the United States to integrate diverse peoples into a single nation is in marked contrast to the homeland of the president's father. Kenya has been an independent nation for nearly half a century, but if you stop people at random—even in Nairobi, where traditional customs are weakest—and ask them where their main allegiance lies, they will almost always reply that their tribe is much more important to them than their country. This is certainly the case with the Luo and many other ethnic groups in the country, whose tribal allegiances go back for centuries. These compelling loyalties have inevitably led to much conflict among Kenyans, both before British colonial rule and after independence.

I first worked in Kenya in 1987, the same year the younger Barack Obama first visited his African relatives. Inevitably, Kenya was a very different country back then, but in some ways, very little has changed. Back in 1987, Daniel arap Moi had been president for nearly ten years, and he would remain so for another fifteen. He came to power promising an end to corruption, smuggling, tribalism, and the detention of political opponents, and he enjoyed popular support throughout the country. But his good intentions had not stood the test of time, and by 1987 his government increasingly relied on secret police, human rights abuses, and political assassination to stay in power.[1] He changed the nation's constitution to make Kenya a single-party state, suppressed political opponents, and cleverly manipulated Kenya's ethnic and tribal tensions to weaken and divide the opposition.

In 1999 Amnesty International and the United Nations issued reports accusing Moi of serious human rights abuses.[2] Moi was constitutionally barred from running for another presidential term in 2002, and the following year news of even more human rights abuses began to surface, including the use of torture. In October 2006 Moi was found guilty of taking a $2 million bribe from a Pakistani businessman in return for a monopoly of duty-free shops in the country's international airports.[3] In 2009, people told me that in many ways life was better than it had been back in 1987, although I was soon to find out that political intimidation, corruption, and tribalism were still a routine part of political life in Kenya.

As soon as I stepped off the aircraft at Jomo Kenyatta International Airport in November 2008, it was obvious that other big changes had happened since my first visit. When I first came to Kenya in 1987, the population was 22.4 million; today, it is 39 million people (2009 estimate).[4] Nairobi is no longer the genteel colonial city that it was in 1987; 60 percent of the population live in shantytowns. The city's largest slum, Kibera, is said to be the biggest in Africa, with more than a million inhabitants. Traffic clogs the streets, and air pollution has become a serious problem. The number of vehicles on the road has doubled in ten years, and Kenya now has one of the worst road safety records in the world. Yet despite the large number of Mercedes cars and Land Cruisers on the streets, the majority of people still earn less than $2 a day.

On the other hand, the strong tribal divisions have not diminished in the last twenty years. The country accommodates more than forty separate tribal groups, with the Kikuyu the biggest group, by far with 22 percent of the population, followed by the Luhya with 14 percent, the Luo with 13 percent, the Kalenjin with 12 percent, and the Kamba with 11 percent. Smaller tribes make up a further 27 percent of the population; Kenyans of European, Asian, and Arab descent account for just 1 percent. Religious beliefs are equally divided: 45 percent of Kenyans are Protestant, 33 percent are Roman Catholic, and Muslims and traditional religions make up about 10 percent each.

As the most populous tribe, the Kikuyu have dominated Kenyan politics ever since the country gained its independence from Britain in 1963 and Jomo Kenyatta, a Kikuyu, became the country's first president. (The similarity of his name to his country's is coincidental.) The Kikuyu also have a reputation for being very successful in trade and commerce. The traditional Kikuyu lands are in central Kenya, in the fertile highlands to the south and west of Mount Kenya—this was the region that attracted the white colonists in the early years of the twentieth century. As a consequence, the Kikuyu (along with the Kalenjin and the Maasai) suffered extensive displacement as the whites took over their traditional lands and turned their farms into large plantations growing coffee, tea, and cotton.

The Luhya are the second-largest tribe, with a population of over five million, but they are widely spread around the country and much more diverse than any other ethnic group in Kenya, with around sixteen or eighteen subgroups. Many of these subgroups speak their own dialect of Luhya, some of which are so different from one another as to be considered separate languages altogether. Because of their diversification, the Luhya have a much smaller political voice in the country than might be expected from their numbers.

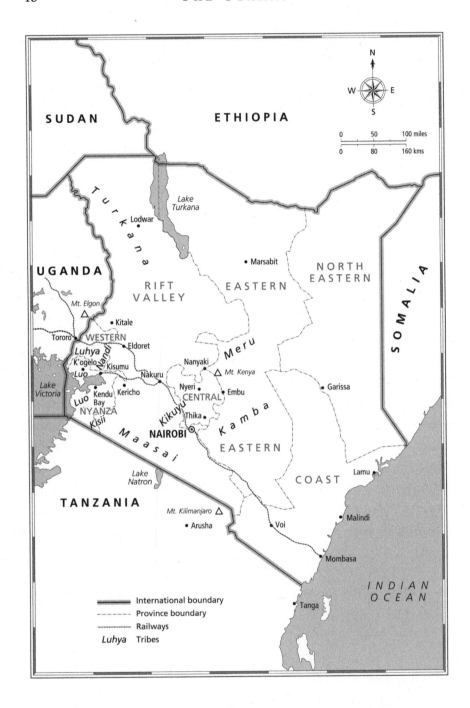

Major towns, provinces, and main tribal areas in Kenya.

The Luo, Kenya's third-largest tribe, has a population of just under five million. This is the tribe of Barack Obama's ancestors. They traditionally place much emphasis on education and have produced many scholars in Kenya, some of whom have graduated from prestigious colleges around the world (including Barack Obama senior, who graduated from the University of Hawaii in 1962, and later took a master's degree in economics at Harvard). As a result, Luo professionals dominate almost every part of Kenyan society and frequently serve as university professors, doctors, engineers, and lawyers.

One such Luo professional is Leo Odera Omolo, a respected journalist based in Kisumu, Kenya's third-largest city and the center of the Luo homeland. Leo has spent all of his life reporting from around Africa and has been on first-name terms with practically every African president in the past fifty years. He once told me that Idi Amin of Uganda challenged him to a wrestling match—not once, but three times. He was very proud to have beaten him on each occasion.

In explaining what made the Luo different from other Kenyans, Leo first pulled down his lower lip to reveal six missing front teeth. Most African tribes traditionally circumcise boys to mark the onset of manhood. But the Luo (and some other tribes whose ancestors migrated south from Sudan) mark the end of childhood of both sexes in a different but still painful way: by removing the six bottom front teeth. "I am a Luo," he said with a cheeky grin and a twinkle in his eyes, which belied his seventy-three years:

> I have twenty-three children by five wives, and another three children by women who were not quite my wives. We are tall, very black, and very intelligent because we eat lots of protein, lots of fish.
>
> The Luo are fair and they are democratic people. They want to discuss issues. They don't want secrecy. They don't have "night meetings." If they call a meeting, they will reveal it outside when they've done.
>
> They also squabble and fight, but the fight can be resolved very quickly. The next day, if nobody is killed, you are friends again.

That is a trait of the Luo. Some of them are hot-tempered—they come up and down quickly—but they don't hold a grudge after a disagreement.

There are also so many parties with the Luo. At a funeral—a lot of it; marriage—a lot of it. [Luo] spend a lot of their energy and resources in parties. A funeral will deplete a family and leave them poor . . . they slaughter all the cows they have, goats, everything. They will even clear their grain store.

When Kenya became independent in 1963, the Kikuyu and the Luo inherited most of the political power. Their mutual distrust, stemming from intertribal rivalry, continues to lie just below the surface of Kenyan politics. Immediately after the last presidential elections in late December 2007, this antagonism degenerated into riots against President Mwai Kibaki, a Kikuyu. After Kibaki unilaterally declared that he had won the election, the Luo opposition leader, Raila Odinga, accused Kibaki of vote rigging.

Although the worst atrocities during the postelection violence took place in the Rift Valley, protesters also took to the streets in Kisumu. Roy Samo, a local councilor in Kisumu, experienced the postelection carnage at close quarters:

They were counting the figures and Raila Odinga was leading the president by more than a million votes. Then there was [an electrical] blackout, and the next minute [President] Kibaki was leading Raila by 1 million votes. Nobody could believe it! We have a town with an 80,000 maximum electorate, so how can the president get 150,000 out of a possible 80,000 votes?

I remember when they announced [that Kibaki had won]— I was here in my house watching the result. People from all their houses and in the bars, they started screaming and shouting and a cloud of death could be seen hanging around Kisumu. . . . People were watching their TVs and they started seeing how people in Nairobi were reacting. Like in Kibera [Nairobi's biggest slum], they started burning tires, uprooting the railway . . .

Around 8 p.m., Kisumu also started going up in flames—it was about looting and the burning of property. So many people rushed into supermarkets to loot. Sixteen people were burned [to death] and fifteen people were shot dead. In my area, ten people were shot dead, because by now the police were shooting people. [The violence] started on the twenty-ninth of December, 2007, up to February 28, when Raila [Odinga] and Kibaki signed an agreement.

The government figures say that 1,500 were killed, which we dispute. It's ten times more than that, and 500,000 people were displaced. But now, as we are talking [in May 2009], 220,000 people are still living in tented camps.

Tribalism remains strong in Kenya for several reasons. Primary schoolchildren usually learn their tribal language first, before moving on to Swahili and then English. Even today, young people usually marry within their own tribe, especially if they stay within their tribal area.

Although tooth extraction is now mostly a thing of the past, other religious and traditional customs still strengthen the tribal bond of Kenyans. The ongoing controversy over circumcision demonstrates the continuing hold of tradition on Luo society. Because research has shown that circumcised men are 60 percent less likely to contract HIV, circumcision is now encouraged for all Kenyan males as a way of reducing the disease (which has reached epidemic proportions, afflicting one in five young Luo males).[5]

Not surprisingly, many of the younger, sexually active men support the idea of circumcision, but it has caused a storm of protest from the more traditional Luo, who consider circumcision to be a tribal taboo. I went down to the beach at Dunga, a small fishing village on the shores of Lake Victoria near Kisumu, and talked to some of the fishermen there. Dunga is the only working fishing village left in the Kisumu area, and women walk up to ten miles every morning to buy fish to carry back and sell in their village. The women earn less than 100 Kenyan shillings ($1.25) a day, but the fishermen are traditionally some of the best paid workers in the region, often earning Ksh 500–1,000 ($6.25–12.50) a day or more. Charles Otieno, a local fisherman and a community leader in the Dunga cooperative, explained:

> HIV is a very big problem along the beaches. . . . Most of these women here [at the beach] are widows and most of their husbands have died of HIV. So they come and interact with the fishermen. The men have many girlfriends; they never have one girlfriend. For example, I'm a fisherman. I can fish at Dunga beach one week, another week I go to another beach and I fish there, and then I go to another beach and I have to obtain another girlfriend there. So every time I do that, most of the fishermen do that.

I asked Charles if many of his friends had been circumcised to help prevent catching the HIV virus. He replied, "According to our customs and beliefs—it started from earliest times—our people were not being circumcised. Some of the people have gone for circumcision, but most of the people, they are not going."

About fifty miles west of the main city of Kisumu, almost as far west as you can go in Kenya without ending up in Uganda or getting your feet wet in Lake Victoria, is the tiny village of Nyang'oma K'ogelo. Here lie the graves of President Obama's father, also named Barack Obama, and his grandfather Hussein Onyango Obama. Even during the Democratic primary, media attention on the Obama family in K'ogelo was intense, and it became positively frenzied once Obama won the election. Within a couple of weeks of the election, I was driving to K'ogelo, where President Obama's stepgrandmother Sarah Obama lives. The red dirt road was in much better condition than I expected, and I mentioned this to Roy Samo, my researcher and translator. He chuckled as he cited a Luo proverb: "*Ber telo en telo*—the benefit of power is power." The road had obviously been upgraded very recently, and workers were still putting in culverts to deal with flooding during the rainy season. Alongside the dirt track, more workers were installing wooden electricity poles. For the first time in their history, the residents of K'ogelo who could afford it would have light after dark, at the flick of a switch. The first person to benefit from the electricity would of course be Mama Sarah.

K'ogelo turned out to be a very ordinary, very sleepy Kenyan community, with no running water and a population of just 3,648.[6] Most of the huts are spread across the rolling hillsides, separated by fields of maize. The village center has a handful of shops scattered around an area of hard-baked earth, which serves as the marketplace on Tuesdays and Fridays. In the local shops you can buy a leg of goat from the butcher, a bottle of local beer from the bar, or a simple meal in one of several small "hotels"—tiny drinking and eating establishments with not a bed in sight. Down a small side street are two barber shops—they are usually good places to hang out to get the latest gossip, although in all the time I spent in K'ogelo, I never actually saw anybody having his hair cut. Rather, the two barbers seemed to earn their living from renting out their battery-powered disco equipment for parties. The busiest workers in the village were the two old men who repair punctured tires; they both seemed to have a never-ending row of battered bicycles lined up against the trees. The real action in K'ogelo seems to take place under the shade of a large acacia tree, where the young men of the village spend most of the day sitting around, smoking, and idly chatting.

In this part of Kenya, most people live modestly, working as small-scale farmers growing subsistence crops such as maize, millet, and sorghum, supplemented with the occasional cow and a few chickens. The province of Nyanza, often locally referred to as Luoland, does not have the rich farming land of the central highlands, and therefore this area was less attractive to the white colonists who settled in the region a century ago. The close proximity to Lake Victoria also makes this one of the worst places in Kenya for mosquitoes, and malaria is a common killer, especially among young children; almost three thousand children die every day from malaria in sub-Saharan Africa. (However, the recent introduction of free mosquito nets in Kenya has helped decrease child mortality from the disease by over 40 percent.)[7]

Like the more fortunate villages in Kenya, K'ogelo also has two schools. The land was donated by President Obama's grandfather, and after Barack Obama visited the village in 2006 they were named the Senator Obama Primary School and the Senator Obama Secondary School. These two schools are typically Kenyan: simple brick structures with no window frames and few facilities. Outside, cattle graze on the school grounds; inside, the classrooms are packed with eager young faces. Everywhere in Africa, you will find schoolchildren with an enthusiasm to learn and improve themselves, a commitment that somehow eludes many pupils in the Western world. But here in K'ogelo, the children have a clear pride in their village school for a very obvious reason. The pupils in the Senator Obama schools of K'ogelo seem to have absorbed the campaign slogans of their local hero—"Change we can believe in" and "Yes we can"—just as fully as Obama's most fervent supporters in America.

For Sarah Obama, change was certainly happening. This eighty-seven-year-old woman had hosted the world's media for the previous two years, with all the regal patience and good humor of an African queen mother. Sarah still lives in her husband's compound, which he established when his family moved to K'ogelo in 1945. But within a few months of moving there, Onyango's other wife, Habiba Akumu, left home and returned to live with her parents. (Many months later, I would learn about the extraordinary circumstances behind this acrimonious family squabble, which left Sarah to care not only for her own four children but for Habiba Akumu's three children as well—a young girl also named Sarah, Barack Obama senior, and his younger sister Hawa Auma.) Although Mama Sarah is related to the president only by marriage, she raised Barack Obama senior from a young boy. For this reason President Obama often refers to her as "Granny Sarah." Sarah has only a few words of English and prefers to speak either Dholuo (the traditional Luo language) or Swahili. Nevertheless, on most days when she is in K'ogelo, she sits patiently in her front garden under the shade of a large mango tree planted by her husband. There she holds court, welcoming the dozens of visitors who come to pay their respects.

Being the oldest surviving relative of the U.S. president has been a mixed blessing for Sarah Obama. She certainly welcomes the new borehole that was drilled just outside her front door, which relieves her of the daily chore—shared by practically every woman in Africa—of collecting water from the nearest well or river. But Sarah was less enthusiastic about the ten-foot-high wire fence that now encircles her compound, or the dozen members of the Kenya police force who are now camped at all times in a makeshift security post nearby. "It is God's will," she said. "The electricity and the water are good. But now I cannot go anywhere without being mobbed by all the people. I am like a prisoner in my own house."

Sarah is not the only member of the Obama family who spends time in K'ogelo. Kezia Obama, Barack Obama senior's first wife, also keeps a hut next to Sarah, although she now lives in southern England. Being a large and extended family, other members periodically pass by "Home Squared" to give Sarah their support. Still, most days the visitors and journalists coming to Mama Sarah's house vastly outnumber the few Obama family members in the village.

I was puzzled why the media seemed to show so much interest in such a small, sleepy village as K'ogelo. After just a few days in K'ogelo I had seen everything that there was to see: the Obama compound, the Catholic church, the two schools, the clinic, and the market. Yes, there was grand talk of building a conference center and a modern hotel in the village, but Luo have a reputation for making grandiose plans and I doubted whether anything would change very quickly in this quiet African outpost.

Several of the people I spoke to in K'ogelo had mentioned that there were more Obamas living in another place called Kendu Bay, on the opposite, southern side of Winam Gulf. Barack Obama wrote about visiting this township in *Dreams from My Father*, but he said little about the town, focusing instead on his time in Nairobi and K'ogelo. Now, with only one day left of my visit to Nyanza, I decided to try my luck elsewhere.

I had been warned that the road from Kisumu to Kendu Bay was very poor, so I made an early start. However, like many of the major roads in this part of Kenya, it had recently been resurfaced and driving was really not a problem—except for the appalling driving standards of most Kenyans. Nor was it really that difficult to find the Obama homestead. By now, Obama was easily the most famous name in Africa, and after a few inquiries we were directed off the main road from Kendu Bay and up a dirt track.

Even though Africans tend to be notably relaxed and welcoming to total strangers, even to a *mzungu* who arrives unannounced, I was feeling a little uncomfortable about arriving at the Obama homestead without making any arrangements. I had not been able to phone ahead, and I did not even know whom I should talk to about the family. Yet within five minutes, I was walking through the family homestead with Charles Oluoch, a cousin to President Obama. Charles is a tall, thin, handsome man, just past his sixtieth year. As such, he is one of the family elders, and, as he explained to me in excellent English, he is also chairman of the Barack H. Obama Foundation.

With obvious pride and with grand sweeping gestures, he took me around part of the Obama homestead—K'obama—a large area of sprawling compounds with scores of small brick huts stretching out into the distance among the trees. "Here is the entrance to the Obama home. There are several homes here. It is a big home because the children are many. This one is Joshua Aginga's home. He was the third son of Obama Opiyo. This is his first wife's house, and this is his second wife's house. . . ."

Charles continued telling me an extraordinary history of the Obama family as he guided me through what was only a small part of the homestead. My mind reeled as he recited, in extraordinary detail, the family history—husbands with four or five wives, a dozen children, brothers, cousins, and uncles . . . The complexity of the family tree was mind-boggling.

I soon learned that it is a Luo tradition for the husband and each of his wives to have separate huts, with the first wife having a bigger dwelling than the second wife, whose house is slightly larger than that of the third wife, and so on down the pecking order. Every building here was very modest by any standards, and typical of this part of Africa. Traditionally, Luo huts had round walls made of wattle and daub, and were thatched with a straw roof. But in recent years, as the Luo have begun to add furniture to their households, the round huts have mostly been replaced with a square design so that cupboards and dressers and sofas can be pushed back against a flat wall. Today the huts are also built more permanently of brick or stone, sometimes daubed with mud; the traditional straw thatch has given way to corrugated iron roofs.

Charles took me by the arm and walked me in a new direction. "I want to show you something special," he said. We arrived at a tiny hut, with wooden shutters in place of the windows. "This house is where the president slept in 1987. He came visiting—he wanted to know his roots. So he came up to Kendu Bay, and this is where he slept."

We pushed open the simple wooden door with its faded, peeling paint and noisy, doubtful hinges. Inside, the room was dark and cool, in contrast to the oppressive tropical heat and light outside. On the hard earth floor was a thin straw mat, which had taken on almost mythical status within the family: "This is the mattress he was given to sleep on. We could not afford the big mattresses from the supermarket." Charles lit up the dark room with a broad grin. "He must have been very uncomfortable for the whole night, because he is not used to such things."

I asked Charles how many journalists had come to Kendu Bay. He tensed noticeably at the question. "Very few. Very, very few. They all go to K'ogelo. They don't come here."

"But there is very little to see in K'ogelo, and so many more Obamas are living here," I said. "So why do all the journalists go to K'ogelo?" Charles looked rueful and said nothing.

A couple of months later, when I joined the family to watch the presidential inauguration on television, I began to understand the real reasons for the press's interest in K'ogelo rather than Kendu Bay. First, when Barack Obama came to Kenya in 1987, his half sister Auma served as his guide. As the second child of Barack Obama senior and his first wife, Kezia, Auma was brought up in K'ogelo, even though most of the huge, diverse Obama family lived elsewhere. So it was not surprising that Barack would spend most of his time in K'ogelo, where Auma grew up, rather than the village where most of the Obamas lived.

Second, I learned that Raila Odinga, the Kenyan prime minister and a Luo, is from Bondo, a small town just eight miles southwest of K'ogelo. His family still has very strong ties to the area, and his brother is the local MP. I was told that when President Obama visited in 2006 as a U.S. senator, the prime minister's office had channeled press interest in the Obama family to K'ogelo and not to Kendu Bay. After all, any politician would want positive international or regional attention to come into his own patch, rather than anywhere else in the region.

Time was beginning to run out for me with Charles Oluoch in Kendu Bay. Driving in Kenya is a hazardous business even in daylight, and I was keen to return to Kisumu before it got dark. But Charles had one more thing to show me. He led me around a hedge of small trees to a clearing to one side of the huts. There was a simple grave, not dissimilar to the two I had seen in Mama Sarah's compound in K'ogelo. Here, on a brass plaque screwed to the concrete headstone, was an inscription:

HERE LIES OBAMA K'OPIYO OF ALEGO K'OGELO
FROM WHOM ALL OF US JOK'OBAMA COME.
DEDICATED BY THE BARACK H. OBAMA FOUNDATION,
ABONG'O MALIK OBAMA

I was intrigued and a little confused. Obama Opiyo? Charles explained: "The man who is lying here is Obama Opiyo, our great-grandfather. Obama had four wives, and between them there were eight sons and nine girls, and one of his sons was Hussein Onyango, who is the grandfather to the president now of America."

I did some quick mental arithmetic. If Charles was sixty and Opiyo was his great-grandfather, then Opiyo must have been born around 1830. I was keen to know from Charles what had happened to the family in the intervening years.

"That," said Charles, with another of his big smiles beginning to break out, "is a very long story, and it will have to wait until you come back to visit us next time!"

2

MEET THE ANCESTORS

OYIK BIECHA KALUO KAE

My placenta is buried here in Luoland

FLIGHT JO 831 leaves Jomo Kenyatta International Airport in Nairobi for Juba, in southern Sudan, every morning at 7:30 sharp. It is a short flight, only about 600 miles to the northwest, and it usually takes less than ninety minutes. Yet the cheapest round-trip ticket costs nearly $750. Mile for mile, the Nairobi–Juba route must be one of the most expensive flights anywhere in the world, and I asked the ticket assistant at Nairobi airport why the price was so high. He shrugged. "No other airline really flies there so often," he said with a smile, "and all the aid agencies must go there now."

Between 1983 and 2005 southern Sudan was embroiled in a vicious, bloody conflict between the Muslim government in the north and the Sudanese People's Liberation Army in the mainly Christian south. It was Africa's longest-running civil war; nearly two million civilians were killed, and another four million were forced to flee their homes. Since January 2005 a United Nations–sponsored settlement has brought an uneasy peace to the area and offered a chance to rebuild a region that has been devastated by twenty-two years of fighting. Within a few months of the peace agreement, the Nairobi-based airline JetLink opened its lucrative daily flight into Juba, the historic capital of the south, giving access to hundreds of humanitarian aid workers from the United Nations and other international agencies.

After flying over Kisumu at the eastern end of Winam Gulf, the aircraft crosses over some of the most remote regions of East Africa. To the north is Mount Elgon, Kenya's second highest mountain, which straddles the Kenya-Uganda border. Soon it passes over Lake Kyoga, a vast, shallow lake and swamp in eastern Uganda, and home to large numbers of crocodiles. Another thirty minutes into the flight and the aircraft flies over the White Nile, at 4,145 miles the longest river in the world. Providing there are no delays, the aircraft begins its approach into Juba International Airport before ten in the morning, losing altitude over the foothills of the Imatong Mountains, which straddle the border between Sudan and Uganda. To the north is the Sudd, the world's biggest swamp—a vast and formidable expanse of waterlogged lowland the size of Florida. In the hot season, the smaller rivers frequently run dry; during the wet season in late summer, the waters of the Bahr al-Jabal (White Nile) and its western tributary, the Bahr al-Ghazāl (River of Gazelles), burst their banks. It is an annual pattern of flooding that has recurred for thousands of years, and the locals have learned to use it to good effect.

Historians and anthropologists believe the southern part of the Sudd to be the "cradleland" of Barack Obama's ancestors. These early people, called the River-Lake Nilotes or the Western Nilotes, were mainly pastoralists and fishermen, and they lived a hand-to-mouth Iron Age existence in this part of Sudan more than a thousand years ago.[1] The area is dotted with a series of ironstone plateaus incised by the tributaries of the big rivers that flow north toward Egypt and the Mediterranean. During the wet season when the waters were high, these people gathered on the islands formed by the floodwaters; during the dry season, they moved

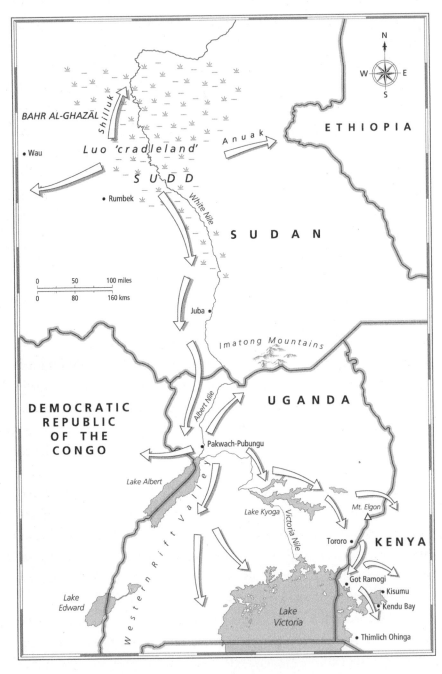

Migration of the Luo ancestors from southern Sudan
from c. 1300 to 1750.

out to the lower land, where their cattle could graze. When they moved away from their villages during the dry season, they lived in temporary huts called *kiru,* which were made from branches and leaves.

Between six hundred and eight hundred years ago, these people left the Sudd and started on a perilous migration south into Uganda and eventually Kenya. This almost biblical movement of people, which took more than a dozen generations to complete, was a long and painful process that in time laid the foundation of the Luo tribe of Kenya. It is a journey that started with a local chief living in a mud hut overlooking the White Nile, and ended seven centuries later with the leader of the most powerful nation on earth living in the White House.

Nobody can be absolutely sure what triggered the migration of the Nilotes from southern Sudan in the late fourteenth and early fifteenth centuries, but one likely possibility is that climatic change gradually forced the pastoralists to move in search of a more hospitable environment. Rock paintings throughout the Sahara portray elephant, rhino, hippo, buffalo, crocodile, and giraffe—animals associated with much wetter conditions than exist today—suggesting that conditions across the northern half of Africa have become progressively drier over thousands of years. In southern Sudan too, the climatic conditions are thought to have been much wetter than at present.[2] Successive years with poor rainfalls would have had potentially catastrophic consequences in this region, where the water floods over a very large area and is therefore highly prone to evaporation.[3]

One elder from Alego, Lando Rarondo, offered me another theory. He thought the Nilotes moved from Sudan because of an anthrax epidemic. His suggestion is entirely plausible; anthrax is one of the oldest recorded diseases, and it is believed to be the sixth plague recorded in the book of Exodus. An acute, lethal bacterial disease that affects grazing animals, including sheep and cattle, anthrax can also be passed on to humans, either through direct contact or through eating the flesh of an infected animal.

Whatever initiated the migration of the Nilotes, whether it was climate change, overcrowding, disease, drought, conflict, or some combination of these, historians are confident that the diaspora began around AD 1400. This was not a grand, organized movement of people but rather a gradual dispersal, as extended families began to migrate south and east from southern Sudan. Over the next four hundred years some of these migrants slowly moved toward what is now Kenya. Over the generations, their language changed and they adopted traditions that made them distinct from other peoples, until a clear Luo tribal identity slowly emerged.

Historians have broken down the Luo diaspora into three distinct phases. The first involved leaving the Sudd. These Nilotic peoples dispersed to the north, west, east—and one group, under the leadership of Obama's ancestors, began a long trek southward toward Uganda, following the course of the Upper Nile.

For any people on the move, there are three essentials for survival: water, food, and shelter. For this reason, the Luo never strayed far from the river; it provided fish to eat, and water for their cattle, and a clear route to follow. This movement up the White Nile likely gave the Luo their name, which is derived from the vernacular saying *oluwo aora*, which means "the people who follow the river."

In many ways the traditional lifestyle these people had followed in the Sudd prepared them perfectly for their migration. They were used to moving their cattle up to higher ground when the Nile flooded every year and then taking them back down during the dry season. The dry-season camps in the Sudd probably provided a model for their temporary migration encampments as they moved along the Upper Nile.[4]

The long migration seems to have prompted a bellicose period in their history, as the newcomers developed a reputation for being aggressive and dangerous. The expertise they had developed in iron-making in their cradleland meant they were probably better armed and more practiced in warfare than the tribes to the south whom they were about to displace.[5] For a period of two or three generations, the Luo effectively became riverine pirates, plundering villages along the length of the Upper Nile; they operated rather as the Viking marauders had along the European coastline some five hundred years previously. Although the Luo canoes were flimsy, they were light, fast, and maneuverable, allowing small bands of young Luo warriors to make daring raids up and down the banks of the Nile, stealing cattle, crops, and women.

The Luo became adept at incorporating captives into their societies, so their numbers increased at an astonishing rate. And as their numbers increased, their military strength grew; but this also put greater demands on their food supply, which in turn increased the rate of their territorial expansion. Father Joseph Pasquale Crazzolara, a Catholic missionary who worked for much of the first half of the twentieth century in East Africa, undertook some of the very earliest research into the migration of the Luo (or, as he chose to call them, the Lwoo). In his epic history of the traditions of the tribe he wrote:

> On the march, as still in big hunts, the tribal, clan and family groups kept closely united. . . . Female prisoners were absorbed and became completely submerged. . . . For male captives the case was different in theory, but scarcely in practice. Prisoner slaves were allocated to a family or clan-group, and treated as blood-relations, and even given wives, or cattle as dowry. But with their children and descendants they started their own sub-clans and social life, as a clan-segment, related and hence exogamous, to the main Lwoo clan.[6]

In these early days of the southward migration, the various communities on the move were based around patrilineal clans, which recognized an aristocratic or "dominant" clan; this was usually the largest clan in the region, or the first to establish in a particular area. The leaders in this hierarchical system were, in descending order of authority, the *ker* or king, the *ruoth* or chief, and the *jago* or subchief. They ruled over both the subjects living in the chief's enclosure—the *jo-kal*—and the *lwak* or "herd" of incoming subjugated people.[7] Over time, the two peoples became one, mainly through polygamous chiefs fathering huge numbers of children with *jo-kal* and *lwak* women alike. As the early Luo society developed, so too did their belief that they were superior to the other tribes in the region. Their leaders believed that their royal lineage and ritual powers gave them the right to rule over others who did not have these special attributes, foreshadowing a conceitedness and arrogance that many Kenyans would claim is characteristic of the Luo today.

As the Luo moved south along the length of the Upper Nile during the fifteenth and early sixteenth centuries, they entered what is now northern Uganda. It had taken several generations for the Luo to cover the 220 miles from southern Sudan to the site of Pubungu, near Lake Albert. Here they built a great military encampment beside the river, about ten miles downstream from where the Nile exits the lake.[8] Today, Pubungu-Pakwach is a forlorn little town with a single main street and a stout but simple steel-girded bridge over the White Nile. The modesty of the modern-day town notwithstanding, the early Luo chose their spot well: this bridging point is still an important strategic position on the river, and even today the Ugandan military will try to stop people from taking photographs of the bridge. For the Luo, Pubungu marked a dramatic change in their lifestyle, from nomadic pastoralists to a ruling elite, and for this reason the period is seen as the second major stage in the migration of the Luo.

According to Luo oral history, the leader who helped build Pubungu up to become an impressive war camp was named Podho II. He is said to be the (15) great-grandfather* to President Obama. Podho II's citadel became a springboard for the Luo to radiate outward and dominate the region for several generations. Little remains today of the imposing fortress at Pubungu, but the many old villages and archeological sites in western Kenya that display similar construction methods can give us some idea of what Pubungu was like at its peak. These settlements, with their distinctive dry-stone walling, are called *ohinga* in Dholuo, a name that means "refuge" or "fortress." One particularly fine example in south Nyanza is called Thimlich Ohinga (*thimlich* means "frightening dense forest"). Archeological evidence suggests the site was occupied by Bantu tribes more than five hundred years ago, but it was the Luo who started to build in stone when they occupied the region circa 1700, about two hundred years after the Pubungu period.

Today, Thimlich Ohinga is preserved as a national museum, but its remote position in an isolated part of south Nyanza means that it gets very few visitors—a pity, because the fortress is built on a low hill that gives a magnificent view across the region. *Euphorbia candelabrum*—a great, spiky succulent that is traditionally found in many Luo homesteads—towers above all the other vegetation here. The curator, Silas Nyagwth, took me around the site, which covers more than ten acres and includes six large stone enclosures nestled among the trees and shrubs on a gentle slope.

Inside the stone compound, the wall was reinforced with stone towers where guards kept watch over the flat plain below. In the early days the main tribe here was the Maasai, who had a formidable reputation for fighting; the stone walls, between three and ten feet thick, were well constructed from loose stones and large blocks to protect against both hostile neighbors and wild animals. Inside the stone enclosures the

---

*Numbers in parentheses are used throughout as shorthand where there are large generational gaps; (3) *great-grandfather* signifies great-great-great-grandfather, and so on.

original huts have long since disappeared, but the outlines of house pits and cattle enclosures can still be seen.

Pubungu's considerable size—it was probably substantially larger than Thimlich Ohinga—suggests that the Luo made a conscious decision to halt their migration, at least for a time, and establish themselves in northern Uganda on the banks of the river Nile.

Before the arrival of the Luo, the region around Pubungu had been the land of the Madi tribe, whose homesteads extended on both sides of the White Nile. Soon the Luo were sending out raiding expeditions, and their warriors brought back plunder and captives from the Madi and other local tribes. The Luo also attacked the prosperous kingdom of Kitara, home to several tens of thousands of people and hundreds of thousands of cattle, and routed the pastoralist Chwezi people who lived there.[9]

It was during this belligerent period that the events in one of the most powerful and enduring Luo legends are claimed to have occurred. I heard the fable of the lost spear and the bead from several different people in Nyanza, and it takes on many forms among different African groups who originated in southern Sudan.[10] Although the story cannot be true in all its variations, the legend nevertheless gives us a fascinating insight into the centuries-old beliefs and customs of the Luo.

One common version of the spear and the bead story begins with two brothers, Aruwa and Podho II, who lived in Pubungu in the second half of the fifteenth century. When their father, Ramogi I, died (perhaps around 1480–90), his eldest son, Aruwa, took over the chiefdom and the two brothers lived in relative harmony.[11] However, one day an elephant came into their fields and began to trample the crops. One of Aruwa's nephews was sitting on a raised platform watching over the millet field. When he sounded the alarm, Podho rushed out to protect his son and chase away the elephant. As he did so, he grabbed the nearest weapon, which happened to be a spear belonging to Aruwa. Podho wounded the elephant, but not fatally, and it escaped into the forest with Aruwa's spear still hanging from its side. What Podho had not realized was that in the rush to protect his son, he had grabbed Aruwa's sacred spear in error. He confessed his mistake to his brother, but Aruwa was furious; he refused any substitute and insisted that Podho should go and retrieve the missing weapon. Podho had no choice but to honor his brother's demand.

The next morning, at the first crow of the cock, Podho set off alone for the forest, taking with him his own spear and shield, and food prepared by his wife: some *kuon anang'a* (ground maize cooked in milk), grilled meat, and sweet potatoes. It was a dangerous journey for anyone to undertake alone, and he decided the best course of action was to follow the setting sun. After traveling west for several days, Podho left behind the land of human beings and entered the kingdom of the animals. He roamed the remote forest for many days and became worn and weary, miserable at his failure to find the spear. One afternoon, exhausted, he dozed off under a tree and woke to find an old woman watching him: the queen of the elephants. She led Podho to her *kiru,* where she fed him and allowed him to rest. Then she took him to a larger *kiru,* where she kept all the spears that had been hurled at her elephants at various times in the past. The old woman told Podho that he would find his brother's weapon among them. Podho spent several days looking for the sacred spear before he eventually found it. As he thanked the woman and prepared to leave, she presented him with a handful of magnificent beads, unique in pattern and color.

Podho's return journey was difficult, and he was sick with exhaustion by the time he reached Pubungu. He called a village meeting and ceremoniously presented his brother with his sacred spear. His family was concerned about the dispute between the two brothers, but everyone hoped that now the spear was found, the animosity between them would diminish. Time passed and the argument seemed to be forgotten until another confrontation opened the old wound. Aruwa's children were playing with Podho's prized beads when one of Aruwa's daughters accidentally swallowed one. Podho, still feeling aggrieved about being forced to recover his brother's spear, demanded that Aruwa return his bead, refusing any substitute or replacement. Aruwa waited for three days to allow nature to take its course, but the bead did not emerge. Podho continued to insist that the bead should be returned, until the infuriated Aruwa took a knife and cut open his own daughter's stomach to recover it.

After this traumatic event, the brothers realized they could no longer live together, and their families would have to separate or risk civil war. Together they walked down to the Nile at Pubungu and drove an axe into the riverbed as a symbol of their separation. Aruwa went west with his family from Pubungu, and Podho traveled east of the Nile toward western Kenya. A third brother, Olak, is said to have remained behind in Pubungu, where his descendants became farmers and fishermen.

The legend of the spear and the bead is of course apocryphal; similar stories are told by many tribes as far afield as the Congo. Often the names of the participants change when the story is told by other tribes, sometimes a python takes the place of the elephant, and in other versions the stories of the spear and the bead are told as separate events. These stories of migration, lineages, and clanship often contain threads of historical detail, but they are really as much about the present as they are about the past; they played an especially important role in societies that had no written language and where a society's morals and principles needed to be well defined. And at the most simplistic level, the story of the spear and the bead is a reminder of the historic separation of the clans at Pubungu and the new migration that eventually brought Podho's people to western Kenya.

According to the oral history of the Luo, when Podho II left Pubungu he took his whole extended family, traveling east from what is now Lake Albert. This was the third stage of the Luo diaspora, which consisted of several pulses of Luo migration into western Kenya between about 1450 and 1720.[12] The movement of the Luo during this period has been compared to the shunting of a freight train in a marshaling yard; as one car is pushed, it knocks into another, which in turn pushes a third and fourth, and so on. In this way the Luo clans nudged their way into Kenya, and as more people came later, the early settlers were pushed farther east.

Reverting to form when they left Pubungu, Podho's clan stayed close to the waterways to the east of the settlement. First they followed what is now known as the Victoria Nile from Lake Albert, through the forest that today makes up the Murchison Falls National Park, before arriving at the swamplands at the western end of Lake Kyoga. From here they followed the northern shore of the lake, always making sure to secure water, food, and shelter.[13] Along the way they built temporary *kiru* from branches and leaves. They lived off their cattle, caught what fish they could in the rivers and lakes, and hunted in the forests. The younger men, the clan's warriors, scouted ahead for game and suitable places for their next stop. The migration from Pubungu to western Kenya took at least three generations, and the Luo speakers settled for a period at a place called Tororo, close to the present-day border between Uganda and Kenya. On the way from Pubungu to Tororo, Podho II fathered at least six sons. The eldest son, Ramogi II, in turn produced a son, Ajwang', who would at last lead the Luo into Nyanza.

Ramogi Ajwang' and his clan finally made their historic crossing into Nyanza in the early part of the sixteenth century, perhaps around 1530. (For further details, see "Notes on Methodology," page 249.) Ajwang's people, the Joka-Jok, were pioneers, the first of three main waves of Luo-speaking people who moved into western Kenya. Here Ajwang' built his first defensive stronghold on a good strategic high point: the ridge that is now called Got Ramogi.

The region that Ramogi Ajwang' chose for his new settlement resembled the swampy landscape which the Luo left in Sudan some half dozen generations before. The densely forested ridge of Got Ramogi towers above the snake-infested swampy grasslands of Gangu like a vast, sprawling medieval fortress, and the highpoint provides a perfect view of the surrounding countryside. The hills here rise to more than 4,300 feet above sea level, and they are protected on three sides by water: the Yala swamp to the north, the Yala River to the east, and Lake Victoria (which the Luo call Nam Lolwe) to the south. In addition to its natural defenses, Got Ramogi was a good position from which to mount offensives into new territory. And the region was fertile, with plenty of water for their cattle, space to establish their farms, and abundant wildlife in the forest for hunting. The Luo had been migratory for two centuries before Ramogi Ajwang' established this settlement in western Kenya, and for this achievement he has taken on a mythical status among the Luo. Today every schoolchild learns about the famous warrior ancestor; if Ramogi is their King Arthur, then Got Ramogi became his Camelot.

Life was not easy for the newcomers. Ramogi and his clan faced a hostile reception from the indigenous tribes, which soon turned into open warfare; granted, the conflict was caused mainly by the Luo getting up to their old tricks of raiding the Bantu homesteads for cattle and women. The indigenous Bantu were a farming people of medium stature, and they were no match for the tall, powerful Luo with their long history of warfare. The Bantu fled the region; in some cases the tribes moved to another location only to find themselves being displaced again by new waves of Luo invaders a generation or two later. In this way the Luo consolidated their hold on this part of western Kenya over several generations.

Scattered around the flatlands today at the foot of Got Ramogi are clusters of small, isolated traditional homesteads: simple Luo houses with mud walls and thatched roofs, and a sprinkling of cattle grazing lazily in the hot tropical sun. William Onyango, a local farmer in the hamlet of Dudi, explained to me that this is no longer good land to cultivate:

> In the past, this place used not to be swampy. Here it used to be very good. There came some very big rains about 50 years ago that made this place become swampy.

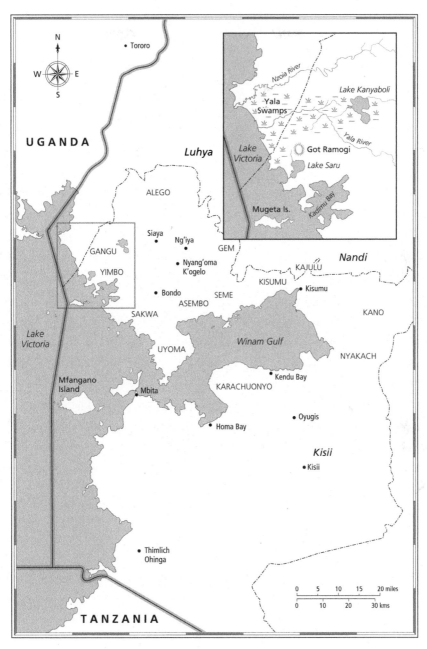

Nyanza Province (Luoland) and the region into which the Luo ancestors migrated between 1530 and 1830; also showing the adjacent Luhya, Nandi, and Kisii tribal areas.

Today, Onyango struggles to make even a basic living from his land:

> In this place I grow my maize—you can see my maize here. You
> call it corn—corn on a cob. Then we have cabbages, onions, and
> all this. That is what I do here to survive. I have ten children to
> look after—I'm not like you who might have two children. I am
> a real African! I have one wife and ten children: six boys and four
> daughters.

Like most subsistence farmers in Kenya, William Onyango struggles to find the money for even the most basic necessities in life. He can
feed his family adequately with the food that he grows himself, but he
can earn cash only by selling his surplus at the market. But competition
is fierce from other farmers in a similar position, and his surplus crops
rarely earn him very much income. And a lack of money is only one of
William's concerns in this very remote part of western Kenya, which
lies just a few miles from the Ugandan border and is accessible only
along rough dirt tracks:

> We have many animals here . . . warthogs, antelope, gazelles, and
> we have lots of hare. We also have hyenas and leopards—these are
> the most common ones. And the snakes—we have lots of snakes
> here. We have the puff adder, the cobras and the spitting cobras,
> the rock pythons, the green and black mambas. We really fear the
> three main ones: the cobra because they can spit a long distance and
> blind you, the puff adders because they are so aggressive, and the
> mambas because they are so poisonous.

It struck me that in many ways William's lifestyle has changed little
from that of his ancestors, all descended from Ramogi Ajwang', who
first settled in the area some four centuries previously:

> Ramogi is my very great-grandfather. He passed through the river
> Nile to this place, Got Ramogi, and he settled at the topmost part

of the hill. I asked my grandfather what is the significance of the top of Got Ramogi. He told me that in those times, there used to be many enemies. So he liked this place because it was like a castle, and he could use this to view all parts of these lower lands.

We have different *gots* here, different hills, but it has only one major name, which is Got Ramogi. When Ramogi conquered here and settled, he allowed his sons to take other hills. Then they could help him to see what was happening if the enemies were coming.

This hilltop is considered to be the ancestral home of both the Kenyan and the Tanzanian Luo; as such, it is a sacred place of pilgrimage for believers in the traditional Luo religion. They come to see features such as Muanda, the sacred tree; Asumbi, the rock of rain; and Rapongi, the whetstone used by Ramogi and his warriors to sharpen their knives. Many rare plants used in traditional medicine can also be found at Got Ramogi. Traditionally the area is guarded and maintained by William Onyango and other direct descendants of Ramogi Ajwang', but the Kenyan government has also now established a national museum here, which is charged with managing and protecting the Ramogi Hills.

According to Luo oral history, in his later life Ramogi Ajwang' decided to leave Got Ramogi and return to his birthplace, Tororo. Ramogi had been a strong and powerful leader, and he left behind in Got Ramogi the greatest gift of all—fifteen sons, who went on to consolidate their hold on the region and to establish a powerful clan. These young warriors spread out in small groups on scouting expeditions to test the region, reporting back about other tribes and natural resources in the area. If an area looked promising, then whole families and subclans would move out and establish new homesteads.

One of the new settlements in the area was situated just north of Lake Gangu, only a few miles from Got Ramogi and still in the Luo's sacred spot—that golden triangle wedged between swamp, river, and lake. At Gangu, archeologists have excavated seven trench and wall settlements thought to date from around 1600, firmly in the early decades of Luo settlement in the region.[14] Even today, broken shards of earthenware pots may be seen scattered around the site, all dating from the early days of the Luo in Kenya. These settlements were called *gundni bur,* ancient fortified communities which were built by Ramogi's ancestors, each with an earthen wall ten to fifteen feet high and about three feet thick. In this respect they resembled the fortifications in Thimlich Ohinga, except that the defensive wall was made of earth, not stone. This wall was surrounded by a ditch six to ten feet deep, and inside the compound were scores if not hundreds of huts, home to large numbers of men, women, and children. The girls and women cultivated the land immediately around the homestead, while the elders and male warriors grazed their herds further away from the homestead. Nearby, overlooking the settlement, a large rock outcrop served as a lookout post for warriors and sentries. These *gundni bur* were compact settlements, providing an element of security for hundreds of people, together with their stores of foodstuffs and cattle.

Each of the seven settlements at Gangu likely experienced a series of short-term occupations by different clans, for the arrival of Ramogi Ajwang' and his descendents was only the beginning of the movement of Luo into the region. From the early sixteenth century to about 1720, scores of families and subclans left the Pubungu area and spread eastward through Uganda and into western Kenya.[15] Many of these migrants passed through Got Ramogi on their way to more permanent settlements. Over time, Ramogi Ajwang's great hill evolved from a defensive medieval fortress to something more resembling Ellis Island, through which generations of immigrants passed on their way to a new life.

As new people moved into the area, the established groups moved on. This was no great, organized transcontinental migration, but rather a gradual, disjointed drift of families and subclans, moving on when it suited them, and with very little coordination with like-minded Luo. Not until the eighteenth century would the Luo begin to organize themselves into anything resembling an established tribe, as subclans gradually went from a group of disparate families into larger groups who cooperated and felt loyalty toward a common leader.[16]

In the early years of the seventeenth century, the Joka-Jok—the clan of Ramogi Ajwang'—were followed by two more distinct waves of Luo people. The main expansion along the northern shore of Winam Gulf occurred between about 1590 and 1790, when the second major group of Luo migrants arrived, the Jok'Owiny.[17] Their leader, Owiny the Great, was a venerated warrior and the great-great-grandson of Podho II. The Obama family trace their ancestry through Owiny's lineage and believe that President Obama is the (11) great-grandson of Owiny.

Despite their success in suppressing other tribes, the cantankerous Luo frequently squabbled among themselves, and one infamous confrontation occurred within the Jok'Owiny in the middle of the seventeenth century. The dispute arose between the sons of Kisodhi, who was the eldest son of Owiny the Great and (10) great-grandfather to President Obama. At the time of the feud Kisodhi's family was living at a place called Rengho, very close to Got Ramogi. Kisodhi—who was in many ways a classic example of the powerful and successful Luo warriors who helped consolidate the tribe's hold on the region—had two wives, Nyaika and Jong'a, and between them they bore him eight sons and an unknown number of daughters. When Kisodhi died, sometime around 1660, his eldest son, Ogelo, naturally assumed that he would take his father's position as head of the family. But as the extended family gathered at the funeral, a serious confrontation broke out among the eight brothers. The resulting split in the clan lasted for generations. To get the full story, I traveled to Got Ager, the site where Kisodhi's second son, Ager, had established his fortification.

At the foot of the steep, wooded ridge I found a single hut, home to Zablon Odhiambo and his wife and three children. Zablon, who claims to be directly descended from Ager himself, acts as keeper of the ancestral home. Together we climbed up to the steep upper slopes of Got Ager, where the view of the flat grazing land, the swamp, and the lake has changed little since Ager lived there 350 years ago. I asked Zablon what he knew about the infamous family dispute:

> It is traditional with the Luo that a family goes into mourning for four days following the death of a male elder. On the fourth day, the family must have their heads shaven as a mark of respect, and to show to others that they are in mourning. I know that when Kisodhi died, he was the father and he had two wives who gave him eight sons. Ogelo was the eldest. When he had been sat down to be shaved, the sisters of his two wives started talking to him. They were saying that because he was sitting down to be shaved, everybody else was going hungry.
>
> They hadn't finished [shaving Ogelo] when he stood up to distribute food to all these women. All his brothers became furious at this, because the women were praising Ogelo as the man with a good heart, as it was only him who got up to give people food. Ager, who was Kisodhi's second son, was leading this onslaught against him.
>
> Now Ager was a very harsh man, and when Ogelo went off for food, Ager sat down and was shaved. When Ogelo came back, he found that his brother had taken his traditional birthright [of being the first to be shaved], and he was furious.

Tempers flared and insults were exchanged as different members of the extended family took sides in the dispute. Throughout all this turmoil, the drummer continued his performance at the funeral, seemingly oblivious to the family fracas going on around him. This infuriated Owiny Sigoma, the youngest son of Kisodhi's second wife, and he drew his spear and killed the ill-fated drummer on the spot:

> People started fighting and Ogelo ran away, taking all the family's cattle. When Ogelo heard that Ager was after him, he kept going, past Siaya [a town about twenty miles to the east]. The people who went there with him became known as the Jok'Ogelo. That is why the place today is still called K'ogelo, the village where the stepgrandmother to the president, Sarah Obama, still lives.

In many ways, the altercation at Kisodhi's funeral is a typical Luo story, combining as it does pride, arrogance, family arguments, and bloodshed. Following the great family confrontation and the challenge to Ogelo's succession, Kisodhi's youngest son, Owiny Sigoma, became the undisputed leader of the clan. He was by far the most aggressive and belligerent of the local leaders—it could even be argued that he was a psychopath. As Owiny Sigoma expanded his territory east, he transferred his power base from his father's settlement in Rengho to a site he named after himself.

But this area was already controlled by the Seje people, another Luo clan who claim descent from the followers of Ramogi Ajwang'. They had been settled in the area for a couple of generations under their leader, a *ruoth* named Seje. Owiny Sigoma was not the type of man to meekly accept the leadership of Seje, and a civil war soon erupted between the two Luo clans. At first Owiny Sigoma was successful, and for a short period he became the undisputed ruler of the whole region. But he ruled by fear, and his repressive leadership style made the inter-clan rivalry worse than ever. Legend has it that Owiny Sigoma would feed the bodies of his enemies to hyenas, thus denying them a traditional burial and condemning their roving spirits to haunt surviving clan members.

Eventually his people tired of Sigoma's dictatorial style and rose up against him. Owiny Sigoma and his close entourage escaped from the region in order to regroup. When Sigoma returned to Alego, he attempted to impose his ruthless rule again on the local population, but he was challenged by the Ugenya people and a full-scale war broke out again between opposing Luo clans. This time Owiny Sigoma's warriors deserted him and he was killed on the battlefield, speared through the chest by an opponent. His death finally brought a measure of peace to the region.

Meanwhile, President Obama's (9) great-grandfather Ogelo, after fleeing the family dispute at his father's funeral, had settled on a low hill called Nyang'oma, overlooking the Yala River. In time, the village became known as Nyang'oma K'ogelo, and today the village of K'ogelo is recognized as the ancestral home of President Obama's family.

At the same time, the Luo continued to migrate into Nyanza from eastern Uganda. Sometime between 1760 and 1820, a third major group called the Jok'Omolo, under the leadership of Rading Omolo, started to move into western Alego. This new wave of migration caused a rapid increase in population, and in little more than two hundred years or so after the arrival of the first Luo people, the area north of the Winam Gulf became overpopulated. This problem was further compounded by a severe drought and famine in most parts of northern Nyanza during the early and middle parts of the eighteenth century.[18] Between 1750 and 1800 the feuding among the Luo became so acute that the clan structure began to disintegrate, and many of the subclans adopted the same solution as their ancestors several generations before: they packed their bags and moved on. This time the Luo moved across the Winam Gulf into south Nyanza, which was still a relatively underpopulated part of western Kenya.

In the Obama family, Obong'o, who was (3) great-grandfather to President Obama, left his ancestral home in K'ogelo and established a homestead in Kendu Bay, on the southern shores of Winam Gulf. Obong'o's original settlement was on the shore of Winam Gulf; later, his people moved to a new site a little inland, and it was either Obong'o's son or his grandson (both named Obama) who gave their name to the new settlement. Obong'o was probably born around 1802 and he is thought to have left K'ogelo before he was even married. Charles Oluoch, who showed me around K'obama, explained to me how his ancestor took the drastic step of leaving the ancestral home in K'ogelo for south Nyanza:

> At that time there was a lot of wrangling, and there were various people fighting within the family. The K'ogelo people were many now, and they came looking for land. Some people thought it would be easier to come this side [of the Gulf], because this particular place, there were not many people.

Obong'o crossed to this side when he was around thirty years old. I heard he came before he was married. It was very hard to carry your family to go to a foreign land. And he came and found that the place was good, so he decided to find a family and settle.

There was forest everywhere, wild animals. The Kalenjins were up there in the mountains. They used to just come down, maybe to bring their cows to drink water sometimes when it was dry. But most of the time this land was not inhabited.

Late in his life, after he had established a family and three sons in Kendu Bay, Obong'o returned to his family compound in K'ogelo, where he died sometime during the second half of the nineteenth century.

Obong'o had at least three sons: Obama, Opiyo, and Aguk. All three were born in Kendu Bay, and they stayed to establish the Obama presence there. It was Obong'o's second son, Opiyo, who would become the ancestor of the Obamas of Kendu Bay, and the great-great-grandfather of the president of the United States.

3

THE LIFE AND DEATH
OF OPIYO OBAMA

ADONG AROM GI BAO MA KANERA

May I grow as tall as the eucalyptus tree in my uncle's homestead

SOMETIME AROUND 1830, in a homestead to the south of Winam
Gulf in what is now Nyanza in western Kenya, a young woman
gave birth to a boy behind her simple mud hut. By tradition, she was
probably alone for the birth, but older women were at hand in case she
got into difficulty. The baby was the second son of Obong'o, who was
by now well established in the Kendu Bay area. Nobody can recall the
name of the baby's mother, nor the names of his sisters, for the Luo
are a patrilineal society and women don't figure in genealogy. Nor does
anybody know the exact year the baby was born, least of all the month
or the day. Yet we know that young Opiyo was the firstborn of twins,[1]
for the Luo have a tradition of bestowing on their children names that
describe something about their birth. *Piyo* means "quick," or in this
context, the quicker of two twins to emerge. Opiyo's family have no
record of the name of the second-born twin, who would, by tradition,
have been called Odongo if a boy, or Adongo if a girl (*dong* means "to
be left behind"). If the twin was a girl, then her name would not be

recorded in the oral history of the family, and if the baby was a boy, we can only assume that he died as an infant.

Opiyo grew to be a strong and respected leader among the Luo of south Nyanza and his family went on to prosper in their settlement in Kendu Bay. However, his arrival into the world was not greeted with the universal joy usually associated with a newborn son. In Luo society, twins are considered a bad omen for a family. As is customary among the Luo, the local women wailed and cried following the announcement of his birth; this was intended to scare away the evil spirits that had brought about the double birth. His mother's parents, who lived in a village nearby, were also quickly given the unwelcome news, for it was important that they too know about the calamity that had befallen the family. The new parents also subjected themselves to a variety of rituals that were intended both to protect their children in their vulnerable first few days of life and also to relieve themselves of the taboo and social stigma attached to bringing twins into the world. Obong'o and his wife had to give up their normal clothing, wrapping tree-vines around themselves for several days after the birth. Obong'o's wife was confined to her hut for several days, and she relieved herself in a large earthenware pot hidden at the rear of her hut. If Opiyo's younger sibling did in fact die during these early days, then its body would have been callously tossed into the pot as a form of penance. This period of taboo could not be broken until the family performed a special ceremony several days after the birth.

These complex and elaborate ceremonies surrounding the birth of the twins were only the beginning of a lifetime of rituals for young Opiyo. These traditions are an essential part of Luo life, and to ignore them would leave a person vulnerable to the omnipresent forces of evil—not to mention ostracism by family and neighbors. Although Christianity now exerts a powerful influence on the lives of most Luo, many of these rituals are still as important and relevant today as they were when Opiyo was born, more than 180 years ago.

Traditionally, a Luo woman marries long before she reaches her twentieth birthday and usually gives birth to her first child within a year of marriage. Although Opiyo was his mother's second son, she was likely to be still young when she gave birth to him. Opiyo's father, Obong'o, had three wives, and he spent three or four nights with each woman before directing his attentions to another. He was expected to have sex with one of his women every night, and his wives frequently competed among themselves for his attention.

Aloyce Achayo, a retired headmaster and a Luo cultural historian, explained the subtle ways in which the wives might have vied for Obong'o's attention:

> Let's say that you have four or five wives, and you come back to your homestead at the end of the day. As you are coming in, an astute wife will send her children to help her husband. In this way, the children will bring their father back to their mother's hut, and so the man will now go to that home first.

Children are prized in Luo society, and women were expected and encouraged to have many children. It was something of a collective effort: setting aside her rivalry with the others, Obong'o's first wife, Aoko, would sometimes advise him to sleep with a younger wife if she knew one of them was coming into the fertile stage of her monthly cycle. Like all Luo men, Obong'o slept in a small hut called a *duol,* and he would creep out after dark to discreetly visit the wife of his choice for the night—always returning to his *duol* before daybreak.

After Opiyo was born, his mother cut the umbilical cord with a piece of sharpened corn husk called a *muruich* and then smeared her newborn son with butter—a tradition that was both symbolic and practical, as the grease reduced the baby's loss of body heat. Next she dug a shallow pit and buried the placenta within the family compound—another important symbolic gesture to tie the child to the family and the tribe, and an act that was even more significant because he was a male.

The Luo believed that anybody with bad intentions toward the family could harm the baby through witchcraft in the days after the child's birth, so following the burial of the placenta, mother and child were confined to her hut for four days. This period inside her hut also had the practical advantage of allowing the baby and his mother to rest and bond before the celebrations began. Although no one except for Obong'o was allowed to enter, people still brought copious quantities of food to the hut because it was believed that mothers who had just given birth needed lots of food; in fact, new Luo mothers are called *ondiek* (hyena). For the next six months Opiyo was breast-fed; eventually his mother would gradually wean him off her milk and begin to feed him a gruel made from finely ground millet flour and water. By the time he was two years old, Opiyo would be eating the same food as adults.

On the fourth day after his birth, Opiyo was brought out at dawn and placed just outside the door to the hut, carefully watched by his parents, who sat a safe distance away. This ceremony is called *golo nyathi*, literally "removing the baby," and it represented Opiyo's introduction to the world. *Golo nyathi* usually marks the start of a great celebration, particularly for a healthy newborn male. But as Opiyo was the firstborn of twins, the family participated in a different type of ritual. Several days after the birth, Obong'o and his wife joined the rest of their extended family in a ceremony where large quantities of beer were consumed. By tradition, the dancing that accompanied the revelry was intentionally licentious, and the family referred to the couple in the foulest and most obscene language imaginable. The proceedings were intended to lift the taboo from the parents, although the ignominy of being a twin would haunt Opiyo for the rest of his life.

On the fourth day after the birth, Obong'o had sexual intercourse with his wife. The couple carefully placed Opiyo between them before making love, a ritual that is called *kalo nyathi*, literally, "jumping over the child." Many events in Luo life need to be consummated by sexual intercourse; in this case it symbolized that the child belonged to the couple. The ritual was also a form of cleansing after the birth, in the hope that another baby would soon follow. If Obong'o had sex with any of his other wives before *kalo nyathi,* the Luo believed that Opiyo's mother would never conceive again. To be safe, Obong'o would sleep with the new mother for several weeks after the birth. Opiyo's final birthing ceremony occurred a few weeks later. It was called *lielo fwada,* "the first shaving of the child," when all of the baby's hair was removed. In many parts of Luoland, this ceremony is still practiced today.

The names of Luo children can tell you a lot about the individual and their family. Traditionally, babies are given two names (and sometimes more), and nicknames are also commonly used. The first, personal name says something about the child's birth: Otieno is a boy born at night, Ochola is born after the death of his father, Okoth is born during the rainy season, Odero is a boy whose mother gave birth by the grain store, and so on. The child also takes the father's personal name as a surname, so Opiyo's full name was Opiyo Obong'o.

(Of course, the Luo may adopt other names when it suits them, which can cause some confusion. The name Obama was frequently used across generations; Opiyo's elder brother and Opiyo's second son both had it as their personal name. The name is thought to have originated in the early eighteenth century. Opiyo's great-great-grandfather was called Onyango Mobam—*Mobam* means "born with a crooked back," indicating that he was probably born with curvature of the spine—and the name presumably became corrupted to Obama.)

A girl's personal name usually begins with an *A,* so Atieno is a girl born at night, Anyango was born between midmorning and midday, Achieng' is a girl born shortly after midday, and so on. When a woman marries, she becomes known by her husband's surname.

The vast majority of Luo, probably more than three-quarters of them, use this unique form of naming. However, when missionaries brought Christianity to Luoland in the early twentieth century, some people began taking Christian names when they were baptized. Therefore Charles, Winston, Roy, and David are all common first names for boys, and Mary, Sarah, Pamela, and Magdalene are typical girls' names. Barack (which means "blessed one" in Arabic) is unusual, and it comes from President Obama's grandfather, Onyango Obama, who converted to Islam while in Zanzibar after the First World War. (When Barack Obama defeated John McCain in 2008, practically every child born in Nyanza that night was called either Barack or Michelle, and both names have remained very common ever since. It is something that will cause chaos in Nyanza's primary schools in about three years' time!)

Opiyo's younger brother, who was probably born around 1835, was called Aguk. Normally this is a female name (the male version being Oguk, meaning a boy born with a humped back; together with the name Mobam, this hints at some genetic abnormality in the family). However, a boy is occasionally given a female name (or a girl a boy's name) to indicate something significant or prestigious about the birth. For example, the only boy born into a large family of girls might be given his mother's name to mark the honor of giving birth to a male heir; conversely, a girl could be named after her grandfather if he was particularly respected within the community, or if he was a renowned warrior and hunter. This reversal of names confers a special status on the individual. A woman with a man's name, for example, will often be offered a chair to sit in when she is waiting in line, or she might receive a small discount when she is out shopping.

One final layer of naming that is very common in Luoland is the use of nicknames, which are always related to where the individual lives. A man from Kendu Bay might be referred to as "Jakendu"—in this case the preface *Ja-* is used in combination with the village or township of a man. A woman from the same location might be nicknamed "Nyakendu."

As a young boy, Opiyo grew up in a large, extended family, with many brothers and sisters. The family homestead was also home to any widowed grandmother in the family, and the girls would gather in her hut, called the *siwindhe*. Girls usually moved out of their mother's hut at a relatively young age, so as not to disturb their mother and father when he visited at night. In the *siwindhe* they learned about appropriate behavior for a Luo girl, the mores of the clan, and the sexual and social duties expected of them; it served as a classroom in a society without formal education.[2] Opiyo's grandmother also presided over storytelling and verbal games in the *siwindhe*. Friendly arguments often broke out over the precise interpretations of *ngeche* (riddles), such as "Which is the pot whose inside is never washed?" (The standard answer is "Your stomach.") Sometimes the children were asked to solve a riddle that had several potential answers: "What is the four-legged sitting on the three-legged waiting for the four-legged?" The standard answer would be a cat sitting on a stool waiting for a rat, but children vied to find alternative answers. The girls stayed in the *siwindhe* with their grandmother until they married.

The most important area in the compound for Aoko, Obong'o's first wife, was the *agola,* or veranda outside her hut, where the thatched roof extended beyond the mud wall, supported by pillars. Most of the domestic activities took place on the *agola,* including grinding flour, cooking, and tending to the chickens; a traditional hearth sat here, consisting of three large stones that raised the pots above the fire. Obong'o's wives used traditional earthenware pots of varying sizes to prepare meals, with each pot kept exclusively for one particular food. Even today, the Luo will tell you that cooking in an earthenware pot is far superior to using aluminum saucepans.

After the day's work was finished, Opiyo and his brothers would join their father in his hut for their evening meal. (Single men slept in their own bachelor huts, known as *simba*.) The men always ate separately from the women and girls, and Obong'o's three wives would cook in the evening and bring the food to his hut. This was one of the few occasions on which they would ever come to his *duol,* which was always the preserve of the male members of the clan. The staple food was *kuon* (called *ugali* in Swahili), a dough made from hot water and maize flour; it is usually rolled into a lump and dipped into a sauce or stew. Everyone ate with their fingers (and still do), and *ugali* is used in a variety of creative ways when eating; sometimes a thumb depression is made in the dough to create a scoop, or it is flattened into a thin pancake and wrapped around pieces of hot meat. Fish, either fresh or sun-dried, was also popular, eaten stewed or roasted. The meal was supplemented with vegetables and legumes from the home garden, or anything that could be collected in the forest, including mushrooms, fruit, honey, and even termites.

Traditionally, certain foods were not eaten by certain members of the family; women, for example, would not eat eggs, chicken, elephant, or porcupine, and men would never eat kidneys. Obong'o, as head of the household, was served the best meat, such as the cuts from around the chest of the animal, the tongue, liver, and heart. The women ate the intestines and other offal. The skin of the carcass would then be tanned and used for clothing or bedding. After the meal, Opiyo's father would talk to his sons about Luo legends and stories of their ancestors. The discussions in his *duol* would dwell mainly on heroes, battles, bravery, and hunting, and in this way the oral traditions of the tribe were passed down through the generations. Like the girls, the boys too would play verbal games, asking riddles and telling stories. After their anecdote, each of the storytellers would close with the phrase *Adong arom gi bao ma kanera*—"May I grow as tall as the eucalyptus tree in my uncle's homestead."

The Luo have a long tradition of entertainment and partying, and even today, Luo are some of the best musicians and dancers in Kenya. During important ceremonies such as weddings and funerals, Obong'o would invite a musician to play the *nyatiti,* an eight-stringed wooden lyre. This was played either as a solo instrument or with an accompanist on the drums or some other percussion. *Nyatiti* sessions were great social occasions, and people would make requests or ask the player to repeat a piece. Any request had to be paid for, often with a chicken or a useful household object. Other musical instruments included the *ohangla* (a drum made from the skin of a monitor lizard), horns, and flutes.

Beer drinking was also an important part of these social events. The best Luo beer is called *otia,* and it is brewed from sorghum flour that has been fermented, dried in the sun, cooked and fermented again, and finally strained. The men drink the beer warm, sipping from a large communal pot with a long wooden straw called an *oseke,* sometimes up to ten feet long. The men always use their right hand to hold the straw, because this is the hand that represents strength and integrity. (Left-handedness is viewed with suspicion by the Luo, and left-handed children are forced to use their right hand for eating and to greet people.) Another type of beer is *mbare,* which is made from brown finger millet flour, called *kal.* This is not cooked but, like *otia,* is dried and refermented. (The fermented grain left over from beer making is a useful by-product that the Luo leave outside for wild guinea fowl to eat. The residue, which is still potent, intoxicates the birds and makes them much easier to catch.)

Often the adults also smoked tobacco or took snuff during these social events, and they smoked *bhang* (marijuana) from calabashes. Opiyo would have played games with his siblings and neighbors at these parties. One popular game that is still played in Luoland is *ajua,* which uses small pebbles on a board with two rows of eight holes; *adhula,* a form of hockey, was also popular; and sometimes the young men would play a type of soccer using a ball made from rolled banana leaves. Another sport was *olengo* (wrestling), which gave the young men a golden opportunity to show off their strength and physique to the girls from neighboring villages.

When he was around fifteen, Opiyo faced one of the most important ordeals of his life: the traditional removal of his six lower teeth. Both boys and girls underwent this ceremony known as *nak*, which was performed by specialists in the community called *janak*. By tradition, Opiyo's parents were not given advance notice that their son was being prepared for his initiation into adulthood. The practice was widespread in Luoland until the middle of the twentieth century, when both the government and missionaries tried to discourage it. Despite this, *nak* is still performed today in some rural villages in Luoland, and even in certain churches in the main city of Kisumu.

It is still very common to see older men with their lower teeth removed. Joseph Otieno, a retired farmer in his late sixties, lives in a remote community in Gangu in western Kenya. He still remembers with total clarity the day of his *nak:*

The ceremony was usually done during the summer in August. The night before the ceremony, I crept into my mother's granary and stole a basket full of millet. This was my reward.

My sister came to my hut, and she escorted me the next morning to the ceremony. That morning when I went, I felt brave because it was my initiation into manhood . . . because all the Luos go through the same thing. I had to kneel down, my sister held my shoulders, and I opened my mouth. The way they did it was to use a thin, flattened nail to remove my teeth. They forced the flattened nail into my gums to loosen each tooth. You can't be afraid—you must be strong.

You could not reach the age of twenty without your teeth being removed. There were some people there who were afraid, so they put a stick in their mouth to keep it open. If you are too fearful, which some people were, then a group of boys would come and hold you down.

I asked Joseph what the significance was to the Luo of having their front six teeth removed:

> Number one, the reason why they were removing this is that sometimes people can get sick, and this would be a gap where they could feed you food or drink.
>
> Number two, if you die anywhere [away from home], then people would know you were a Luo.
>
> The third one, it was an initiation into adulthood, and it shows that you are now no longer a child. Luos are not circumcised, so this was our initiation. If you didn't do it, then your agemates would not walk with you. If it wasn't done, I would have to stay in the house all day. It was painful, but we had to go through it.
>
> Afterward, my mouth bled for eight days.

Joseph made the whole experience sound straightforward and perfectly normal, but I knew that the *nak* ceremonies didn't always go quite so smoothly. Leo Odera Omolo is a Luo journalist who lives in Kisumu. He too had his lower teeth removed, but against his will:

> When I was young, I lived away from home a lot of the time, and I did not want my teeth removed. When I was about eighteen, I returned to my parents' house one day for a short visit. That night I was grabbed by several young men from the village and they dragged me from my bed. My parents insisted that I should have my teeth removed, otherwise it would bring shame to my family. It was done forcibly. The boys held me down and the *janak* pulled out my six lower teeth with pliers.

As a young boy, Opiyo spent most of his days tending his father's growing herd of cattle, taking them out to the pastures in the morning and returning with them every evening. But once he had undergone *nak,* Opiyo became an adult and an important member of his clan. As he grew older, his father, Obong'o, and his uncle Ogola taught him to hunt. Wildlife was still very common around Kendu Bay during the middle part of the nineteenth century, and the animals—antelope, buffalo, warthog—were an essential food source for the family. Opiyo learned how to throw a spear and shoot a bow and arrow, and he went off on regular hunting trips with his brothers. These hunting expeditions were not without danger; the African or Cape buffalo (*Syncerus caffer*), for example, is one of the most unpredictable and thereby dangerous animals in Africa, often turning and attacking with little provocation. (Today, only the hippo and the crocodile kill more humans in Africa.) Lions, leopards, hyenas, and poisonous snakes also made Opiyo's hunting forays risky affairs.

Opiyo now also had the opportunity to really make a name for himself as a warrior. One of the reasons the young men did not marry until they were nearly thirty was because of their responsibilities as fighters; the defense of the clan was a priority, and being a warrior was a form of "national service" expected of all young men. (Only sons whose family lineage depended on them to produce an heir were exempted; such boys might be married as young as fifteen and would not be expected to fight.) The young Luo were always prepared for war, and frequently skirmished with other clans and tribes over land, cows, resources (such as grazing rights for cattle), and sometimes women. Disagreements also arose during social gatherings, such as the succession fight between Owiny Sigoma and his older brothers at their father's funeral.

Platoons of warriors were organized for battle along family lines, based on the principle that kinship strengthens the bond between combatants. The clan leaders called the fighters by blowing a small sheep's horn called a *tung'*, which made a high-pitched wailing sound that could be heard a long distance away. Once the warriors were assembled and ready to fight, the *oporo* was blown; this was a low-pitched booming horn from a bull or buffalo. This sounded the attack, and the young men of the clan, often high from smoking *bhang*, would advance on the enemy. The fighters were armed with spears (*tong'*), war clubs (*arungu*), and arrows (*asere*). For protection, the men carried a shield (*okumba*).

The *kuot,* an even larger, body-sized shield, was made from three layers of African buffalo skin and would deflect even the most powerful spear or arrow. A village elder would select a spear and fold its blade in on itself; this was the first missile to be thrown at the enemy, in the belief that this act would render the enemy's spears ineffectual.

The battles could be bloody affairs, and in the aftermath the job of recovering the dead and wounded fell to the women, who remained safe from attack by the enemy under widely accepted rules of warfare. The women carried the dead and injured back to the homestead, where they were greeted with loud wailing. If the clan had been victorious in battle, the returning warriors would stomp their way back to the compound in elation, thrusting their spears skyward and chanting the *agoro*—the victory song. It was taboo for those fighters who had killed in battle to enter the homestead through the main gate; instead, they waited outside the compound until a new opening was made in the thick euphorbia hedge for them to enter. Inside, their wives and mothers waited for them, smeared with dust, to celebrate their safe return. The fighters then underwent a cleansing ceremony that involved swallowing tough strips of raw lung from a billy goat; the goat skin was also cut into strips, which were tied to the wrist of the successful warrior and around his spear, one strip for every man he had killed in battle. The goat's heart was then removed and the warriors also ate this raw before their heads were symbolically shaved as a mark of victory.

The next major episode in Opiyo's life was his marriage. Every member of the Luo community is expected to marry, and anybody who remains unwed is viewed with suspicion. Usually Luo men take their first wife in their late twenties, and very few men are unmarried by the time they reach thirty-five. As with all Luo ceremonies, Opiyo's marriage followed a strict protocol that was designed to strengthen family ties. A suitable girl was selected by an aunt or a marriage maker, called a *jagam* or "pathfinder." The Luo are strict about this selection and do not allow marriage with any relative, however distant. Opiyo's first wife, who was called Auko Nyakadiang'a, came from the Kardiang' clan several miles away. Opiyo visited the family and met the chosen girl; either one of them could refuse the union at this stage. Traditionally the girl is coy about the approach and is expected to play hard to get. After several refusals, she eventually agrees to the marriage.

The lineage of a prospective partner is keenly scrutinized by both the family and the village elders. If, for example, the prospective bride's father was a known liar or practitioner of witchcraft, then a marriage into that family would be considered unwise. Likewise, any hereditary conditions such as epilepsy would have negative connotations for the union. As with all Luo betrothals, final approval for Opiyo and Auko's union rested with the village elders.

The next stage is the negotiation of the bride-price, which would have been paid by Opiyo's father to Auko's family, and which can take up to three years to organize. It is often paid in installments, but the total typically involves twelve cows or more, and at least one goat (for ceremonial purposes). Once the bride-price was paid, Opiyo could claim his bride in yet another elaborate ritual. One day he stole off to Auko's village with his two brothers, Obama and Aguk; their intention was to kidnap his intended in a ritual known as "pulling the bride." Having moved out of her mother's hut when she reached puberty, Auko was now living in her grandmother's *siwindhe* in preparation for her marriage. Opiyo most likely bribed Auko's grandmother to be conveniently away from her hut when the crucial time came for him to claim his bride. As part of the ritual the girl must always resist the attempt to be taken, and there is every chance that her screams will be heard by her brothers, in which case a fight will ensue. This was no token skirmish—the young men in the girl's village are determined to prove their mettle by putting up a serious resistance to the kidnapping, and in return, the kidnappers are expected to show their determination to take the girl.

Opiyo was successful in "pulling" his bride, and he took Auko back to his *simba,* inside his father's compound. That night they consummated their marriage, again according to ritual, as Aloyce Achayo explained:

> The very day the lady is brought back, they are married. What will happen now is that a group of girls [from the bride's village] will come at night, maybe forty or fifty girls, following this girl who was pulled. And that is called *omo wer.* If those girls don't come, there is no sex.
>
> The bride and the bridegroom come into the house for their first experience, and the consummation has to be witnessed by two or three girls who are almost the same age as the one who is being married. Outside, the other girls are singing all night. They don't sleep. If this particular girl is found to be a virgin, there is very big joy from the girl's side. A big, big joy.
>
> Very early in the morning, these girls will go back [to their village] with the news that she was or wasn't a virgin. During our olden times the majority used to be virgins. On their first meeting, the blood will show. She will sit on a stool, which will then be carried back to the girl's home to be shown to the mother.

The third stage of the wedding ceremony occurs on the morning after the consummation. As the *omo wer* girls return to the village, they meet the older women coming in the opposite direction to celebrate the marriage. This is called the *diero,* the wedding celebration of the women. The next day the men—including those who forcibly resisted the pulling of the bride—have a *diero* of their own at the husband's home.

The final ceremony occurs a few weeks after the wedding day. After the marriage has been consummated, the bride asks a handful of her friends to remain behind in the village to keep her company in her new home; they stay for as long as a month. Then the bride's girlfriends return to their village for a final celebration, the *jodong.* Opiyo and Auko returned to her home to visit her family, with Auko leading a goat behind her. Once they reached her parents' home, the animal was slaughtered, its neck cut from behind in the traditional Luo manner, to mark the beginning of the *jodong*. As many as sixty people would have gathered for much eating, drinking, dancing, and singing.

The homestead where Opiyo grew up in Kendu Bay was laid out in exactly the same way as that of all the neighboring clans. The huts were ringed with a thick euphorbia thorn hedge to keep out enemies and wild animals. A typical Luo compound had two entrances through the hedge: a formal, main gate that was always used by visitors, and a smaller gap at the rear of the compound that allowed people to take a shortcut to their fields. The largest hut in the compound, perhaps fifteen feet in diameter, belonged to Opiyo's father's first wife, and the door to this hut faced the main entrance to the compound. Any visitors to the homestead were directed to introduce themselves at this hut, for it was the first wife who always ran the compound. To the left of the big hut was the house of Obong'o's second wife, identical in every way to that of his first wife, but slightly smaller. To the right of the big hut was the home of Obong'o's third wife, again slightly smaller still. In this way, the huts of all the wives were built on alternate sides of the first wife's hut, each slightly smaller in size. Each wife also had her own granary or *dero* next to her hut, but generally they would work together to cook meals for the whole family.

Obong'o's hut was smaller even than that of his youngest wife, but as he spent most nights elsewhere, there was little point in having anything too grand. As head of the homestead, he used his hut for holding council with his fellow elders and for discussing family business with his three sons. Women never came to Obong'o's hut unless they were summoned or to bring food to the men.

Once Obong'o's sons reached puberty, they moved out of their mother's hut and built their own shelter inside the compound. Obama was Obong'o's eldest son, and he built his *simba* first, close to the main gate to the compound and just to the left of the entrance. When Opiyo came of age, he too built his own *simba,* but this time to the right of the main gate; his younger brother Aguk built his *simba* to the left of the entrance to the homestead, thus following the same pattern as the women's huts. In this way, the young men of the family guarded the entrance to the family compound. The wives' huts in the upper part of the compound and the sons' houses near the entrance to the compound were deliberately arranged to be a respectable distance apart.

Before he was married, Opiyo enticed local girls into his *simba.* This was expected of him, and periodically Obong'o would pass quietly by his son's *simba* at night to check that his son's social (and sexual) development was on course. Although both boy and girl gained sexual experience in this way, the girl would almost always draw the line at full penetrative sex, for virginity was, and still is today, expected of all brides.

The sons also had to get married in order of seniority, and once Obama took a wife, she moved into his *simba.* In time, each of the sons would marry, and their respective wives would move in to start a family of their own. Only when Opiyo had a son could he leave his father's compound and establish a homestead of his own.

Opiyo's hut, just like all the others in the compound, was circular, with thick mud walls and a pointed, thatched roof. Visitors had to stoop low to enter the doorway, and the inside was cool and very dark, as the huts had no windows. There was no furniture to speak of: a raised mud platform served as a bed, and scattered animal skins and blankets gave a little comfort for sleeping. A small fire gave some warmth, and the smoke rose into the rafters and helped to fumigate the thatch.

The reaction to an article in one of Kenya's leading national papers in early 2008 shows the lasting significance of the *simba* among the Luo. At the time, Barack Obama was running against Hillary Clinton for the Democratic Party nomination. The *Standard* ran a front-page special, with the headline "Exclusive: Obama's One-Day Visit to Kenya":

Senator Barack Obama, the man who has caused a sensation in the presidential nomination race in the U.S., is in Kenya for a one-day visit. . . . Obama will make a public appearance at KICC [Kenya International Conference Centre] where he will sign autographs and speak on peace.

He is later scheduled to leave for his father's home in Kogelo, Siaya District shortly after midday.

Within minutes of the paper hitting the news stands, crowds were flocking to the conference center in Nairobi to hear the great man speak, and hundreds of callers jammed the switchboards of the local radio talk shows. The rumor soon spread that Obama had been advised that he could greatly increase his chances of success in the election by returning to Kenya and building himself a *simba*. This, people claimed, would show that he was a true Luo, and somehow impress the American voters. What nobody seemed to notice was the date on the top of the paper: April 1.

For almost every young male Luo, there comes a time when he moves out of his father's homestead and establishes his own compound. The young men leave their father's compound in strict order of seniority, so Obama had to move out first before Opiyo could do the same. The youngest son in the family, in this case Aguk, never leaves. Instead, he stays behind to look after his aging parents, and in time he inherits his father's compound.

Certain other young men also did not qualify to start their own compounds. A man without a family of his own could never move out; nor could he if he had only daughters, as some of the complex rituals involved in establishing a new homestead require both a son and a wife. Nor can a left-handed person set up his own home; the Luo believe that if a left-hander were to establish his own compound, it would lead to the death of his siblings. (Traditionally, left-handed people were also thought to be easy prey for their enemies, and they were vulnerable to magic and witchcraft. According to strict Luo tradition, then, President Obama would never be allowed to establish his own homestead in Luo-land on two accounts: he has only daughters, and he is left-handed.)

For several weeks before setting out to build his own compound in Kendu Bay, Opiyo surreptitiously looked around for a suitable loca-tion, but he had to be careful not to be seen to be too interested, in case others moved there first or put a curse on the site. The area to the south of Winam Gulf was still relatively sparsely populated in the mid-nineteenth century. In those days, thick tropical forest still covered most of the land; wild animals too were common, and encounters with leopards, cheetahs, and hyenas were frequent.

On the eve before he set out to build his new home, Opiyo had ritual sex with Auko, his first wife. The next morning, he rose before dawn and walked out of the family compound, accompanied by his father, Obong'o; his uncle Ogola; his wife, Auko; and Obilo, his eldest son. Everyone had his or her own specific roles to play that day. Opiyo carried a large cockerel; Obilo a new axe; Auko had a small fire smol-dering in an earthenware pot. Upon arriving at the chosen place, his uncle Ogola selected the precise location for the new home, then drove a forked pole into the ground where the very center of Opiyo's hut would be. Ogola hung a birdcage on one branch of the forked pole, and at the base of the post he carefully placed a piece of soil taken from an anthill they had passed on the way. The bird cage contained a selection of items to bring good fortune to the homestead: a rotten egg to dispel sorcery, stargrass for prosperity, and stalks of millet and maize to attract wealth. Finally, Opiyo's uncle took blades of *modhno* grass, tied them into a knot, and cast them down on to the ground; the grass symbolizes a blessing for a new home, and protects against evil forces.

Now the real work could begin on the new hut. First Obilo, Opiyo's eldest son, cut a pole using his father's new axe. Opiyo then cleared the site of undergrowth and dug the first hole, into which he placed the pole which his young son had cut; this first hole in the ground always coincides with the sleeping side of the house. Next, Opiyo marked out the outline of his circular *duol,* and the rest of the party joined in to dig holes for the remaining poles; these would form the main reinforcement for the mud walls. Opiyo took care to put cow dung, *modhno,* and *bware* (a medicinal plant) into the holes for the door poles. For the door post, he cut down a *powo* tree and removed the bark, leaving a smooth surface that would protect the family from the evil effects of witchcraft; negative forces would simply roll off the post to the ground and never enter the house.

With the door pillars in place, the rest of the family and the neighbors joined in to help Opiyo complete his house before nightfall. All day there was a steady supply of help. Women carried water and cooked food for the men, and they also helped carry some of the lighter building materials, such as reeds. The men did all the heavy construction work, such as softening mud to build the walls; they also climbed up and thatched the roof. The house had to be finished by the end of the first day, and when it was completed, Opiyo lit a fire and placed the cockerel inside the *duol* to crow the next morning. Meanwhile, the family returned to the old home, leaving Opiyo and his son to spend the first night together in their new hut. Opiyo spent four nights in his new *duol* with his young son, Obilo, which gave him time to build a grander hut for Auko. On the fifth day, his wife moved in and the couple consummated the new hut by having sex that night.

In time, Opiyo took a second wife; her name was Saoke from the Wasake clan and she came from a village fifty-five miles away, on the border between Kenya and Tanzania. Saoke's home was a long way from Kendu Bay, which suggests not only that Opiyo was wealthy enough to take a second wife but also that his good reputation must have been widespread throughout south Nyanza. When Opiyo married Saoke, he built a hut for her in the family compound. In time, Opiyo fathered three sons, Obilo, Obama, and Agina, and at least two daughters. His middle son, Obama, was born around 1860 and he became the great-grandfather of President Obama.

Living as we do in the twenty-first century, it is difficult to fully appreciate just how independent and self-sufficient Opiyo and his family had to be to survive. They lived in a remote part of western Kenya during the middle and latter part of the nineteenth century, a full fifty years before white colonists introduced any form of modern technology. Opiyo and his family grew all their own food, built their own houses, and made their own clothes (such as they were), as well as many of their farming implements and weapons.

Opiyo's family cultivated two plots of land. The kitchen garden or *orundu* was usually located behind the family compound and was accessible through the secondary opening in the hedge. The *orundu* was fenced off to keep animals away from the produce, and Opiyo's two wives, Auko and Saoke, grew vegetables here, as well as legumes (peas and beans), peanuts, *simsim* (the Arabic word for sesame), maize, millet, cassava, and African sweet potatoes. The food grown here was usually for immediate consumption. Further away from the compound was their main farm. This was the preserve of Opiyo himself, and here he grew cereals and pulses for long-term storage, creating a strategic reserve for his family to use during times of drought and famine.

In addition to the crops, the family reared cattle, goats, sheep, and chickens. Cattle were, and still are, considered to be the most important livestock for an East African and the main measure of a man's wealth. The head of the family has to accumulate cattle to pay the bride-price for his sons, although he also receives animals when his daughters are married off. The importance of cattle to an East African can never be underestimated; apart from their prestige value, they also represent an invaluable resource for the family, for they provide milk, meat, skins, and fuel. Sheep are also prized by the Luo and are used mostly as food or as gifts for friends. Responsibility for looking after the livestock falls on the young males in the family, and Opiyo's sons took turns caring for the animals, usually for three days at a time. (President Obama's father, Barack senior, is often referred to as having been a "goatherd" during his youth. In fact, he looked after all of his father's livestock.) The women always looked after the chickens and other fowl, and they would take cone-shaped fishing baskets down to the nearest river to catch what they could.

· Opiyo traded surplus food for items he could not produce himself, such as knives and salt. Money would not be introduced until the early twentieth century (by the British); instead, the Luo economy functioned on a sophisticated system of bartering. Not only were there specific exchange rates between commodities such as grain and meat, but when an owner slaughtered a bull to exchange for cereals, each part of the animal was valued differently. The Luo also had a special form of barter called *singo,* which was a form of promissory note. If a man needed to slaughter a bull for a specific ceremony such as a funeral but did not have one of his own available, he would strike a deal with a neighbor to exchange one of his cows for a bull. Under the *singo* system the neighbor would keep the cow until it produced a calf, which the neighbor then kept for himself.

One important area of expertise in the Luo community was traditional herbal medicine, which was used to treat both physical and psychological illnesses. Common medical problems included fractures and other physical injuries from accidents or battles; parasites; snakebite; eye infections; and tropical diseases such as malaria, sleeping sickness (trypanosomiasis), and bilharzia. Snakes are very common in the region and the Luo have a wide variety of treatments, which include mystical therapies as well as concoctions made from as many as twenty-four different herbaceous plants. The most common treatment involves cutting, sucking, and binding the injury, followed by the application of a poultice made from leaves or roots and held in place with strips of cloth or tree bark.

Before the coming of the Christian missionaries at the start of the twentieth century, the Luo believed in a supreme God or life force called Nyasaye, the creator. Nyasaye is all powerful, and he intervenes directly in the daily activities of humans, bringing disease and disaster when displeased. The mystery of Nyasaye is all-encompassing, and he can be found not only in the sun and moon but also in rivers, lakes, mountains, large rock structures, trees, and even snakes (especially the python)— all of which are natural conduits for his divinity. Some devotees even kept a large goat in their house as a living embodiment of Nyasaye. In this sense, the Luo are traditional animists.

The Luo believed that the sun could appear to people in dreams. When this happened, the sleeping individual would become very agitated and might have to be physically restrained as he or she reached out to ask for the sun's blessing. The individual might also dream of throwing cow dung, human excrement, or seeds toward the sun, and in return he or she would be blessed with wealth in the form of a good harvest or many cattle. Believers also invoked the power of the moon: old men prayed for more wives, young men for a bride, young women for a husband, and married women for satisfaction. Many consulted celestial bodies to help forecast the weather and to predict the future. A ring appearing around the sun signified that an important person had just died, and solar or lunar eclipses were viewed with awe as harbingers of a major event. When these portentous signs appeared, the village elders would gather and deliberate over the most appropriate action to take to avoid disaster.

Belief in the power of Nyasaye is still common among the Luo. In 2003, the appearance of a twenty-foot-long python in a village on the

banks of Lake Victoria exposed rifts in the community, pitting tradi-
tionalists against modernists. The snake was found by a thirty-five-year-
old mother of five called Benta Atieno, who considered it her divine
duty to ensure that the female python safely hatched its dozens of eggs.
When she first discovered the snake, she ran to tell other people in the
village about her find. The elders and other locals considered this to
be a special snake, an *omieri*. If the *omieri* was cared for, they claimed,
good things—healthy livestock, bountiful harvests—would ensue, but
if it was harmed, then bad luck would befall the village. They recalled
that seven years previously another large python had been killed in the
village and a severe drought subsequently struck the area. However,
some people, including senior church leaders, called for the snake to
be destroyed, fearing that it would take livestock or even harm small
children. The appearance of large pythons in Kenyan villages is a common enough event, especially during the rainy season, and so the Kenya
Wildlife Service removed Benta Atieno's snake and released it well away
from human habitation.

A spirit can become a demon, *jachien,* when the circumstances of
his death and burial are not honored correctly. For this reason, the strict

The Luo also worship their ancestral spirits, both male and female.
They believe that man is made up of visible and invisible parts; the
invisible part, known as *tipo* or shadow, combines with the visible part
(the human body) to create life. When an individual dies, their body
becomes dust and the *tipo* becomes a spirit, which retains the individual's mortal identity but becomes even more powerful and more
intelligent in the afterlife. Thus the most potent spirits were those of
important people, and powerful male ancestors were usually the most
respected and the most feared. Spirits can haunt only the living members of their own clan, and the Luo believe that an ancestral spirit continues to exist for as long as those who recognize it are still alive. People
perceive these spirits to be agents of both good and evil, and they might
claim to see, hear, or smell them when awake, or encounter them in
their dreams.

A spirit can become a demon, *jachien,* when the circumstances of
his death and burial are not honored correctly. For this reason, the strict

rituals and customs of the tribe must always be followed to avoid the creation of a *jachien*. The Luo sacrificial ritual involves the consecration of an animal before killing it and sharing the meat among the members of the clan. If the spirits are offended, the head of the family must seek expert help from someone who can best advise what course of action to take.

Within Luo society, there are both sorcerers and healers who claim to have unique spiritual powers and who can call upon *juok*—a supernatural force—to use in their spells. It is a battle between good and evil, between the *jajuok* or witch doctor who uses *juok* against the good of society, and the *ajuoga*, a diviner or healer, who can offer protection against these evil spells. Opiyo knew that if he needed advice about the future or had worries about his ancestral spirits, he should turn to an *ajuoga* for help: he is an expert in dispensing medicine and magic for positive reasons; he can diagnose illnesses, prescribe cures, and appease the spirits using sacrifice or other cleansing rituals. Whenever Opiyo visited an *ajuoga*, he took with him a present, or *chiwo*. The diviner might contact the ancestral spirits using a number of different techniques, including *gagi*—literally, "casting pebbles"—or *mbofwa*, meaning "the board." This last method involves rubbing two flat wooden blocks together, one of which is much bigger than the other, and summoning the spirits by name. The *ajuoga* knows that he has contacted the spirit when the smaller piece of wood begins to stick to the bigger piece. For *gagi*, the diviner tosses wild beans or cowry shells onto the ground and interprets the message according to the pattern they make. These methods help the *ajuoga* to identify the rebellious spirit that is causing the problem. Most diviners rely on the ancestral spirits for their knowledge, and any consultation with the dead is done in darkness; only the *ajuoga* can see and talk to the spirits.

However, Opiyo not only feared ancestral spirits; his neighbors could pay a *jajuok* to use witchcraft and sorcery to bring harm or death to him and his family. (In witchcraft, practitioners use mystical powers to harm or kill others, whereas sorcery achieves the same objective through the use of material objects.) Throughout his whole life, Opiyo lived under the constant fear that a curse could be cast on his family, and he took elaborate precautions to guard against evil. A neighbor might engage a *jajuok* for a number of reasons; for example, rivalry over land or a woman, or resentment toward a successful neighbor. The Luo believed that by cursing and killing a successful neighbor, you could benefit from their death. Whatever the reason for the dispute, the *jajuok* acted as a hired hand who could bring death or pestilence, for a fee (usually three cows). An individual could also protect themselves against a *jajuok* by finding a practitioner at least as powerful as the protagonist, who (for another fee) would conjure up an antidote to the spell.

Jajuok inherited their powers from their fathers and grandfathers, and their techniques varied; some could simply stare at or point the dried forearm of a gorilla at a person to bestow a fatal curse. Others could summon lightning to strike an individual, or slaughter a black sheep or a cockerel to produce a curse to strike morbid fear into their target. Some would mix the blood of a sheep with secret ingredients and leave the concoction in front of the hut of the targeted individual, or alongside a path where they would be sure to pass. In many respects, these techniques are similar to those used in other African societies, and also in Haitian vodou; when they work, it is because people believe in the power of the magic.

Unsurprisingly, practitioners of magic and sorcery were the most feared individuals in Luo society, for they literally had the power of life and death over ordinary people. (The fees they received for their services also made them among the wealthiest.) However, they were also considered to be outside the normal social structure of the Luo tribe and could not live a normal family life.

Belief in witchcraft persists today. Roy Samo is a local councilor in Kajulu, a sprawling village north of Kisumu. He told me how people in the village feared witchcraft and how only recently somebody had directed a bolt of lightning onto a neighbor's house. I know Roy well, and I asked him almost jokingly what he thought about these traditional beliefs. I was astonished at his response. "Oh, I fully believe in them—they have the power of good as well as evil." "But Roy," I said, "you're an educated man, a devout Christian and a pastor at your local church!" "Yes," he laughed, "but I am also an African!"

As recently as May 2008 in Kisii district, south Nyanza, eleven elderly people—eight women and three men between eighty and ninety-six—were accused of being witches and burned to death by a mob. Villagers told reporters that they had proof the victims were witches: they claimed to have found an exercise book that contained the minutes of a "witches' meeting," including details of who was going to be targeted next. In 2009 Kenya's *Daily Nation* claimed that on average, six people are lynched in Kisii district every month on suspicion of witchcraft.

Sometime around the end of the nineteenth century, Opiyo Obong'o died. Like many Luo men, he reached a good age due to a combination of a high-protein fish diet and a lifetime of physical labor that kept him lean and fit. Indeed, it is not unusual for men in this part of Africa to live to be a hundred years or more. For the Luo, there is no such thing as a natural death; there must always be a cause. An old man dies not of old age, but because he has been called by his ancestors to join them for further duties in the afterlife.

Opiyo's death marked the beginning of his last ritual on earth, an elaborate rite of passage for both the deceased and the family who survived him. Even in death, Opiyo was expected to conform to certain traditions. First, it was considered a very bad omen to die at any time other than between two o'clock and seven o'clock in the morning. Today it is possible to preserve a body with formalin; failing that, the body is placed on a bed of sand covered in banana leaves to keep it cool. But in the past, a corpse had to be buried very quickly, and certainly on the day of death before the midday heat emerged. If Opiyo died in the evening and his body lay in his hut overnight, then three goats had to be sacrificed to dispel the bad omen and the evil spirits that would otherwise haunt the family. The goats would be provided by close members of his family, either his brothers or his cousins, and they would be brutally bludgeoned to death instead of having their throats cut. Only by killing the goats in this gruesome way could the evil influences that had caused the man to die be dispelled.

The first that the villagers heard of Opiyo's death was when his first wife, Auko, began wailing—a high-pitched howling cry called *nduru.* By tradition, she stripped naked and ran from her hut to the entrance of her compound and back again. Auko then dressed in her husband's clothes, which she would continue to wear throughout the protracted mourning period. This was the first ritual, which only the first wife could perform. Opiyo's other wife, Saoke, also showed respect toward her dead husband by wearing his old clothes. Saoke joined Auko in *nduru;* alerted by the noise, people soon began to congregate outside Opiyo's hut. Meanwhile, Opiyo's two married daughters had been told about their father's death, and they came to the family compound as quickly as possible. By tradition, the eldest daughter had to arrive first; her younger sister could not enter the compound until after the older daughter had arrived.

Long before his death, Opiyo had prepared the skin of his biggest bull for his funeral. He had not only killed the bull himself but also lavished great care in curing the skin, readying it for the day when it would be wrapped around his naked body as a burial shroud. A man never used the skin of a cow—that would only ever be used for a woman. (This practice largely died out over the years from the influence of European missionaries, and most Luo are today buried in wooden coffins.) Opiyo's body lay inside his *duol* to the right of the door until later that morning, when he was buried within the confines of his homestead.

On the day of Opiyo's burial, his relatives built a bonfire next to his grave to honor the deceased. The fire was called *magenga,* and the big logs burned for several days as friends and relatives came to pay their respects. The *magenga* always has to be lit by a cousin and the eldest son of the dead man. Like the skin of the bull, Opiyo kept an old cockerel in his hut ready for the day of his burial. During the lighting of the *magenga,* the cockerel would be killed and then roasted on the flames to signify that the man has now gone and can no longer offer the household his protection. Along with the bird, Auko also prepared a traditional dish of *ugali* for the visitors.

By the evening, all Opiyo's relatives and his two married daughters had congregated by his grave, and for the next four days neighbors brought food to the house to help feed the visitors. The morning after the burial his family brought out Opiyo's three-legged stool, his fly whisk, and his clothes and placed them on his grave to accompany him to the next life. During the four-day mourning period, the women wailed and danced to chase away the "death spirits." They left the houses in the compound uncleaned until the last day, when his two wives performed *yweyo liel*—the "cleansing of the grave." This marked the start of a spring clean throughout the whole compound. On the fourth day, Opiyo's three sons, their wives, and his daughters also had their heads shaved in a symbolic act called *kwer,* which indicates to others that a person is bereaved. Opiyo's wives too had their heads shaved, and they continued to wear his clothes for several more months.

On the fourth day the mourners prepared to leave. As with other ceremonial functions with the Luo, seniority and sexual consummation were all part of the ritual; Opiyo's eldest son, Obilo, returned to his homestead and had sex with his wife before his two younger brothers could leave their father's compound; the other brothers also had to consummate the mourning period by having sex with their respective wives. If this is not done correctly, the Luo believe, you might become sick or bear a child with physical or mental problems. (Most Luo Christians, even those living in the cities, still practice this custom today.) Meanwhile, Opiyo's two wives continued to mourn their dead husband, rising early in the morning at dawn to sing and praise him, extolling his virtues to anyone who was listening.

Opiyo's widows, Auko and Saoke, were now restricted in what they could do and where they could go. After his death they were considered to be unclean—tainted by his death and capable of putting a curse on people. They could not enter another's hut for fear of bringing bad luck to the owner, nor could they shake hands with their friends, eat with them, or pick up their children. They could not stroll by a river for fear of it drying up, nor walk through a field of maize for risk of it shriveling. These women were in *chola,* and they could be released from this restriction only once they were "inherited."

During the first four days of mourning after Opiyo's death, his two brothers and his male cousins gathered in the family compound to decide which of them would inherit his wives. Inheritance is a process by which a dead man's wives are literally shared among his immediate relatives. It might be several weeks or even months before the women are finally inherited, but on the day of the inheritance, it is essential for the man to consummate the event with his new wife. Sometimes a man might inherit more than one wife, or even all of them, and he would be obliged to have sex with all of the women on that first night, in strict order of seniority. Any woman toward whom the man failed in his obligation on that first night was required to remain confined to her hut until another husband could be found to rise to the occasion.

If her married sons had not already established their own homestead before their father's death, then they could not do so until after their mother had been inherited. This rule placed pressure on women to agree to inheritance, no matter how much they might prefer otherwise. There are some restrictions over who can inherit a woman; for example, a woman could not be inherited by a man with whom she had previously had an extramarital affair. The woman might also object if she considered the man to be "of bad character," so there has always been some element of choice. However, in the past, the women would always be inherited by somebody. This tradition of wife inheritance might seem bizarre, but in a society or environment where survival is tough and tenuous, it does guarantee that any widowed woman and her children will be looked after and not abandoned.

In rural areas wife inheritance is still the norm and its modern-day practice is partly responsible for the high incidence of HIV/AIDS among the Luo population. Due to the great social stigma attached to being HIV positive, a man will often keep his illness hidden from his family and take his medication only at his place of work. When he dies, his wife might be quite oblivious to the fact that she is carrying the virus, and when she is inherited, she can pass it on to her new husband, and thence to his other wives.

Sometimes a woman will resist inheritance: Hawa Auma, aunt to President Obama, told me that when her husband died she refused to be inherited. Auma is a practicing Muslim, and many people in her mosque supported her firm stand. In the end, she agreed to a token inheritance but refused to allow the union to be consummated. Auma is a very strong-willed woman, but others are not quite so fortunate. In the village of Kajulu on the outskirts of Kisumu, there was recently a case of a widow, devoutly Christian, who spurned all attempts to be inherited. Her own son then died quite suddenly, leaving the woman's daughter-in-law widowed as well. Luo tradition forbids two widows from living in the same compound, so in order to bring pressure on the woman to be inherited, the village elders refused to bury her son. Within a matter of weeks, the woman relented.

On the day that Auko and Saoke were inherited, the family slaughtered a bull in celebration and the women discarded their dead husband's apparel for new clothes. They were now free from the taboo of Opiyo's death. The restrictions placed on other members of the family were now also lifted. Within a few months of Opiyo's death, all of the huts of his wives were destroyed and new ones built in a ceremony called *loko ot,* literally "changing hut."

Today, most Luo are Christians, and their families have been so for more than a century. Nevertheless, traditional rituals still play an important part when a Luo dies. Although most people are now buried in a shroud or a suit and their body is placed in a coffin rather than a bull's hide, every Luo insists on being buried in his or her own homestead. In 1987 the Nairobi courts heard a landmark case to determine the final resting place of a prominent Luo lawyer, S. M. Otieno. The trial held the attention of the nation for months. Otieno's widow, Virginia Wambui Otieno, was a member of the Kikuyu tribe, and their marriage in 1963—one of the first between a Kikuyu and a Luo—was considered to be shameful at the time. Mrs. Otieno argued that because her husband had led a modern life and had no regard for tribal customs, she had the right to bury him in a place of her own choosing; in this case, she wanted a nontribal burial on their farm near the Ngong Hills on the outskirts of Nairobi. The lawyer for Otieno's Luo clan argued that without a proper tribal burial in his homestead in Luoland, the ghost of Otieno would haunt and torment his surviving relatives.

Otieno's body lay in a Nairobi mortuary for more than four months while the dispute worked its way through the courts. Finally, the Nairobi Court of Appeal ruled in favor of the Luo tribe, arguing that it was impossible for a Kenyan citizen to disassociate himself from his tribe and its customs, especially those of a tribe such as the Luo, who still retain such strong traditions. The court ordered that Otieno's body be given to his fellow tribesmen for a traditional committal in his homeland near Lake Victoria. Although the judges said that tribal elders owed it to "themselves and their communities to ensure that customary laws keep abreast of positive modern trends," this significant legal ruling highlighted the power that tribalism still exerts in Kenya. To this day, neither Otieno's widow nor his children have visited his grave in Nyanza.

Otieno was an exceptional case; nearly every Luo wants and expects to be buried in his homestead. Even if an individual dies overseas after living abroad for many years, he or she would still want the body returned to the family compound. Many Luo now live and work in other parts of Kenya, especially Nairobi, so when there is a death in the family, relatives and friends can sometimes take several days to return to the family homestead. It has therefore become customary to preserve the body, either in a hospital mortuary or at home, to allow people time to pay their last respects.

Leo Odera Omolo said that as a boy, he always looked forward to a death in the village. "We would look at the old people, waiting for them to die. That way there was lots of singing and dancing, and plenty for people to eat and drink. It was a good excuse for a party, and we enjoyed ourselves!"

I have been to several Luo funerals, and it is clear that people attend them for many different reasons. The immediate family is grief-stricken, while others are in tears because the deceased owed them money and they know that now they will never be repaid. Local politicians use the events as an opportunity to press the flesh and make promises to the electorate that they are likely never to keep, and most of the rest of the company are there to eat, drink, and dance, or maybe just to pick a fight with somebody. After more than a hundred years of Christianity, the indigenous Luo traditions have been absorbed and integrated into Christian rituals, and the tribal influence still colors these major life events.

Many other strong Luo traditions persist to this day, even among modern city dwellers. Husbands and wives have to respect rigid taboos when visiting the compound of their in-laws. For example, when one of a Luo's in-laws dies, the person cannot visit the in-law's homestead until after the burial; to view the corpse would effectively be "to see them naked." If a man visits the house of his wife's parents, he must never look at the ceiling. If a man's in-laws come to visit him, they must never sit opposite the door leading to the marital bedroom. Nor would someone ever accept (or be offered) food in an in-law's homestead, or sleep there. To do so would break an indissoluble taboo.

Recently in Kajulu, a bad tropical storm prevented a couple from returning home after visiting their daughter and son-in-law. They had no option but to stay the night; this was quite acceptable providing the parents-in-law sat upright and stayed awake all night. Unfortunately it was a long night, nature took its course, and both parents fell asleep. This serious breach of protocol had only one possible solution: the house had to be destroyed completely.

This rule raises serious problems, of course, for the president of the United States. When he moved to Washington, D.C., with his family in January 2008, he invited his wife's mother, Marian Robinson, to live with them and help raise their two daughters. By Luo tradition, there is only one way to break the taboo created by such a rash decision—and that is to knock down the White House.

4

THE WAZUNGU ARRIVE

RIEKO LO TEKO

Brain is mightier than brawn

SWAHILI IS an East African Bantu language that has been greatly influenced by Arabic; its very name comes from the Arabic *sawāhilī* (meaning "of the coast"). Swahili has always been a lingua franca, enabling people with different native tongues and different origins to come together, to communicate, and especially to trade. In the nineteenth century, Swahili-speakers had to find a new word to describe the increasing number of European traders who were appearing on the shores of East Africa. It did not occur to them to choose an obvious word linking the Europeans to their color, because in their eyes, the odd-looking strangers could be anything from white to pink, red, or brown, depending on how much time they spent in the sun. Instead, the Swahili-speakers coined the word *wazungu* (*mzungu* in the singular) to describe the newcomers as "people who move around."

The East African coast had welcomed many foreigners long before the first Europeans arrived at the end of the fifteenth century. Attracted by the lucrative profits to be made in gold and ivory from the African continent, Arabs traded along the coast as early as two centuries before the Christian era. Commerce with India came later, around the seventh century, and then in 1414 a huge fleet of sixty-two Chinese trading galleons and 190 support ships under the command of Zheng He crossed the Indian Ocean and landed on the African coast.[1] Fourteenth-century Chinese maps show the East African coast in great detail, suggesting that they had been sending trading missions to the region for some time before Zheng He's armada arrived. This trade with both the Arabs and the Chinese disproves the myth that Africa—the "Dark Continent"—had little or no contact with the outside world until it was "opened up" by Europeans.

Toward the end of the fifteenth century, just as the Luo were leaving their cradleland in Sudan and migrating south up the Nile valley toward Uganda, the Portuguese landed on East African shores. On July 8, 1497, just five years after Columbus set sail for the New World, the Portuguese mariner Vasco da Gama departed from Lisbon with a small fleet of four ships. Like Columbus, he hoped to find a sea route to the spices and other riches of the Orient. Da Gama, however, chose to sail east around the southern cape of Africa—a longer and much more challenging task than crossing the Atlantic. As he sailed into the Indian Ocean, da Gama was entering unknown territory, where no white-skinned European had yet traveled. By the time da Gama's fleet reached Mombasa on the east coast of Africa, the Arabs—who dominated trade in the Indian Ocean—were waiting for him. They launched a seaborne attack to cut the Portuguese anchor ropes. Da Gama retreated and sailed farther north to Malindi (Melinde), where he finally found a friendly sultan. The association between the Portuguese and the town lasted almost two hundred years; the Church of St. Francis Xavier was built during da Gama's visit, and the building survives to this day as one of the oldest churches on the continent.

Da Gama signed a trade agreement with the local rulers in Malindi, which heralded the onset of European involvement in East Africa. Two years later, in 1500, the Portuguese sacked Mombasa in retaliation for the earlier snub and established a series of trading posts and forts along the coast, including the construction of Fort Jesus in Mombasa in 1593. By skillfully manipulating the rivalries between Malindi and Mombasa and other independently governed towns on the coast, the Portuguese successfully dominated much of the coastal trade in the region for a century.

Trade between East Africa and the rest of the world continued to flourish; Indian cotton, Chinese porcelain, and metalwork from the Middle East were traded for slaves, ivory, and gold. However, several environmental factors in sub-Saharan Africa inhibited trade and travel. The prevalence of the tsetse fly (which carries the parasite that causes trypanosomiasis, affecting both humans and animals) in large areas of highland savannah severely limited the use of pack animals for transporting goods. Unlike other parts of coastal Africa, East Africa has no large rivers running inland and the highland tributaries are too shallow and fast-flowing for the extended use of boats and canoes. As a result, any exploration or trade inland relied on human porterage. Before the British built a railway at the beginning of the twentieth century, the only route inland from the coast to Lake Victoria was a meandering track through dense tropical jungle; a return trip could take as much as six or seven months. Food had to be purchased or hunted en route, tolls paid to ensure safe passage, and the loads were limited to what could be carried by human porters—effectively no more than about sixty-five pounds. Therefore the trade to and from the interior mostly involved items of high value and low weight: rare skins, ivory, copper and gold, glass beads, cotton textiles, and, in later years, tobacco, guns, and liquor. Slaves were also traded, and they had the additional advantage of being able to walk.

Ever since the Spanish opened up the New World at the beginning of the sixteenth century, the European nations had been on an imperialist binge around the globe. But given the difficulties of accessing the interior, they paid scant attention to East Africa—at least at the beginning. The Spanish and Portuguese colonization of the Americas in the 1500s was soon emulated by Great Britain, France, and the Netherlands.

India and other Asian countries became absorbed by the burgeoning European empires, which sought new spheres of influence around the world, and sources of raw materials to fuel the rapid industrialization back home. Only in the late nineteenth century, after they had carved up most of the rest of the world, did Europeans turn their attention to the division and colonization of Africa.

After the Portuguese left the East African coast for good in 1720, bloody and bowed by repeated conflicts with local rulers and the Arabs, the sultan of Oman became the undisputed ruler of the coastal region. However, he proved ineffectual, appointing governors from rival families in Pate, Mombasa, and Zanzibar who soon began to fight among themselves. In 1822 the new ruler of Oman, Seyyid Sa'id, finally sent a fleet of heavily armed warships to subdue the querulous city-states. The Mazruis in Mombasa had no defense except for their puny muskets and the massive stone walls of Fort Jesus. At the time, two British survey ships, HMS *Leven* and HMS *Barracouta,* were on a Royal Navy mission to survey the east coast of Africa. The Mazrui chief pleaded with Captain Fitzwilliam Owen to make Mombasa a British protectorate and defend them against the sultan's fleet. In return for British protection, the Mazrui agreed to assist the British in ridding East Africa of the scourge of slavery.[2] With imagination and foresight, Owen realized what Britain could achieve in this part of Africa. On February 7, 1824, the Royal Navy hoisted the Union Flag over Fort Jesus; it was the start of Britain's domination of East Africa, which would last for the next 140 years.

The European exploration of the interior of East Africa began in earnest in the middle decades of the nineteenth century. In early 1844, Dr. Johann Ludwig Krapf, a German Protestant missionary and accomplished linguist, arrived in Zanzibar. His ambition was to link the east and west coasts of Africa with a chain of Christian missions. He soon moved on to Mombasa with his wife, Rosine, and their newborn daughter; tragically, both mother and child soon died of malaria. In spite of his deep depression from this shocking introduction to the privations of nineteenth-century Africa, he persevered and moved inland to establish his first mission on higher ground at Rabai. But his spirits did not fully recover until the arrival of a Swiss Lutheran missionary, Johannes Rebmann. Together they became known, not for their missionary work, nor for their translation of the Bible into Kiswahili (the name of the language in Swahili), but for their expeditions into the interior.

Together, Krapf and Rebmann became the first Europeans to see the snow-capped Mount Kilimanjaro in 1848, and then Mount Kenya the following year. (Krapf recorded it originally as Kenia, which he learned from the indigenous tribes who live around the mountain.) The local Embu people told Krapf that they did not climb high on the mountain because of the intense cold and that "white matter" rolled down the mountains with a loud noise. Noting that the rivers on the slopes of Mount Kenya flowed continuously, unlike other rivers in the area, which dried up after the rainy season had ended, Krapf and Rebmann deduced that glaciers existed on these equatorial mountains—a correct deduction that was initially greeted with derision by the scientific community.[3]

From information gleaned on their travels, Johannes Rebmann also co-created the "slug map"—an ambitious but ultimately misleading representation of East Africa, showing a single huge lake in the center of Kenya. The map, which was presented to the Royal Geographical Society in London in 1855, did much to stimulate further interest in the region, as armchair travelers who had never set foot in Africa argued fiercely about Krapf and Rebmann's findings.

The travels of Krapf and Rebmann pioneered the early exploration of East Africa, but their travels only highlighted how little was known of the African interior and other adventurers soon followed. Next into the region were the British explorers Richard Burton and John Speke, eager to find the great lakes which were said to exist in the center of the continent and to locate the source of the White Nile. Burton and Speke mounted their expedition in 1856, a year after the "slug map" came to London. Like Krapf and Rebmann before them, they found the travel arduous, and both men fell ill from a variety of tropical diseases. In 1858 Speke sighted a vast lake, which he named after the British queen, and claimed it to be the source of the Nile. This infuriated Burton, who was too ill to travel at the time and who considered the matter still unresolved. This very public quarrel between two of Britain's greatest explorers only generated even more interest among geographers back home, encouraging others who were keen to either confirm or disprove Speke's claims.

By the middle of the nineteenth century, finding the exact location of the headwaters of the White Nile had taken on an importance that is difficult to comprehend today. It resulted not only from the excitement of exploring a continent hitherto unknown, but also from the British government's obsession with gaining strategic control over large parts of the world. East Africa became even more important in 1858, when the Compagnie Universelle du Canal Maritime de Suez started work on a canal to connect the Mediterranean to the Red Sea. The British considered this French-backed project to be a threat to their geopolitical and financial interests in the region, even though the canal was intended to be open to all nations. They instigated a revolt among the workers, bringing the construction to a halt.[4] Despite these setbacks, the canal opened to shipping in November 1869, and it played an important role in speeding up the European colonization of East Africa by offering a quicker route to the Indian Ocean.

Even before the Suez Canal was opened, David Livingstone, the Scottish medical missionary and explorer, began his own search for the headwaters of the Nile. Livingstone had worked in South Africa since 1840, but now in January 1866 he arrived in Zanzibar to mount his first expedition in East Africa. He believed the source of the Nile was farther south than the great lakes; assembling a team of freed slaves, he set off inland and reached Lake Malawi in early August. However, his mission was not a great success; one by one, his porters deserted him, and most of his supplies and all of his medicines were stolen. Livingstone then traveled north through difficult swampy terrain toward Lake Tanganyika, but with his health declining, he had to join a group of slave traders to stay alive. Livingstone was ill for most of the last four years of his life, suffering pneumonia, cholera, and tropical ulcers on his feet.

Livingstone was appalled by the scale and barbarity of the slave trade in East Africa, which had continued despite Captain Owen's attempts to contain it more than forty years previously. His reports back to England referred to what he called the "great open sore of the world":

> To overdraw its evils is a simple impossibility. . . . We passed a slave woman shot or stabbed through the body and lying on the path. [Onlookers] said an Arab who passed early that morning had done it in anger at losing the price he had given for her, because she was unable to walk any longer. We passed a woman tied by the neck to a tree and dead. . . . We came upon a man dead from starvation. . . . The strangest disease I have seen in this country seems really to be broken heartedness, and it attacks free men who have been captured and made slaves.[5]

Slavery was not new in Africa, where the use of forced labor goes back more than five thousand years. The Egyptian king Sneferu recorded in the third century BCE that he had attacked neighboring Nubia and brought back 7,000 black slaves and 200,000 head of cattle.[6] The Arabs too traded extensively in human labor, and although the Prophet Muhammad laid down precise rules about the ownership of unbelievers, the Qur'an does not explicitly forbid human bondage.

Elikia M'Bokolo, a renowned Congolese historian, has written passionately about this international crime from the perspective of an African:

> The African continent was bled of its human resources via all possible routes. Across the Sahara, through the Red Sea, from the Indian Ocean ports and across the Atlantic. At least ten centuries of slavery for the benefit of the Muslim countries (from the ninth to the nineteenth). Then more than four centuries (from the end of the fifteenth to the nineteenth) of a regular slave trade to build the Americas and the prosperity of the Christian states of Europe. The figures, even where hotly disputed, make your head spin. Four million slaves exported via the Red Sea, another four million through the Swahili ports of the Indian Ocean, perhaps as many as nine million along the trans-Saharan caravan route, and eleven to twenty million (depending on the author) across the Atlantic Ocean.[7]

Even by the end of the nineteenth century, an estimated fifty thousand slaves still passed through the slave-trading center of Zanzibar every year; from here, they were bound for the markets of Turkey, Arabia, India, and Persia. The Arab traders in East Africa had a reputation for being more brutal than the Europeans and made less effort to keep their slaves from dying. It has been estimated that for every five Africans taken prisoner in the continental interior, perhaps only one reached the slave markets in the Middle East, while the rest died en route. Nor could the Arab slave traders have been quite so successful without the assistance of the Africans themselves. Since it was easier to buy slaves brought to the coast than to hunt them down and capture them inland, the Arabs relied heavily on Africans, and especially the Kamba people, who lived between the coast and the central highlands in Kenya, to act as middlemen and organize huge caravans to bring slaves and ivory from the interior.[8]

The Luhya people of western Kenya also helped the traders. Their leader, Nabong'o Shiundu, was particularly keen to find allies who could help him build his power in the region, and he became notorious for capturing other Africans, including Luo, and selling them to the Arab slave traders.[9] The island of Zanzibar and the nearby port of Kilwa on the mainland became the largest African shipping points for the trade, and as demand continued, Arab slavers penetrated farther and farther inland, even as far as Uganda and Congo, in search of new sources of slaves. Eventually in 1873 the British forced the ruler of Zanzibar to close his slave market and to forbid the export of slaves from the regions under his control. (Enforcing this rule was not easy, and even as late as the 1970s the United Nations received complaints of a thriving trade in black slaves from East Africa.)

Leo Odera described some of the personal encounters that his Luo ancestors had with the slave traders:

> It used to be very common in this part of the world. It caused chaos and whole families would move on to evade the traders. Many years back when my family was still in Busoga in Uganda, the slave traders took many people, including Chwanya, one of my ancestors. The family did not expect him to return and they even held a mock funeral to mourn his passing. However, his son Onyango Rabala followed the Arabs. Onyango found them feasting by the lake and with the slaves in chains in a dhow. The slavers were cooking a long way from the water because of the danger from crocodiles, so Onyango swam up to the boat and pushed it into the lake—and it had all their weapons on board too! In Dholuo, we have a saying: *rieko lo teko*—brain is mightier than brawn. The Arabs ran away too frightened to retaliate, and Onyango rescued his father and two other slaves chained to him. When he returned, there was a great taboo because he had been mourned as dead and there were many rituals to be performed. He had to sleep in the granary for three days and eventually his second wife took him back.

Meanwhile, David Livingstone was still on his quest to find the source of the White Nile; however, by 1870 his reports back to London had ceased and the journalist Henry Morton Stanley was sent by the

New York Herald newspaper to find the missing explorer; he arrived in Zanzibar in March 1871. Stanley was a Welshman, born in Denbigh; his father was either John Rowlands, the town drunk, who later died from delirium tremens, or James Vaughan, a married lawyer from London and a regular customer of Stanley's mother—a nineteen-year-old prostitute. The baby's name was entered into the birth register of St. Hilary's Church as "John Rowlands, bastard," and Stanley spent his life trying to live down the shame of being born illegitimate. As a five-year-old, he was given up to a workhouse; when he was released at seventeen, he fled Wales for America, where he changed his name in an attempt to erase his past. Stanley landed in New Orleans in 1858, and during the American Civil War he fought for the Confederacy before being taken prisoner, whereupon he changed sides and fought for the Union. He covered the Indian Wars as a journalist and gained a reputation for taking on risky assignments, but the thought of going to Africa terrified him. He called it an "eternal, feverish region" and had nightmares about what he might experience—even contemplating suicide.

Nevertheless, he assembled one of the biggest expeditions ever to set out from Zanzibar; his party was so large that he divided it into five separate caravans and staggered their departure to avoid attack and robbery. Hearing rumors in Zanzibar that a white man had been seen in the region of Ujiji, about 750 miles inland, he set off for the interior at the end of March with some 190 men, armed guards, and a guide carrying the American flag. On July 4, 1871, Stanley sent his first dispatch back to New York from Unyanyembe district, in modern-day Tanzania, in the form of a five-thousand-word letter. The resulting piece, which filled the front page of the *Herald,* quoted Stanley's letter extensively, and ended with a promise from the journalist:

> Our explorer says (July 4):—"If the Doctor is at Ujiji, in one month more and I will see him, then the race for home will begin"; but that "until I hear more of him, or see the long-absent old man face to face, I bid farewell. But wherever he is be sure I shall not give up on the chase." Good words these from a trusty man.[10]

In one of the great encounters in history, Stanley found Livingstone
in Ujiji, on the shores of Lake Tanganyika, on November 10, 1871. Stanley greeted the explorer with the now famous words, "Dr. Livingstone, I
presume?" to which Livingstone apparently responded, "Yes, and I feel
thankful that I am here to welcome you." There is no direct record of
this exchange—Stanley tore the pages describing this encounter out of
his diary, and Livingstone does not mention these words in his own
account. However, they do appear in the first description of the meeting, published in the *New York Times,* dated July 2, 1872:

> I noticed in the center of a group of Arabs, strongly contrasting
> their sun-burned faces, a hale-looking, gray-bearded white man,
> wearing a naval cap, with a faded gold band, and a red woolen shirt,
> preserving a calmness of exterior before the Arabs. I enquired, "DR.
> LIVINGSTONE, I presume?"
>
> He, smiling, answered yes.[11]

Stanley urged the missionary to return to the coast with him, but
Livingstone was determined not to leave until his task—that of finding
the source of the Nile—was complete. However, it was not to be; Livingstone died in Zambia, in the village of Ilala, on May 1, 1873, from a
combination of malaria and internal bleeding caused by dysentery. Two
of Livingstone's loyal servants buried his heart at the foot of a nearby
tree. Then they dried and wrapped his body and carried it back with
his papers and instruments to the island of Zanzibar—a trip that took
them nine months to complete. In April 1874 Livingstone's remains
reached England by ship, and he was buried in Westminster Abbey in
London.

Henry Stanley was inspired by the expeditions of Livingstone and others, and in 1874 the *New York Herald* and the *Daily Telegraph* in London

partnered to finance a return trip. He had several objectives: first, to circumnavigate Lake Victoria and confirm Speke's claim that it was a single body of water and the source of the White Nile; second, to finish Livingstone's work of mapping the Lualaba River, which Livingstone thought might be the Nile itself; and finally and most ambitiously of all, to traverse the continent from east to west and thereby trace the course of the river Congo to the Atlantic. In circumnavigating Lake Victoria, he almost certainly became the first European to make direct contact with the Luo of western Kenya.

The challenge that Stanley set himself can hardly be overstated, even considering the extraordinary precedents set by other explorers. His preparations back in England for the expedition were hopelessly rushed, and he later wrote: "Two weeks were allowed me for purchasing boats—a yawl, a gig, and a barge—for giving orders for pontoons, and purchasing equipment, guns, ammunition, rope, saddles, medical stores, and provisions; for making investments in gifts for native chiefs; for obtaining scientific instruments, stationery, &c., &c."[12] Stanley left for Zanzibar on September 21, 1874.

By this time, the Luo had long finished their great migration. Rapidly increasing their population throughout the nineteenth century, the clans had spread both north and south of the Winam Gulf. Although other tribes lived in the area, the Luo were the dominant group, having very effectively assimilated many of the indigenous people into their tribe. In Alego, to the north of the Gulf, the descendants of the great leaders Owiny and Kishodi were still living in K'ogelo; Obong'o, (3) great-grandfather to President Obama, had left Alego some forty years before to establish a new subclan in the less crowded Kendu Bay area of south Nyanza. By 1874 his three sons, Obama, Opiyo, and Aguk, were in their prime and their families were well established on the southern shore of Winam Gulf.

Back on the coast, Stanley left Zanzibar on November 12, 1874, for the mainland and began his remarkable trek across Africa, with his porters carrying his boats in sections overland to Lake Victoria. This first stage of his expedition took 103 days and his pedometer recorded a distance of 715 miles through dense equatorial jungle. When the expedition eventually reached Kagehyi on the southeastern shore of Lake Victoria, their first task was to assemble their boats. The biggest vessel in his fleet was a steam-powered sailing sloop, the *Lady Alice,* which had been carried from Zanzibar in four parts. On March 8, 1875, Stanley wrote in his diary:

> At 1 p.m. after vainly endeavouring to persuade Kaduma Chief of Kagehyi to accompany me as a guide as far as Ururi, I sailed from Kagehyi with 10 stout sailors of the Expedition in the *Lady Alice,* a cedar boat 24 feet long and 6 feet wide which we have carried in sections from the Coast for the purpose of exploring the Lakes of Central Africa. The men were rather downhearted and rowed reluctantly, as we have had many a grievous prophecy that we shall all drown in the Lake, or die at the hands of some of the ferocious people living on the shores of the Nyanza.[13]

In little more than two weeks, the expedition had sailed up the east coast of the lake and Stanley was approaching Luoland. At this point, his main concern was hippos in the water—they are still considered to be one of the most dangerous animals in Africa. On March 22, he stopped at what he called Bridge Island and wrote:

> The island is covered with mangrove trees, whose branches extend far into the water, under which our boat might be screened by their deep shade. . . . From the summit of the island which is easy of access we obtained a fine view of lofty Ugingo Island and the tall steep mountains of Ugeyeya with the level plain of Wagansu and Wigassi.

From this point onward, Stanley was off the coast of Nyanza—Luoland. He wanted to go ashore to learn the names of some of the villages, but a large gathering of men carrying spears caused him to think better of it. A small, unpopulated island a safe distance away seemed a wiser choice to spend the night. Two days later, on March 24, the group landed at a place Stanley called Muiwanda, and he negotiated with the people to bring food to them:

> We anchored within an arrow's flight from the shore and began to persuade the natives to bring food to us, by holding out a bunch of beads. . . . Finally trade was opened, and while trading for food I found the people very friendly and disposed to answer all my questions. They spoke the language of Usoga with a slight dialectic difference. Neither men nor women wore anything, save a kirtle of grass, or plantain leaves which the latter wore. Men had extracted two front teeth of lower jaw, had bracelets of iron rings, rings above elbows and in ears. Shaved their heads in eccentric fashion . . .

The Usoga people (now known as the Wasoga) result from intermarriage between the Luo and the Luhya. (The Luhya remove two lower teeth as an initiation, unlike the Luo's six.)

Stanley's map of Lake Victoria shows that he completely missed the extent of Winam Gulf, assuming instead that the narrow entrance to this large bay was only the mouth of a small river. Three days later, on March 27, Stanley made contact with another group, this time on the northern side of Winam Gulf:

> They came to repeat the request of Kamoydah, the King [to come ashore], but we begged to be excused from moving from our present safe anchorage, the waves were rough, the wind was strong. They begged, they implored and all but threatened. Three more canoes now came up loaded with men, and these added their united voices to invite us on the part of the King to his shore. Finding us still obstinate, they laid hands on the boat, and their insolence increased almost to fighting pitch.

The following day, they had another couple of unsettling encounters with the locals:

In the morning while sailing close to the shore we were stoned by the people. Two great rocks came near to crushing the boat's sides, but a few revolver shots stopped that game. Arriving between the islands of Bugeyeya and Uvuma, we had the misfortune to come across a nest of Lake pirates who make navigation impossible for the Waganda. Ignorant of their character we allowed 13 canoes to range alongside and commenced a friendly conversation with them, but I was soon informed of their character when they made an indiscriminate rush upon the boat. Again I beat them off with my revolver, and having got them a little distance off opened fire with my elephant rifle—with which I smashed three canoes, and killed four men. We continued on our way hence immediately to the Napoleon Channel, and after a look at the great river outflowing northward [the Victoria Nile at the Ripon Falls], sailed to Marida where we rested secure and comfortable.

Stanley's violent confrontation with the locals was an inauspicious start to British involvement in western Kenya, and back in Britain, people were beginning to be outspokenly critical of his actions. In his later years, Stanley was obliged to defend himself against the charge that his African expeditions had been marked by cruelty and gratuitous violence; he argued that "the savage only respects force, power, boldness, and decision."[14] In many ways, Henry Stanley was an enigma. From his writings, it is clear that he had a benevolent attitude toward many of the Africans he traveled with, to whom he owed both his success and survival on the continent. This included Kalulu, his boy servant who loyally stayed with Stanley from 1882 to 1887—Stanley even wrote a children's book about Kalulu's life, and dedicated it to the end of slavery.[15] On the other hand, he was capable of using excessive violence, racial abuse, and condescending language toward Africans. He was, essentially, a man of his time.

Stanley succeeded in circumnavigating Lake Victoria, a voyage that took him two months, before heading west to trace the course of the river Congo to the Atlantic. He eventually reached a Portuguese outpost at the mouth of the river in August 1877, 999 days after leaving

Zanzibar. Crossing central Africa was a remarkable feat, and of the 359 people who started on the expedition, only 108 survived. Stanley's three British companions, Frederick Barker and Francis and Edward Pocock, all died during the expedition, as did his trusted servant, Kalulu.

Stanley's expedition resolved the long-standing question of whether Lake Victoria really was the source of the Nile (something the Arabs had long known); the lake is clearly shown on a twelfth-century map drawn by the cartographer Al Idrisi. (Strictly speaking, Lake Victoria is only a feeder lake to the Nile; the true source of the Nile is the Luvironza [or Ruvyironza], which is the longest river to flow into Lake Victoria, and which bubbles up from high ground in the mountains of Burundi.) Although the lake is not quite as impressive as depicted on the "slug map," it is still a vast body of water with a surface area of 26,600 square miles—making it bigger than the state of West Virginia and the second-largest freshwater lake in the world, after Lake Superior.

By 1880 a new imperialism was beginning to emerge among the industrialized nations. Germany, the United States, Belgium, Italy, and, for the first time, an Asian power, Japan, were all beginning to compete for what little "unclaimed space" remained in the world. As the rivalry among colonizing nations reached new heights, the nations with established empires—primarily Great Britain and France—consolidated their territorial gains. Technology too began to have an effect: the Suez Canal was now open and modern steamships could sail from Europe to East Africa in a fraction of the time previously required to sail around the Cape of Good Hope. The railway and the telegraph were revolutionizing transport and communication on land, and new advances in medicines to treat tropical diseases—especially quinine as an effective treatment for malaria—now allowed vast regions of the tropics to be accessed more safely by Europeans. The time was ripe for the biggest land grab in history.

The division of Africa—the last continent to be carved up by the European nations—was essentially a product of this "new imperialism." Prior to 1880, the colonial possessions of European nations in Africa were relatively modest and were mainly limited to the coastal areas, leaving almost all the interior still independent. By 1900, almost all of Africa had been placed under the administration of various European nations.

Colonial powers had been particularly slow to establish a real presence in East Africa, which is no surprise considering the privations experienced by the early missionaries and explorers and the lack of easy river access to the interior. Furthermore, the reports of Krapf and Burton suggested that the East African region consisting of modern Kenya and northern Tanzania was ill-suited to peaceful infiltration, since this was the province of the Maasai and other warring tribes, through whose land even the armed caravans of the Arab traders feared to travel.

The first traders from overseas who were interested in neither slaves nor ivory had been American merchants from ports in New England and New York. By 1805, forty-eight trading ships from Salem, Massachusetts, were reported to have sailed around the Cape of Good Hope into the Indian Ocean, and the first American vessel is believed to have reached Zanzibar in 1817. The United States dominated the East African trade until the Civil War, when the country lost its preeminent trading position to British, German, and Indian traders. However, trade in the region was generally slow, and by the middle of the nineteenth century East Africa was still a backwater.

Livingstone's emotional reports about the Arab slave trade, which touched the public mood back home, provided the great stimulus in Victorian Britain to opening up East Africa. In particular, his last journey to Africa and his subsequent death in 1873 fired the imagination of missionaries to come and work in Africa. In the mid-1870s, Anglican missionaries began establishing new mission stations deep in the interior. A missionary who arrived with a few dozen porters to establish a mission in a native village had to set up what amounted to a small independent state, where he was recognized as a kind of chief by the other local headmen.[16] By 1885 most of the nearly three hundred Europeans living in East Africa were Catholic or Anglican missionaries.[17] Initially they won few converts. Islam had long been established on the coast, and the Arab traders had helped bring it into the interior. After 1880, however, Christian missionaries made significant inroads in the Buganda region, and by the end of the century Christianity was beginning to spread quickly throughout the region.

Around the middle part of the nineteenth century, the perceived wisdom in London held that African territories were too expensive to run and the potential yields too low to make a profit. As Europe's foremost imperial power, Britain was keen to maintain an influence in the region, but it was not really interested in exercising any real power.[18] Instead, Britain had three priorities on the continent, none of which required direct governance: closing the slave trade with the Middle East, encouraging the expansion of Christianity, and allowing legitimate trade to flourish. Missionaries tried to encourage British merchants and ship owners to establish a commercial presence in East Africa, but the response was mostly limited to Scottish entrepreneurs inspired by their countryman David Livingstone. William Mackinnon, a Glaswegian ship owner and member of the Free Church of Scotland, was one such businessman; he started out in life as a grocer's assistant and rose to become one of the wealthiest men in Britain, running vessels from his British India Steam Navigation Company to and from Zanzibar from 1872 onward.

Up until the 1880s, 80 percent of the African continent remained under traditional and local control, with foreign interests confined almost entirely to the coastal areas. Then in 1885, in one of the most cynical and avaricious moves ever undertaken by colonial powers,

5

THE NEW IMPERIALISM

KIK ILAW WINY ARIYO

Don't chase two birds at once

THE INDIVIDUAL responsible for changing much of the face of East Africa in 1885 was a reckless, hot-headed young German student called Karl Peters. The son of a Lutheran minister, Peters was born in the small north German village of Neuhaus, on the banks of the river Elbe. In 1879 he left Berlin University with a degree in history and moved to London, where he stayed with a wealthy uncle. During his four years in London, Peters studied British history and its colonial policies, developing a deep contempt and loathing for the British; at the same time he became passionate about the new opportunities for German imperialist expansion. In 1884 his uncle committed suicide and Peters returned to Germany. Fired up with nationalistic zeal, and supported by like-minded contemporaries, the twenty-eight-year-old established the Gesellschaft für Deutsche Kolonisation—the Society for German Colonization. At its first executive committee meeting, the group clearly defined its objectives: "the founding of German plantation and commercial colonies by securing adequate capital for colonisation, by finding and securing possession of regions suitable for colonisation, and by attracting German immigrants to those regions."[1]

The express aim of their society was to propel Germany headlong into rivalry with the two leading imperial nations in Europe—Britain and France—and it did not take long for them to realize their ambitions. By 1884, Chancellor Otto von Bismarck of Germany had reversed his previous declaration that he had no wish to acquire overseas colonies.[2] That year, Germany made its first real bid for membership in the colonial club when it announced territorial claims in South West Africa, in Togoland and Cameroon, as well as part of the East African coast opposite Zanzibar. Germany was joined by Belgium and Italy—two small European nations with no previous colonial ambitions—which declared an interest in Congo and the Red Sea region, respectively. Even Portugal and Spain once again became interested in claiming bits of African territory.

Fearing that the stampede to claim African territories could easily get out of hand and lead to military confrontation, Bismarck readily agreed when the Portuguese asked the Germans to convene a meeting of European powers to resolve their interests in Africa. The conference opened in Berlin on November 15, 1884, and a plethora of ambassadors and politicians attended from fourteen European countries. Few of the participants, if indeed any at all, had ever set foot in Africa. For a full three months the European nations haggled over the partition of the continent, completely ignoring any of the cultural or linguistic boundaries already established by the indigenous populations.

By the end of February 1885, Africa had been carved up into fifty irregular countries. In this new "imperial" map of Africa, borders were often drawn arbitrarily, with little or no regard for ethnic unity, regional economic ties, migratory patterns of people, or even natural boundaries. The only logic or reason that applied to the map was that of political expediency around the conference table in Berlin, and the boundaries established there have created tribal tension and conflict in Africa ever since.

On November 4, 1884—just two weeks before the negotiations began in Berlin—Karl Peters and his two companions, Karl Ludwig Jühlke and Count Joachim von Pfeil, arrived in Zanzibar intent on realizing their imperial ambitions. All three were still under the age of thirty. Their trip had not been sanctioned by the German government, and the German consul in Zanzibar showed Peters a communication from the German Foreign Office stating that Peters could expect from the government "neither Imperial protection nor any guarantees for his safety."[3] Undeterred, they disguised themselves as mechanics and crossed over to the mainland at Bagamoyo, where they began to establish a German colonial presence in East Africa. Within days, they succeeded in negotiating their first treaty with an African chief on behalf of the Gesellschaft für Deutsche Kolonisation. Encouraged by their first audacious success, the three young Germans pushed on and made several more treaties with neighboring tribes. Msovero, a local chief in Usagara, agreed to offer "all his territories with all its civil and public appurtenances to Dr. Karl Peters . . . for all time," while in return, Peters agreed to "give special attention to Msovero when colonising Usagara."[4] Peters later wrote about this initiative:

> As the Gesellschaft wanted to found independent German colonies under the German flag, its activity naturally was limited to those areas which at that time had not yet been taken. In fact, only Africa was suitable. . . . Already in November 1884 this task basically had been fulfilled by the expedition sent via Zanzibar. On December 14th 1884 I found myself, as representative of the Society for German Colonisation, as the rightful owner of 2,500 square miles of very lush tropical land, located to the west of Zanzibar.[5]

By the middle of December—after just six weeks in East Africa—Peters had signed a total of twelve agreements with the "sultans" of four inland regions, which gave him theoretical control of more than sixty thousand square miles of the East African mainland. In practice, of course, these treaties were hardly worth the paper they were written on, as it is unlikely that the Africans had any idea of what they were actually ceding; their real value, however, was to demonstrate to other colonial powers that Germany had prior claim to the region. The young German had achieved exactly what he needed.

Peters returned to Germany as quickly as possible, and on February 12, 1885, two weeks before the conclusion of the Berlin Conference, he founded the Deutsche Ost-Afrika Gesellschaft—the German East Africa Company—to which he assigned all his African territories. With the Berlin Conference coming to a close, Bismarck refused at first to accept responsibility for the new acquisitions in Africa. But Peters had a very strong fallback position: he threatened to cede the land to King Leopold II of Belgium. On February 17 Bismarck agreed to issue an imperial charter—a *Schutzbrief*—that placed all the territories acquired by the German East Africa Company under the protection of the emperor, Kaiser Wilhelm I. This impudent but brilliant move by the young German adventurer inevitably provoked vociferous complaints from established overseas interests in the region. The British had previously acquired treaties inland around the foothills of Mount Kilimanjaro, and a group of entrepreneurs had ambitious plans to build a railway between the coast and Lake Victoria. Now they had some real competition.

In response to Karl Peters' inspired initiative and the creation of a German protectorate, the British formed the British East Africa Association (BEAA). After several months of saber-rattling in London and Berlin, the Anglo-German Agreement was signed in 1886, followed by a second treaty in 1890 that consolidated the arrangements. With these two treaties, Britain and Germany agreed on their spheres of influence in East Africa. The dividing line ran from the coast south of Mombasa to a point on the eastern shore of Lake Victoria, cutting straight across East Africa in a northwesterly direction, except in one place where it kinked around Mount Kilimanjaro. (Queen Victoria wanted her grandson, the German kaiser, to have his own "big mountain" in Africa.) Everywhere north of the border became the Protectorate of British East

Africa, and Germany took the area south of the line. This left the Luo who lived around Winam Gulf under British rule, although a small number of Luo living farther south fell under German control.

In 1891 Peters was made *Reichskommissar* (imperial high commissioner) to German East Africa, but within a few years rumors began to reach Berlin of his cruel and inhumane treatment of Africans. He is said to have used local girls as concubines, and when he discovered that one of his lovers had had an affair with his manservant, he had them both hanged and their home villages destroyed. This earned him the name *mukono wa damu*—"the man with blood on his hands." He was recalled to Berlin, where a judicial hearing officially condemned him for his violent attacks on African natives; he was dismissed from government service and deprived of his government pension. Ironically, Peters sought refuge in London, where he continued to develop further interests elsewhere in Africa. Back home in Germany many people still considered him to be a national hero; Kaiser Wilhelm II later reinstated him as imperial commissioner and awarded him a pension from his own private budget. Twenty years after his death in 1918, Peters was officially rehabilitated by the personal decree of Adolf Hitler, who feted him as an ideological hero, even commissioning a Nazi propaganda film in 1941 about Peters' life. He remains a controversial figure to this day.

The creation of British East Africa took place on two levels. The first, on paper, had already been hammered out in diplomatic meetings in London and Berlin. Now the second stage was about to begin, as Britain came to terms with taking control of an area that was bigger than metropolitan France and nearly twice the size of German East Africa.[6] In 1888, with an investment of £240,000, the British East Africa Association received a royal charter and was renamed the Imperial British East Africa Company (IBEAC). The ambitions of IBEAC were impressive—at least superficially; the company would act as both a trading and a development agency with a special emphasis on improving the well-being of ordinary Africans. However, neither the British nor the German government had any intention of spending state funds on colonial administration. Rather, the British government hoped to devolve responsibility for governance to a chartered company.

Like the Deutsche Ost-Afrika Gesellschaft, the Imperial British East Africa Company started badly. In German East Africa, Karl Peters' personal misconduct focused attention on German arrogance and overbearing contempt toward Africans. In British East Africa, the problems were incompetent management and lack of business acumen. William Mackinnon—the Scottish ship owner who had been inspired by Livingstone to open trade in Zanzibar in 1872—was made chairman of the IBEAC, and he was blamed for the company's mismanagement. Every visitor to Mombasa seemed to comment on the disorganization of his administration. The Foreign Secretary, Lord Salisbury (who never had much faith in Mackinnon), once commented that he "had no quality for pushing an enterprise which depends on decision and smartness."[7] By 1890, even his fellow directors had lost faith in Mackinnon's unrealistic ideas and had become frustrated with his poor planning.

That year a young man called Charles William Hobley arrived in Mombasa to begin work on the coast as an IBEAC transport superintendent. First-Class Assistant Hobley would later join the colonial government and become the provincial commissioner of the Kavirondo region near Lake Victoria, the homeland of the Luo, but he came to Africa in 1890 as an inexperienced twenty-three-year-old. His memoirs give a fascinating insight into what Mombasa was like toward the end of the nineteenth century:

> It could not have been healthy, for it was surrounded on three sides by the native town, and the mosquitoes were very trying to a newcomer. A mosque stood about fifty yards away, and the frequent calls to prayer, by the muezzin, were at first a novelty, but soon

became tiresome monotony. Shortly before my arrival it was said that the wailing tones of the call to the faithful so frayed the nerves of a young assistant who was confined to bed with fever that he hurled a bottle at the muezzin, an injudicious act which took much explaining.[8]

Mombasa had long been a strategically important harbor on the East African coast. Its local name, Kisiwa M'vita, means "island of war"—a reference to centuries of bloody battles between the Portuguese, Arabs, and Africans—and the old town appears on a map by Ptolemy dated AD 150. Now that the British government had decided to keep strategic control over the Upper Nile valley, it was essential to maintain the lines of communication from Uganda to the coast. The government and the IBEAC were both mainly interested in Buganda (now part of central Uganda) rather than Kenya. But with Zanzibar ceded to the Germans, Mombasa became the gateway to East Africa for the British, and the city was placed under colonial rule on July 1, 1895.

The old town is still a maze of narrow coral-pink streets with whitewashed houses on either side, each with a traditional heavily carved wooden front door and a balcony overhead; it is little changed from Hobley's time, except for the unsightly power lines that festoon the alleyways. The old town's narrow streets give some relief from the sun, and it is here that the traders set up their stalls, selling anything from fruit to carpets to brassware—forerunners to the tourist curio shops that continue to turn a profit for their Muslim owners today. In 1895 countless dhows from Oman, Arabia, Somaliland, and India jostled for position in the old harbor, ready to take on their cargoes of ivory, gold, frankincense, mangrove poles, and slaves. The modern port still serves Kenya and Uganda, with shipping containers stacked high, waiting to be dispatched inland.

As the nineteenth century came to a close, the IBEAC had two major objectives: to organize trading caravans into the interior and to collect customs revenues from a string of seven company agents stationed along the coast from Vanga in the south to Lamu in the north. It also faced two major obstacles: the lack of profitable mineral resources and the absence of large navigable rivers reaching inland. Not much had changed in terms of infrastructure since Krapf had penetrated the interior fifty years before, and a round-trip from Mombasa to Lake Victoria remained a perilous, six-month-long undertaking. Human porterage was expensive here at £250 a ton, and with the abolition of the slave trade in the region, the only financially viable export from the interior was ivory.[9] It was a recipe for economic disaster.

During the 1890s, the IBEAC made several attempts to find cost-effective alternatives to the Zanzibari porters who brought goods out from the interior. Donkeys and camels were brought in from the Middle East and used as pack animals, and Cape oxen were imported from South Africa to pull carts. Construction began on a few roads, and a steamer was chartered for use on the small rivers that were navigable for a short distance inland. In one particularly pathetic attempt to open up the interior, workers even laid a few miles of narrow-gauge tramway from the port of Mombasa, the wagons pushed by Africans. The tramway never served any useful purpose other than what one visitor referred to as carrying "occasional picnic parties."

Increasingly desperate about the financial viability of British East Africa, the directors of the IBEAC began to lobby the British Tory government for a subsidy to build a proper railway. Political resistance to this "gigantic folly" arose immediately, with opponents claiming that the railway "started from nowhere" and "went nowhere." Furthermore, Liberal politicians argued that the British government had no right to build a railway through land owned by African tribes. In response to objections that the venture would also be a monumental waste of tax-payers' money, the IBEAC found support from an old ally; in an article published in September 1891 the *Times* of London declared: "It is not, after all, a very serious matter to build four or five hundred miles of railway over land that costs nothing."[10] The editorial could not have been more misguided, but the IBEAC won the day. Agreeing to fund the enterprise, the minority Tory government contended that it would bring an end to the East African slave trade, secure British control over the headwaters of the White Nile, and advance "the cause of civilisation throughout the interior of the continent."

The estimated cost of the construction was just over £3 million, equivalent to over $450 million today.[11] The final cost was nearly double.[12] Soon after the inaugural plate-laying ceremony on May 30, 1896, the British tabloid newspapers began to call it the "Lunatic Line," and not without good reason. In order to build the railway, the British shipped in some 32,000 workers from India, conveniently overlooking the paradox of using indentured laborers to build a railway to rid Africa of slavery.[13] The workers received a pittance for their labors in intense heat and poor working conditions. Twenty-five hundred workers died during the construction, an average of nearly five deaths for every mile of track laid. The company also imported an additional five thousand educated Indian workers to service the project, including clerks, draftsmen, drivers, firemen, mechanics, stationmasters, and policemen.[14] An estimated 20 percent of these workers remained in East Africa, where their descendants form a substantial part of the small Asian community now living permanently in Kenya.

The railway was intended as a modern transport link to carry raw materials out of the Uganda colony and to carry manufactured British goods back in. The senior British diplomat in Uganda, Sir Harry Johnston, described the enterprise as "the driving of a wedge of India two miles broad right across East Africa from Mombasa to the Victoria Nyanza." The British started their railway line at the new station on Mombasa Island, extending to the mainland over Salisbury Bridge— diplomatically named after the British prime minister of the day. Once on the mainland, the first challenge was to cross the waterless Taru plain. The Scottish explorer Joseph Thomson first visited the region in 1878 and was the first traveler to write about the desert:

> Weird and ghastly is the aspect of the greyish-coloured trees and bushes; for they are almost destitute of tender, waving branch or quivering leaf. No pliant twig or graceful foliage responds to the pleasing influence of the passing breeze. Stern and unbending, they present rigid arms or formidable thorns, as if bidding defiance to drought or storm. To heighten the sombre effect of the scene, dead trees are observable in every direction raising their shattered forms among the living, unable to hold their own in the struggle for existence.[15]

As the workers built the railway across the Taru plain, every drop of fresh water had to be transported from the coast to the camps. By 1898, the line reached the Tsavo River, 125 miles from Mombasa, where the construction was delayed for nine months by two lions who hunted together, mainly at night. The lions had developed a taste for human flesh and terrorized the Indian workers, causing hundreds to desert the construction camps. The pair killed at least 28 Indian and African laborers, and some accounts put the number as high as 135.[16] Eventually the lions were hunted down and shot by Chief Engineer John Henry Patterson, who sold the skins to the Field Museum of Natural History in Chicago for $5,000. The curators laboriously repaired the skins and stuffed the two animals, and they are still on display in the museum today.

Lions proved to be a recurring disruption to construction. A year after Patterson's successful hunt, a road engineer called O'Hara was dragged from his tent near Voi and killed by a lion, and in June 1900 Police Superintendent C. H. Ryall was sleeping in his observation saloon at Kima station when a lion entered his carriage and killed him, dragging his body through a window and into the bush. In general, man-eating lions are a rare occurrence in Africa; one explanation suggests that many of the railway workers who died of injury or disease were poorly buried, or not buried at all. Scavenging lions, stumbling across an easy meal, developed a taste for human flesh.

By 1899 nearly 300 miles of track had been laid and the line reached the foothills of the Kenya highlands—an area of swampy ground that the Maasai called En Kare Nyrobi. Here, over halfway from the coast to Lake Victoria, the company decided to build a railway depot to facilitate further construction up into the highlands. The railway headquarters relocated from Mombasa, and what started out as a tented encampment built on a fetid swamp soon became a permanent township, with proper houses for the staff. The settlement attracted Asian merchants who supplied goods and services to the workforce, and a year later the spelling of the town was changed to Nairobi. Kenya's capital city was born.

The railhead finally reached Lake Victoria, 575 miles from Mombasa, on December 19, 1901. The terminal was called Port Florence after the wife of the chief foreman plate layer, who had tenaciously stayed with her husband during the whole of the five-year construction period. (Port Florence was later renamed Kisumu.) Several branch lines followed, and in 1931 the line was extended to both Mount Kenya in the highlands and Kampala in Uganda.

Throughout the construction of the railway, opposition arose from the tribes through whose land the track was being laid. Leading the fight were the Nandi of central Kenya. A subtribe of the Kalenjin, they were known for defending their independence and were particularly fearsome during the late nineteenth century. Many years before the railway line to Lake Victoria was even started, a Nandi *orkoiyot* or spiritual leader called Kimnyole arap Turukat predicted that a big snake would emerge from the eastern lake (interpreted as the Indian Ocean), belching smoke and fire, and would go on to quench its thirst in the western lake (Lake Victoria). Kimnyole also prophesied that foreigners would one day rule the Nandi lands. These forecasts only reinforced the Nandi's fear of foreign intervention, and for years the tribe harassed anyone who tried to cross their lands—the Arab caravans generally took a long detour either north or south of Nandi territory to avoid trouble. The Nandi would not even allow individual Europeans to pass through their country without the correct papers, and in 1896 they killed a British traveler called Peter West and his twenty-three porters when he attempted an unauthorized crossing—an event that sparked an eleven-year war between the Nandi and the British.

By 1900, a year before the railhead reached Lake Victoria, the Nandi had a new *orkoiyot,* supreme chief Koitalel arap Samoei.[17] They still fervently believed the railway was the snake from Kimnyole's prophecy, and they united behind Koitalel to oppose the last stage of the line. They proved to be excellent guerrilla fighters in the dense forests and steep valleys of the Rift Valley, where the superior firepower of the Europeans was less effective. Even after the final track had been laid, the Nandi kept up their harassment and regularly stole the shiny copper telegraph wire to wind around their necks and arms as body ornaments.

Charles Hobley, who had now been promoted and moved to Nyanza, later commented: "The Wanandi [Nandi], with the exception of a few in the vicinity of the station, have all along viewed our presence in the country with veiled repugnance. . . . We were unwittingly living on the edge of a volcano."[18]

The constant provocations were too much for the British, and in October 1905—four years after the line was finished—a military intelligence officer, Colonel Richard Meinertzhagen, was sent to negotiate with the Nandi leader. Unfortunately, one of Koitalel's other prophesies—that British bullets would turn to water—proved not to be correct.[19] According to tribal legend, as Meinertzhagen moved forward to shake hands with the Nandi leader, he drew his pistol and shot Koitalel dead. This was a signal to British troops hiding nearby to open fire on the assembled tribesmen, killing at least twenty-three more.

Some reports claim that Meinertzhagen beheaded Koitalel as he lay on the ground. Other British officers complained, accusing Meinertzhagen of treachery, and the colonel was called before a military inquiry. Meinertzhagen claimed the shooting was in self-defense; the tribunal found him not guilty, although he was later transferred out of the area. In any case, Koitalel's death had exactly the result the British had hoped for: the Nandi's resistance was broken, and they were no longer a threat to the safety of the railway.

However, the railway was not the only object of African opposition, and the British found that the imposition of colonial rule was opposed practically everywhere. Between 1895 and 1914 the British organized a number of military raids—"punitive expeditions"—against what they called "recalcitrant tribes." Everywhere, the British used well-armed soldiers and crack-shot mercenaries against the spears and arrows of the Kenyan tribes. For the next couple of decades, British rule in East Africa could be maintained only by the use of force.

In the Luo heartland of Nyanza, the arrival of the British could not have come at a worse time. In the early 1880s the region had been hit by a series of natural disasters that drastically reduced many of the tribal populations in the area, including the cattle-raiding Maasai. When Johann Krapf first encountered the Maasai in 1848, he wrote that the Maasai "are dreaded as warriors, laying all to waste with fire and sword, so that the weaker tribes do not venture to resist them in the open field, but leave them in possession of their herds, and seek only to save themselves by the quickest possible flight."

But the diseases that devastated East Africa in the 1880s, including rinderpest and bovine lung disease, were particularly hard on those whose livelihoods depended on cattle, such as the Maasai and to a lesser extent the Luo. A generation after Krapf explored central Kenya, the

Austrian explorer Oscar Baumann traveled extensively through Maasai lands, and in 1891 he witnessed at first hand the devastation that had been wreaked on the region: "There were women wasted to skeletons from whose eyes the madness of starvation glared . . . warriors scarcely able to crawl on all fours, and apathetic, languishing elders. Swarms of vultures followed them from high, awaiting their certain victims."[20] By one estimate, two-thirds of the Maasai died during this period. Weakened by disease and famine as well as the loss of their cattle, the Maasai never recovered their numbers.

In western Kenya, the Luo too were suffering. The livestock diseases were joined by a succession of locust invasions between 1885 and 1890 that devastated the crops in Luoland and brought the onset of the *ong'ong'a* famine of 1889.[21] These devastating pressures on the population created a virtual civil war throughout Luoland, as clan fought neighboring clan over cattle, land, and grazing rights.

Although no Europeans were present to witness the catastrophic effects of disease and famine, among the Luo the memory of such traumatic events has been faithfully passed down by word of mouth, from one generation to the next. John Ndalo, a close Obama relative from Kendu Bay, vividly recalls the stories of cattle plague and famine that his father and grandfathers had experienced:

> Many homes lost their family. People were fighting, and if you had even a little food, people would come in a great number and invade your family and take everything away. For those whose cattle survived, we organized raids and went in big numbers with spears and arrows . . . and bring back all their cattle.
>
> When we had exhausted the food within the other clans of the Luo, we went to attack other tribes, including the Luhyas, who are our immediate neighbors, and even some of the cattle we got from the Maasai . . .
>
> The famine also led to more wars and the invention of the buffalo shield. The buffalo skin was very strong, and we knew it would resist any spear, so it led to a lot of rearmament in the African society. So we were looking everywhere for the buffalo, everywhere,

because there used to be many more here in this area. So the young men had to kill them.

Weakened by famine, the Luo were struck down by smallpox, which had also ravaged the Maasai. The death rate in Luoland was so high that it led to widespread depopulation throughout the lake region, forcing thousands of people to reconsolidate and move to new areas. This migration reintroduced the tsetse fly in areas previously free of the insects, spreading an epidemic of human trypanosomiasis that killed at least 250,000 people between 1902 and 1908. John Ndalo remembers the days when trypanosomiasis was common around Kendu Bay:

> The sickness name in Dholuo is called *nyalolwe*—sleeping sickness. We were taught to clear all the bushes where the animals were, because the tsetse fly was in the bushes and if they bit the cattle, the cows would die.
>
> When a tsetse fly bites a human being and you are out there tending your cattle, you fall asleep suddenly, and when you are sleeping all the cattle will just wander off!

In 1895, the year that President Obama's grandfather Hussein Onyango Obama was born, the British appointed Charles William Hobley to be the new regional colonial administrator in Nyanza. Hobley was becoming an old hand in Kenya, having worked in Mombasa for the IBEAC since 1890. Hobley soon established his administrative headquarters in Mumias, about forty miles north of Winam Gulf, where he found mixed attitudes toward colonization among the Luo.

Hobley believed that the British could only control the region through force: "The reaction of a native race to control by a civilized Government varies according to their nature, and to their form of government, but in every case a conflict of some kind is inevitable, before the lower race fully accepts the dictum of the ruling power."[22] Starting in 1896, Hobley mounted a series of vicious punitive expeditions against the Luo clans who opposed British rule. He referred to the Luo as "the Kavirondo," and on several occasions between 1896 and 1900 the British confronted what they called "recalcitrant Kavirondo sections" in open battle. The Luo's arrows and spears were no match for the Maxim machine gun and the Hotchkiss cannon, and several hundred Luo warriors were killed in each clash. Usually the British followed up their attacks by confiscating the livestock and destroying the houses of the Luo. In this way the British established a form of colonial dictatorship, imposed and maintained by violence, and totally indifferent to the needs or wishes of the Africans.

Not all the Luo clans were hostile to the British, and the colonists became adept at "divide and rule" as they pitted clan against clan. (The Luo have a saying for it: *Kik ilaw winy ariyo*—"Don't chase two birds at once.") Those groups who accepted colonial authority were treated as "friendlies" and received special privileges. British policy called for colonial administrations to be based on indigenous political systems, so the new administrative borders were designed to mirror the boundaries of the *pinje,* or Luo clan system. However, unlike the traditional Luo *ruoth,* who acted as guardians of traditional laws and customs, the newly appointed chiefs signed up by the British were effectively African civil servants, paid for and given their wide-ranging powers by the imperial authority. In this way, the colonial administrators recruited local labor to impose control in the region and to collect the taxes that were beginning to be levied on the Africans.

One such chief was Paul Mboya, who governed the Kendu Bay area when Hussein Onyango was living there in the 1930s. An important man in the community, Mboya had been the first Luo to be ordained as a pastor in the Seventh-Day Adventist church. Later the British made him chief in Karachuonyo in south Nyanza, and then secretary of the regional African District Council.[23] Sarah Obama's youngest brother,

Abdo Omar Okech, said that his brother-in-law made an enemy of Mboya by standing up to him over forced labor:

> Onyango wanted Africans to walk freely. So he had this argument with Paul, because during those times, there was forced labor, which was introduced by the white men. The chief's representatives would come around and take you to work on the farms. Paul organized this because he was the chief, but Onyango opposed this. Paul was misusing his power. If somebody said they were sick and could not go out and work for the white men, Paul would just take you forcefully because he was a powerful man.

Another favorite of the British was Ng'ong'a Odima, the chief in charge of the whole of the Alego region, north of Winam Gulf. A reliable and enthusiastic supporter of British rule, Odima grew wealthy and powerful from the benevolence of the colonial administration; like many of the new breed of African officials, he also abused his position. The chiefs, who were frequently employed as hut counters and tax collectors, often overcharged villagers, refused to issue them receipts for payments, and forced people to feed them during the course of their administrative duties.[24] The Luo historian Bethwell Ogot believes this early form of patronage ultimately led to the normalization of dishonest profiteering in Kenyan society:

> Thus new allies were co-opted by the British and new pivots of patronage were created at different levels of the social and political system. In this way, corruption began to manifest itself [in Kenya] in various forms such as nepotism, bribery, looting and gradually it became entrenched and tolerated as an essential ingredient of governance.[25]

The system worked effectively, and within a very few years the Luo were pacified, becoming loyal supporters of British rule in Kenya. According to Hobley, the great advantage of the "Kavirondo" was that:

Once they were beaten they readily made peace and, once they had
made peace, it was peace, for within a few hours the women were
in camp selling food, and one had no anxiety about a subsequent
treacherous attack either at night or on the road. Under these circumstances mutual respect gradually supervened and we became
great friends.[26]

Having quelled the opposition of the Luo and other tribes by the
early twentieth century, the IBEAC turned its attention to the finances
of the railway. The final cost of over £5.5 million was 80 percent over
budget, and the British realized that the line had no chance of paying
for itself.

Shortly before the line was completed in late 1901, the British Foreign Office had appointed a new governor. Sir Charles Norton Edgecumbe Eliot was an experienced career diplomat and a brilliant linguist
who had previously served in Russia, Morocco, Turkey, and the United
States. Eliot realized immediately that the Uganda Railway was a
white elephant, but he also insisted that the protectorate had to be self-
financing and that the railway would have to pay its full running costs.
An arrogant, conceited man, Eliot held the indigenous Africans in contempt, calling them "greedy and covetous" and claiming the African "is
far nearer the animal world than is that of the European or Asiatic."[27]

In his search for ways to develop British East Africa and make it
financially viable, Eliot effectively ignored the Africans in his plans,
except as a source of tax. Instead of developing the local population,
he proposed to resolve the fiscal problems of the railway by sending
white settlers to colonize the rich land in the Kenyan highlands, where
they would produce cash crops for export. (Other diplomats and politicians had different ideas about what to do with British East Africa,
none of which involved the participation of the indigenous Africans.
Lord Lugard, then high commissioner of the Protectorate of Northern
Nigeria, suggested that British East Africa be given over to the Indians,
and Harry Johnston, the new special commissioner in Uganda, even

referred to Kenya as the "America of the Hindu." The colonial secretary in London at the time, Joseph Chamberlain, even offered the protectorate to the European Jews as a permanent home.[28] However, none of these competing ideas actually addressed the problem of paying for the railway, so Eliot's plan prevailed almost by default.)

Eliot also introduced what was called a "hut tax"—a duty on every dwelling, payable in hard currency. If a man had several wives and several sons, then a tax was due on each of their houses. This was an iniquitous levy on a society that did not have a cash economy. In addition to raising money for the Uganda Railway, the tax also effectively forced the Africans to work for the British in order to earn the money to pay the colonial administration. The Africans bitterly resented the tax, which the Luo historian Bethwell Ogot claims set off the "beginning [of] rural-urban migration and the breakdown of the closely-knit family structure and values."[29]

Critics in London asserted that Europeans had no moral or legal right to settle or colonize the Africans' land, to which Eliot responded in his characteristically blunt manner:

> There seems to be something exaggerated in all this talk about "their own country" and "their immemorable rights." No doubt on platforms and in reports we declare we have no intention of depriving the natives of their lands, but this has never prevented us from taking whatever land we want for Government purposes, or from settling Europeans on land not actually occupied by natives. . . . We should face the undoubted issue, namely: that white mates black in a very few moves. . . . The sooner [the native] disappears and is unknown, except in books of anthropology, the better.[30]

By May 1901—less than four months after taking up his tenure in Nairobi—Eliot submitted his first annual report to the Foreign Office back in London, in which he greatly exaggerated the agricultural potential of British East Africa. Nevertheless, his report had the desired effect, and the colonization of the richest agricultural land in East Africa soon began. In 1903 the first large grants were made around Lake Naiva-sha in the central Rift Valley, regardless of the rights of the indigenous tribes in the area.

The colonial administration declared the land to the north of Nai-robi and the central highlands around Mount Kenya to be Crown land, and by 1904 white farmers from Europe and South Africa began to arrive, lured by the promise of good farming land being sold off for a pittance. The original occupants of the land, predominantly the Kikuyu, Maasai, and Kalenjin, were moved off their tribal territories, and the incoming foreign white settlers qualified for a ninety-nine-year lease on their new farms. Eliot, eager to speed up the process, pursued even greater independence from London over the allocation of land. He claimed that "the enormous land appetites of the colonists, particularly South Africa, should be considered, and this, without wasting time on African interests."[31] Ever unapologetic, Eliot also wrote to the foreign secretary, Lord Lansdowne:

> There can be no doubt that the Masai and many other tribes must go under. It is a prospect which I view with equanimity and clear conscience. [Masaidom] is a beastly, bloody system founded on raiding and immorality.[32]

Eventually this uncompromising attitude brought Eliot into direct conflict with the Foreign Office back in London, and he was forced to offer his resignation in 1904.

Despite Eliot's departure, the settlement of what became known as the "White Highlands" continued. By 1905, 700 Afrikaner farmers had arrived from South Africa, together with more than 250 British and other settlers. Between 1904 and 1912 the South Africans out-numbered the British, and other Europeans arrived from a number of countries, including Finns and Jews. In contrast to the pattern of colo-nization in other parts of the British Empire, the availability of cheap local labor meant that these newcomers never intended to perform manual labor themselves. Instead, they were determined to become planters—managers who would oversee the Africans doing the hard labor. As John Ainsworth, one of the early colonists, wrote in 1906, "White people can live here and *will* live here, not . . . as colonists performing manual labour, as in Canada and New Zealand, but as planters, etc., overseeing natives doing the work of development."[33]

Wealthy British families used their strong political connections to buy up huge areas of land, and by 1912 just five families owned 20 percent of all the land held by whites. The population of white settler-farmers in British East Africa rose from just thirteen in 1901 to nearly ten thousand in 1921. By then 20 million acres (about one-eighth of the country) had been designated as "native reserves," and more than 7.5 million acres—by far the best-quality farming land—had been taken by the white farmers. The Maasai reserve, for example, was only one-tenth of the area the tribe had occupied prior to 1883.

In the ten years between 1895 and 1905, British East Africa grew from an isolated backwater to a colonial protectorate bigger in area than metropolitan France. Controlled by an administration that was prepared to use ruthless force where necessary, the Africans now paid taxes to live in their own homes, steamboats sailed on Lake Victoria, telegraph lines crossed the land, and a railway connected the ocean to the interior. Into this world of dramatic change a young Luo male was born; his name was Onyango Obama, second son of Obama and Nyaoke, grandson to Opiyo, and later grandfather of the president of the United States.

Onyango belonged to the very last generation of Luo to be raised in an independent Luoland. He started life in an Iron Age society whose people were catapulted into the twentieth century in less than a generation. Onyango would fight in two world wars, witness a bloody national revolt against the colonial rulers, and eventually see his country gain independence from white rule. But for his first few years, he grew up like any other young Luo male, in a world that was tough, uncompromising, and narrowly defined. Already his family's cattle had been decimated by a decade of bovine infections, his father and five wives had struggled through the 1889 famine with young children, and now an epidemic of smallpox was rampaging through the region. Many Luo families had been forced to move on, but Onyango's father, Obama, elected to stay in the family homestead in Kendu Bay.

When Onyango was nine a new influx of white people arrived in Nyanza whose influence on the lifestyle of the Luo would match that of the British administrators: the Christian missionaries. Although Anglican and Catholic missionaries had worked in East Africa for several decades, most of their stations were concentrated in central Uganda. The new missionaries came from a very different branch of Christianity: the Seventh-Day Adventists (SDAs), an evangelical Christian church that observes Saturday as the Sabbath and puts strong emphasis on the imminent second coming of Jesus Christ. The Seventh-Day Adventists were late on the scene in Kenya and only established their first mission in 1906. Under the leadership of a Canadian missionary, Arthur Asa Grandville Carscallen, the Church focused its attention on the region around the eastern shores of Lake Victoria, where it established seven mission stations.[34]

Upon arriving in Kisumu in November 1906, Carscallen did not receive the reception he had been expecting. A colonial official told him that they had missionaries of all shapes and sizes, and with all sorts of labels, and the last thing they needed was any more. Undeterred, he began to scout for a suitable place to establish his first mission, and his first trip took him to Kendu Bay:

> Brother Enns, Brother Nyambo and myself took a small launch here and crossed over to the southern shores of the Kavirondo Bay where we pitched our tent close to the water's edge until we could have a look around the country. After a few days' search we decided

to locate on a hill about two miles back from the bay. From this hill we have a fine view in every direction. . . .

The country here is very thickly settled with a most friendly class of natives. We can stand on our hill and count about two hundred villages, each of the nearest ones sending us a present of at least a fowl. The natives have made friends with us quite quickly, and we now have a good deal of company every day. . . . Whenever [the chiefs] come they bring us some little present. One brought a fine sheep the other day. Another, who wants two boys educated, brought us a fine young bullock, nearly full grown, to pay for the education of the boys. Other missionaries say it is best to take something that way from the chiefs as it makes people feel that the education is worth something.[35]

John Ndalo was born eighteen years after Arthur Carscallen established his mission in Kendu Bay, and like many of the residents of the area, he was baptized as a Seventh-Day Adventist. He recalls his father telling him about the arrival of the first missionaries:

When they first came, there was an old man called Mr. Ougo. He was the first person to see them. So they asked Ougo to give them a place where they could settle. So in that place called Gendia, that's where they put their tent. Mr. Ougo was the owner of all that land, and he gave them a place to stay.

So these missionaries started getting into people's homes, to tell them about this foreign god. Initially, they were very suspicious of these white men. But you know, the white man knows how to go about making friends, giving them sweets and so on. But some of the Africans were very proud, so they said, "Forget about the white man"—some of them were taking *bhang,* so they were very strong-headed.

Then they began by building a small settlement with a school, where they started teaching people the word of God. But there was a language barrier because people couldn't understand them. So they started teaching the older people of about thirty years of age, teaching them English so they could communicate.

An accomplished linguist, Arthur Carscallen soon mastered the Dholuo language (which in itself was no mean feat), and he went on to create the first written language and dictionary for the Luo people. He even imported a small printing press, which he used to produce a Luo grammar textbook, and spent several years translating parts of the New Testament into Dholuo. (This original press is still used today in the SDA mission in Gendia.) With textbooks, the Luo could receive a formal education. The Seventh-Day Adventists also stress the importance of good diet and health, so one of the mission's objectives was to establish a free clinic where they treated malaria, cholera, and other diseases. They even made house calls.

A year after arriving in Luoland, Carscallen was joined by his fiancée, Helen. As an accomplished seamstress, she was less concerned about the lack of a written language and more troubled by the lack of any clothing worn by the locals. Determined to change the situation, she began to grow cotton, and made her own fabric to clothe the Africans. However, John Ndalo recalls that his older relatives found the new clothing provided by the missionaries had several disadvantages over their traditional attire, especially when it came to ease of access for certain bodily functions:

> They used to wear skins, so when the white man came, they started to give them clothes. They had a very hard time with these clothes, because every time they wanted to go for a "long shot," they had a big problem taking off their clothes. It was difficult to handle the European clothes, so we were struggling for a long time. We could not get them on, and they tried very hard to get people to wear them by giving us sweets and sugar. But people refused because they didn't want to wear them, they were cumbersome to us.

The missionaries' stalwart independence and focus on corporeal as well as spiritual matters brought them into conflict with some of the local traders who were trying to establish a presence in the region.

Richard Gethin, the first British trader to settle permanently in Kisii, in south Nyanza, complained that Carscallen and his other missionaries were "more interested in trading in buffalo hides" than in saving souls. He also claimed that their mission houses, far from being havens of spiritual devotion and learning, were used mainly to store skins and other trade goods for export:

> Preaching of the Gospel was conspicuous by its absence. Carscallen would see an old Jaluo [Luo] native asleep in the shade of a tree. He would approach him, put his hands on his head and if he still slept, give him a kick on the backside saying, "Son you are saved and you can thank the Lord it is me who has saved you; if it were one of the others you would be condemned to terrible torture when you died." With this, the convert would be roped into carrying a load on the next safari.[36]

For the young Onyango Obama, the arrival of the white missionaries provided an exciting diversion from the monotony of village life. Onyango was only eleven when Carscallen established his first mission in Gendia, but according to Onyango's last wife, Sarah, he was fascinated by these white strangers from the beginning.[37] Sarah says that Onyango was always different from the others, even as a young boy. As a child he would wander off by himself for days on end and nobody would know where he had been—nor would he tell them anything when he got back. He was always very serious as a child; he never laughed or joked around, or even played games with the other children. He was, and would always remain, an outsider.

But Onyango had a great strength, and that was his curiosity. He wanted to learn about and understand everything around him. This innate inquisitiveness drew him to the white missionaries like iron to a magnet. At a time when most of the Africans were doing their best to ignore these new visitors, thinking that, like the Arab traders, their presence would be only temporary, Onyango went off alone to find out more about these strange new people who had come to live in Luo-land. Nobody in the family can recall how old Onyango was when he left, but he must have been only in his early teens, perhaps fourteen or fifteen—old enough to wander away from home alone, but young enough to return before the outbreak of the 1914 war.

Nobody in his family knew what had happened to him; for all they knew, he could have been taken by a leopard or bitten by a deadly snake. During Onyango's absence, life in Kendu Bay carried on as it had done for generations: the older girls slept together in the *siwindhe* and learned from their grandmother, and the boys tended the livestock and joined their father in his *simba* to talk long into the night about heroic deeds of past warriors. Then, after several months' absence, Onyango returned to his father's compound wearing long trousers and a white shirt. In a household where no one wore more than a piece of animal skin to cover their genitals, a young black boy dressed like a white man was deeply shocking. Onyango's father was convinced that his son had broken a strict tribal taboo and had been circumcised; after all, why would anyone wear trousers except to cover this humiliation? And his shirt? Surely he wore this to cover an illness or sores on his body—after all, venereal disease was not uncommon among the white man, or perhaps he had caught smallpox and was contagious. Sarah claims that Onyango's father, Obama, turned to his other sons and said, "Don't go near this brother of yours. He is unclean." His brothers laughed at Onyango and had nothing more to do with him. Rejected by his family, the young man turned his back on village life in Kendu Bay and returned to Kisumu. Onyango would remain estranged from his father for many years.

By 1914 the new taxes and cash crops had made Nyanza the most successful and prosperous of the provinces in British East Africa, and its few roads and other transportation systems were considered to be the best in the region. In the fiscal year 1909–10, the tonnage shipped along the railway to Mombasa was nearly double that of the previous year, and this grew by an additional 45 percent the following year.[38]

However, in Luoland, people were still bitter over the punitive wars waged against them at the turn of the century, the imposition of the hut tax, and the forced labor on road construction and settlers' farms; these grievances were compounded by the paternalistic attitude of the missionaries. In response, a unique local religious cult was growing in popularity in central Nyanza. Rooted in the traditional Luo religion, Mumboism helped focus local opposition to the white man. At its worst, the movement could be brutal—its followers vowed to sever the arms of those found wearing European clothes, and threatened to transform whites and their allies into monkeys.[39]

According to the religion's followers, the Mumbo spirit serpent used Onyango Dunde of the Seje clan in Alego as a Luo prophet. Onyango claimed to have been swallowed by the serpent which, after a short time, spat him out unhurt.[40] The giant snake then gave Onyango a message to pass on to his people:

> I am the god Mumbo whose two homes are the Sun and in the Lake. I have chosen you to be my mouth-piece. Go out and tell all Africans . . . that from henceforth I am their God. Those whom I choose personally and also those who acknowledge me will live forever in plenty. . . . The Christian religion is rotten and so is its practice of making its believers wear clothes. My followers must let their hair grow never cutting it. Their clothes shall be the skins of goats and cattle and they must never wash.[41]

One Mumbo prediction held that all Europeans would disappear from their country. When German troops crossed the border from German East Africa and attacked the British garrison at Kisii in 1914, the Africans took this as a confirmation of Mumbo's forecast. They rose up and plundered administrative and missionary centers throughout the region—although this particular response came primarily from the Gusii tribe, rather than the Luo. The British were harsh in their suppression of the rebellion, killing more than 150 Africans.

Many of the Mumbo leaders were deported to a detention camp on an island off Kismayo in the Indian Ocean, now part of southern Somalia. However, the threat of expulsion did not deter Mumbo's most devout followers, and despite frequent arrests and deportations by the British authorities, they continued their insurrection throughout the interwar years.

The border with the German protectorate was only seventy-five miles from Nairobi, and the outbreak of war brought panic to the white settlers. Many planters left their farms and fled to the city, carrying any weapon they could lay their hands on: elephant guns, shotguns, sporting rifles. Twelve hundred settlers were accepted for service in the East African Mounted Rifles (EAMR), and the rest were asked to return to their farms. Uniforms were not immediately available, so recruits handed over their shirts and volunteer women sewed the letters *EAMR* on their shoulders.[42] The makeshift army began commandeering horses from farmers. The colony declared martial law, ordering all "enemy aliens" rounded up and incarcerated.

British East Africa was going to war.

6

FIVE WIVES AND
TWO WORLD WARS

PAND NYALUO DHOGE ARIYO

An old knife has two edges

A s THE clouds of war began to roll in over the fields of Flanders in the summer of 1914, there was a widely accepted understanding in East Africa between colonial Britain and Germany that war on the continent was pointless. By 1914 Britain controlled a quarter of the African continent, and the German colonies were five times larger than the Fatherland. Despite the skepticism voiced by both Bismarck and Gladstone in the 1880s about the wisdom of colonizing Africa, by the beginning of the twentieth century both nations were beginning to profit from their overseas ventures. The two colonial nations also faced similar problems in trying to administer large African populations, and open hostility was not in either party's interest. It was a comfortable alliance, and Dr. W. S. Solf, the German secretary of state for the colonies, willingly accepted that his nation's ambitions in Africa would best be served by being "England's junior partner."[1]

Prior to the outbreak of war in 1914, most of the operations by the King's African Rifles (KAR) were little more than "large scale cattle raids" against the native population.[2] The military forces in the two colonies in East Africa were finely balanced in numbers: in the summer of 1914, Britain had 2,383 officers and *askaris* (African soldiers) in the KAR, and Germany had 2,756 troops. One resident of Nairobi wrote that British East Africa "was not prepared. Why should it have been, with a German colony cheek-by-jowl across the border? . . . German East Africa was much too near to be dangerous."[3] However, this peaceful coexistence was not to last, and the first shots discharged in anger during the First World War were fired not in Europe but in Africa.

On August 5, 1914, the day after Britain declared war on Germany, British troops from the Uganda protectorate attacked a German river outpost near Lake Victoria. Ten days later, troops in German East Africa attempted to take the small coastal port of Taveta, a dozen miles inside British East Africa, where a German volunteer soldier called Bröker became the first combatant to die on foreign soil. In south Nyanza in western Kenya, near panic ensued the next month when a detachment of German troops led by Captain Wilhelm Bock von Wülfingen took the undefended British post at Kisii. KAR troops reclaimed the town after fierce fighting and several deaths, but the British now worried that the strategic railhead and port at Kisumu were vulnerable to attack.

By the autumn of 1914, then, German and British forces in East Africa were actively at war, and the conflict continued until after the armistice in Europe. For the first time, ordinary Africans were dragged into a war between European nations, mainly as porters. For weeks and months on end, they were required to march eighteen miles or more a day through the jungle, enduring intense heat and often torrential rain. They survived on meager rations and minimal medical support.

Of the 165,000 African porters who were employed in the KAR Carrier Corps in British East Africa during the war, more than 50,000 died—a much higher casualty rate than on the Western Front. This extraordinary figure represented one in eight of the adult male population in Kenya and Uganda. The war devastated large areas, laid waste to farming land, and brought hunger, disease, and death to ordinary African civilians; thousands more perished in the global influenza pandemic that followed the war. The Afro-American writer and civil rights activist W. E. B. Du Bois wrote in his seminal 1915 essay, "The African Roots of War," that "a great cloud swept over sea and settled on Africa . . . twenty centuries after Christ, black Africa, prostrate, raped and shamed, lies at the feet of the conquering Philistines of Europe."[4]

By 1914 all local insurrections in British East Africa had been suppressed, including the Mumbo rebellion in south Nyanza, and the British had established an effective and comprehensive administration across their territory. Having buckled under colonial rule, the Africans now demonstrated remarkable stoicism in coping with the outbreak of a European war on their continent. Despite the occasional brutality shown by the colonials toward the local people, plenty of Africans admired and respected the organization and stability that British rule brought to the region. In fact, some of the tribes that had been most resistant to British rule in the 1890s contributed many combatants to the KAR—perhaps because the KAR offered an opportunity for young Africans to maintain their warrior status in a society increasingly dominated and controlled by the British. One young African summed up the situation by claiming that the army "was a suitable job for a warrior . . . It showed that we were men."[5] This was particularly the case with the Nandi, who had fought long and hard against the construction of the Uganda Railway at the turn of the century. Ten years later, they contributed a greater percentage of their male population to the KAR than any other tribe in Kenya.[6]

In Nyanza, the Luo had mixed responses to the conflict. Initially, finding volunteers in south Nyanza was relatively easy; the disruption caused by the Mumbo cult had led to high unemployment among the Africans in the region. However, the British soon ran out of willing recruits as young African men started volunteering to work on white farms in order to avoid the Carrier Corps, and their colonial masters had to resort to more persuasive means. In a modern equivalent of the press gang used by the British Royal Navy during the eighteenth century, the authorities rounded up young men when they were at sporting events or other public gatherings or out herding their livestock. To meet their strict quotas, local chiefs sometimes seized unwilling recruits from their homes at night. According to John Ndalo, nobody in the Kendu Bay area wanted to fight, and they were all forcibly conscripted:

> They were using the local chiefs to identify the homes with the young men who were capable of fighting. So the chiefs would come into the locality and say, at such and such a home, we want one young man, or two or three. In the First World War, there were no volunteers—they used to pick young men and take them by force.

However, even these drastic measures did not fulfill the quotas and the colonial government was obliged to introduce legislation to allow the conscription of Africans. In the first twelve months of the war, 4,572 Africans from central Nyanza alone were pressed into service with the KAR, and their numbers continued to increase as the war progressed.

Thousands of young Luo men joined the army, eventually dominating the battalions of the KAR.[7] Of all the major tribes in Kenya, only the seminomadic Maasai avoided active service, although they did provide valuable military intelligence along the border with German East Africa (as did the Maasai living on the other side of the border for the Germans). Hans Poeschel, the editor of the colonial newspaper *Deutsch-Ostafrika Zeitung,* wrote that they must have been reluctant to take up arms on behalf of the British because the Maasai "had grown to know the English . . . as still greater cattle-thieves than they themselves."[8]

For several years running up to the outbreak of war, Onyango Obama had been living away from his family with the white missionaries in and around Kisumu; he was part of the first generation of young Luo boys to benefit from an education in a mission school. Onyango was clever and ambitious, and by 1914 he could read and write both English and Swahili. Sarah Obama claims that he also learned about administration from the British and was familiar with paper records and land titles.[9] Inevitably, Onyango's grasp of administration, as well as his ability to speak Dholuo, Swahili, and English, made him an ideal recruit for the KAR Carrier Corps, because the British desperately needed translators to pass down commands from the white officers to the African porters, scouts, cooks, guards, and wagon drivers. According to Sarah Obama, Onyango's first job in the KAR was overseeing the African teams who were building roads as part of the war effort.

The Carrier Corps was essential for warfare in East Africa. The region had very few roads suitable for mechanized vehicles, and the prevalence of the tsetse fly prevented the use of draft animals, leaving human porters as the only viable means of moving military equipment around the region. John Ainsworth, one of the ablest British administrators in British East Africa, was impressed with the Luo porters during the war:

> A very large portion of the responsibility for producing porters fell on the Nyanza Province. It can be said with truth that they helped to win the war. The Kavirondo porter became a very well-known feature in "German East" during the war. He was usually referred to as omera (a Luo word meaning "brother").[10]

Sir Philip Mitchell, who fought in Togoland, Cameroon, and East Africa and later became governor of Kenya in 1944, claims that it took three porters to support a single armed soldier on the front line in East Africa.[11] He also regretted the terrible loss of life sustained by the Africans in the KAR Carrier Corps: "The heaviest sufferers were the porters, among whom loss of life was greatest and lamentable; faithful men, who did what they had to do with little complaint and great endurance; but who ought never to have been asked to do it, and who suffered much which should have been prevented."

John Ndalo too remembers that the conditions were tough and the casualties high: "During that time, there was no organized form of transport, so the soldiers were walking and many died on the road. So we lost quite a lot of Luo young men. They were working as porters as well as fighting."

In addition to supplying recruits to the Carrier Corps, the inhabitants of Nyanza were required to contribute to the war effort in other ways. In the last year of the war the people of central Nyanza provided more than two thousand head of cattle as well as three thousand goats. The dreaded hut tax was also further increased.

To the Africans, the Europeans were fighting an incomprehensible war. The missionaries and colonial administrators had spent years condemning intertribal wars as sinful and uncivilized, but now the Africans were being recruited for what they saw as just another intertribal war—only on a much larger scale. They could not understand why they were marching for days into a strange and inhospitable country, only to fight an enemy from whom they took little or nothing; why not fight a quick campaign, seize their cattle and women, and then go home? Sir Philip Mitchell understood the Africans' bewilderment:

> The White Men, hitherto seen by the native people in small numbers of superior, almost fabulous, people, all apparently of one tribe, with similar habits and common interests were suddenly found to belong to different tribes which were fighting each other and required African help to do it. Not only was it no longer a shocking and dangerous thing to offer violence to a *Mzungu;* on the contrary, if he was on the other side, it was a soldier's duty to attack him, and kill him if possible or to take him prisoner, and even Chiefs and villages could earn rewards from the other side for what was in fact treason and rebellion against their lawful Government.[12]

The German colonies fought their European neighbors in Africa with varying degrees of success. Togoland, Cameroon, and German South West Africa (Namibia) fell to Allied forces by the early months of 1915, with the exception of the German stronghold of Mora in Cameroon, which held out until February 1916. However, it was a very different story in German East Africa (consisting of today's Tanzania, Burundi, and Rwanda), where the German commander led a brilliant campaign with the support of well-trained *askaris*. Colonel (later General) Paul von Lettow-Vorbeck understood the special demands of fighting a war on African soil, and he also spoke fluent Swahili—this alone helped to earn him the respect and admiration of his African troops. Unlike the British, he also recruited black officers. Von Lettow-Vorbeck understood that, strategically, East Africa would never be anything other than a sideshow during the First World War. His instructions from Berlin were to maintain the defense of the colony at all costs, but he knew he had no real hope of winning this campaign. Instead, he was determined to tie down as many British troops as possible, thereby denying them a place on the Western Front.[13] Through a combination of preemptive strikes on towns such as Kisii and brazen attacks on the Uganda Railway, he not only captured badly needed weapons and supplies but also kept more than 150,000 Allied troops fighting in East Africa throughout the war.

In March 1916 the British launched a formidable offensive against the Germans under the command of General Jan Christian Smuts, who had more than 45,000 troops at his immediate disposal—four times the number of Germans. Hopelessly outnumbered, the German commander nonetheless fought an effective rearguard action as he retreated south through German East Africa. During this campaign Onyango Obama was moved from his road-building duties in British East Africa and transferred to German East Africa to support the growing offensive. For almost a year the Germans and their loyal African *askaris* survived as best they could, alternately living off the land and enjoying supplies captured from the advancing Allied forces. Von Lettow-Vorbeck's army was so successful at acquiring provisions and equipment from the enemy that by the end of the war the German forces had more ammunition than they could carry. Nevertheless, the Germans knew they could not repulse the Allied forces, who pursued them relentlessly across German East Africa and into Portuguese-controlled Mozambique.

By early November 1918 rumors were beginning to circulate among the German forces that the war was nearly over, but von Lettow-Vorbeck remained convinced that any end to the conflict would be favorable to Germany. Chased around East Africa by British forces for the past several years, he and his army had little idea of the real situation in Europe. He expressed disbelief when the British commissioner told him what was happening back home in the Fatherland:

> The Commissioner told me that the German fleet had revolted, and that a revolution had also broken out in Germany; further, if he was to accept a report which was official but had not yet been confirmed, the Kaiser had abdicated on November 10th. All this news seemed to me improbable, and I did not believe it until it was confirmed on my way home months later.[14]

As the commander of German forces in East Africa, von Lettow-Vorbeck had no choice but to offer his surrender to Brigadier General W. F. S. Edwards. Under a storm-laden sky at Abercorn on the border between German East Africa and northern Rhodesia, hostilities ceased at 11:00 a.m. on November 25, 1918—exactly two weeks after the armistice was signed in Europe. Not only had the first shots of the war been fired in Africa, but so too were the last. Von Lettow-Vorbeck's army had the distinction of being the only German forces to have occupied British-controlled soil during the Great War.

Among British imperialists there was an almost palpable excitement about the new opportunities in Africa. For the first time they had the chance to paint Africa "Empire Red" from south to north, and Cecil Rhodes' dream of a "Cape to Cairo" route became a reality. The British could now travel from the extreme south of the continent to the Mediterranean Sea without ever leaving the British Empire; the journey took fifty-three days, traveling 4,456 miles by railway, 2,004 miles on river and lake steamers, and just 363 miles by road.

In 1919, not only did the Treaty of Versailles set out the terms of peace in Europe, but article 22 divided the German colonies between other European nations. This division of territory was just as important as that produced by the Berlin conference of 1885, and once again the Africans were given no voice in their future. Granted, some missionaries were tasked with canvassing African opinion and representing them at the conference in France, but like the politicians, the missionaries had their own vested interests and agenda. The one significant concession made to "African interests" at Versailles was the acknowledgment that, in the words of one historian, Africans "could no longer be bandied about like so many sheep."[15] At the insistence of the United States—which was now beginning to assume a much greater role in international politics—the ex-colonies of Germany were not to be simply handed over to the victorious Allies; instead, they were to become "mandates," administered under the auspices of the newly founded League of Nations. These mandates declared:

> To those colonies and territories which as a consequence of the late war have ceased to be under the sovereignty of the States which formerly governed them and which are inhabited by peoples not yet able to stand by themselves under the strenuous conditions of the modern world, there should be applied the principle that the well-being and development of such peoples form a sacred trust of civilization . . . [and that] . . . the tutelage of such people should be entrusted to advanced nations who, by reason of their resources, their experience or their geographical position, can best undertake this responsibility and who are willing to accept it.[16]

The so-called Class B mandates covered all of the former German colonies in Africa. In German East Africa specifically, Ruanda and Urundi (now called Rwanda and Burundi) would be administered with the Belgian Congo, with the rest of Deutsch-Ostafrika falling under British military rule, consisting of the territory that would become known as Tanganyika.

Despite the grandiose, paternalistic ideals behind the League of Nations, any ordinary African would be hard pressed the see the distinction between a "colony" and a "mandate." As the historian Brian Digre has explained, mandates were simply "imperialism's new clothes."[17] It would take another World War, when Africans again fought and died alongside Europeans, before there was any real progress toward self-governance for Africans. Even so, the end of the First World War marked a turning point in the history of East Africa, and a nascent independence movement was beginning to emerge.

Between 1914 and 1918, Africans fought alongside their white masters, and the experience transformed the image that the black man had of the white. Previously, the European had been feared—he was a superhuman, capable of killing on a whim and curing at a stroke. Now, having spent four long and arduous years living, sleeping, and dying alongside white officers, often advising them in the secrets of jungle warfare, Africans realized there was nothing omnipotent about their colonial masters.

They had also been introduced to the new technology of the European, as one postwar reporter noted:

> Men who a few years ago had never seen a white man, to whom the mechanism of a tap or a doorhandle is still an inscrutable mystery, have been trained to carry into action on their heads the field wireless or the latest quick-firing gun. Men of tribes which had never advanced so far in civilisation as to use wheeled transport, who a few years ago would have run shrieking from the sight of a train, have been steadied till they learned to pull great motor lorries out of the mud, to plod patiently along hardly stepping to one side while convoy after convoy of oxcarts, mule carts and motor vehicles

grazed by them, till they hardly turned their heads at the whirr of passing aircraft.[18]

For some young Luo warriors—as with many of the other African tribes—the white man's war was traumatic. They had long known tribal war and death, but this European conflict was on a scale and magnitude far beyond anything they could have imagined. The rules of the white man's war were also different from those of the African, and the traditional tribal taboos had been broken, leaving a persistent, lingering anxiety about the consequences. The African *askaris* had lived in huts and camps that were obviously cursed with the deaths of others, and they had witnessed horrific injuries and diseases inflicted on their comrades, who were then violated in death by being buried in mass graves with strangers.

Some returning Africans could not face the future and took their own lives—suicide being a rare occurrence in Africa. Others were reluctant to talk about what they had experienced, for fear they would be banished from their community. Military doctors diagnosed the condition among the Africans as a mental illness similar to shell-shock, but circumstances and complaints differed both among individuals and among tribes. The Kikuyu in particular were badly affected, with many young men classified as temporarily insane. The Luo, of course, feared that because the bodies of their fallen comrades could never be buried in Luoland, their spirits would become demons—*jachien*.

Onyango Obama was away from Nyanza for the whole of the war. After road duties he joined the British force that was pursuing the Germans south out of German East Africa. He also spent some time in Zanzibar, which was a British protectorate throughout the war years. There he encountered Islam for the first time. As a young boy he had been brought up to worship the Luo god Nyasaye, who was manifest in everyday things, including the sun, the moon, the lake, and some wild animals. At mission school he had been introduced to Christianity; he was baptized and even took the very English name of Johnson for a short time. But for Onyango, like many Africans at the time, the Christian message of love and compassion toward all men was difficult to reconcile with the white man's apparent willingness to go to war. Onyango saw the Christian doctrine of showing mercy toward one's fellow man as ambiguous, even a sign of weakness—nothing more than sentimental gibberish. So it is not surprising that Islam should have appealed to Onyango, who appreciated the structure and discipline it brought to his life.

Members of Onyango's family think there were other reasons behind his embrace of Islam. John Ndalo thought that at least part of the appeal was the women: "Onyango was an adventurous person and he went to many places, including during the First World War. He met many different people, including Muslims. He even married Muslim wives. So, he had a liking of the Muslim people and he had a liking of the Muslim ladies."

Charles Oluoch thought similarly:

> These Muslim ladies, they know how to treat men. Onyango was attracted to these Muslim ladies because they are different from our women. They are more submissive.
>
> The Christians, when they came, they believed that polygamy was wrong. But Muslims, they gave you the assurance that you can have even five wives. . . . So I think he found it to be more comfortable in Islam than Christianity.

As part of his conversion, Onyango took the Arab name Hussein, which he later passed on to his eldest son, who in turn gave it to Onyango's grandson, President Barack Hussein Obama. However, Onyango's conversion to Islam was anathema to his family back home, who were adopting Christianity under the teachings of the Seventh-Day Adventists. Onyango seems to have taken satisfaction in being different, and no doubt he relished his independence.

Onyango stayed in Zanzibar for a couple of years after the war and did not return to Kendu Bay until 1920. By this time, his family had given up any hope of seeing him alive—after all, he had been away for six years without making any contact. When he eventually returned home, he had to persuade them he was real: "See, this is the real Onyango—it is me!" he is claimed to have said.

Hussein Onyango was still only twenty-five, and under normal circumstances he would have moved back to his father's homestead and looked for a wife. But he was too proud to return, and besides, his faith now made him even more of an outsider in the eyes of his family. Instead he sought to establish a life for himself in Kendu Bay, away from his family. Fortunately, land was still available, so Onyango set about clearing an area some distance away from his father's homestead where he could establish his own compound. He did not initially build himself a traditional *simba,* but chose instead to live in an army-issue tent. People thought that he was crazy, and this only added to his estrangement from his family.

After demobilization thousands of young Africans returned home to find a society in turmoil. East Africa had not seen such a drain on manpower since the 1870s, when Arab slave traders had taken twenty-five thousand Africans a year. For more than four years the normal, supportive African village life had been in limbo; families were dislocated, aging parents neglected, farms abandoned. Young men returned—some of them ill, traumatized, or disabled—to find that their traditional way of life had gone. Meanwhile, their chiefs were rewarded for their loyalty to the British, first for recruiting young men and then for rounding up any deserters. Not surprisingly, the Africans blamed their colonial masters for their postwar problems.

In south Nyanza, the war had disrupted a profitable trade with the region bordering German East Africa, and the population was suffering the consequences. In 1918 the rains had failed in western Kenya, bringing a famine in 1919. The Luo called the famine *kanga,* after the name of the returning soldiers, and an estimated 155,000 people in British East Africa died from starvation that year—three times the number of porters who died in the war. John Ndalo, who was a young child at the time, remembers the locust swarms that exacerbated the food shortages in Nyanza:

> The locusts used to invade this place. They came over the trees and they ate all the leaves and everything, and just left the trees as sticks. . . . There was no food for cattle and there was no food for people.
>
> We devised a method, because they were eating all our food. We said that we must eat them. . . . We'd come very early in the morning and collect them, and then we'd have to boil them for food, and they were very nutritious. Even now, we still eat the locusts—it's called *ongogo* here. You put salt on them so they are tastier.

If famine and locust swarms were not enough, the Spanish influenza pandemic was sweeping the world in the aftermath of war. In the two years between 1918 and 1920 many more died of influenza worldwide than in four years of combat. The Scottish medical missionary Dr. Horace Philp estimated that in south Nyanza district alone five thousand people died from flu, and many more from smallpox and plague.[19] Yet not a single trained medical doctor or pharmacist was available after the war to help the debilitated population of south Nyanza.

The families of the war veterans also received little help from the authorities. Parents and wives who had lost their men hoped for compensation, but nothing was forthcoming. The government announced that unless the men had been officially registered (a procedure that was introduced only in 1915 and was not universal until 1923), no payment would be made, because it would be impossible to trace the relatives.

Still other changes came after the war. In 1915 the government had accepted the white settlers' demand for greater security of land tenure, extending the leases on their farms in the White Highlands from 99 to 999 years. The next year, the British increased the hut and poll taxes on the Africans to help pay for the war. After the end of hostilities, the British government formally annexed British East Africa, declared it to be a Crown colony, and renamed it Kenya* after the mountain in its center. The government also introduced new, onerous demands on the African population: laborers' wages were reduced by a third; a certificate of identification—the *kipande*—was introduced to catch those who ran away from their employers; every male over sixteen was fingerprinted; direct taxation was increased to sixteen shillings a head; and women and girls were compelled to work on white-owned farms. Harry Thuku, a Kikuyu leader who founded the Young Kikuyu Association in 1921 to oppose colonial rule, explained in his autobiography how the women were recruited to work on the new farms:

> A settler who wanted labour for his farm would write to the DC [District Commissioner]. . . . The DC sent a letter to the chief or headman to supply such and such a number, and the chief in turn had his tribal retainers to carry out this business. They would simply go to people's houses—very often where there were beautiful women and daughters—and point out which were to come and work. Sometimes they had to work a distance from home and the number of girls who got pregnant in this way was very great.[20]

The white population too experienced postwar changes, but these were much more favorably received. The introduction of a new soldier settlement scheme was designed to double the European farming population in Kenya. In order to accommodate the anticipated influx of white farmers, the government claimed a further five thousand square miles of the highlands—land taken mainly from the Kikuyu.

---

*The white Kenyans pronounce the name *KEE-nyer,* whereas the black Kenyans prefer *KEHN-yuh.*

By the early 1920s, Hussein Onyango had established his independence by building a proper homestead in Kendu Bay. His neighbors admired the fine hut he had built himself; he kept it scrupulously clean and filled it with fascinating objects that he had brought back from the war. Onyango only added to his mystique when he produced a small wooden box that could speak like a human. The whole community congregated to witness this miracle. One of the elders, his great-uncle Aguk, suggested they should destroy it, as it was obviously their ancestors who had come back to life—the voices could only belong to the much feared *jachien*. Onyango's older brother Ndalo disagreed: instead, he said, they should take the box apart so that they could see the small people talking inside. Onyango patiently explained that the box was called a radio, and it allowed people to talk to one another across long distances. Some of the villagers were not convinced, and they insisted that they would never return to his house until he had cleansed his hut of the spirits with an animal sacrifice.

On a later occasion, Onyango told the skeptical villagers that he could go to an office in Kisumu and talk to people in Nairobi. James Otieno, who is now a very old man living in K'ogelo, was a young boy at the time; he remembers people blowing horns and beating drums to call everyone together. Some of the men were heard murmuring that Onyango had gone completely mad, while others claimed that he had been turned into a witch. Some even accused him of using the story to lure Africans together so that they could be tricked into being sold to the white man. The bravest of the community left Kendu Bay early one morning and accompanied Onyango to the Kisumu railway station. From there he went to the telegraph office, where just as he had promised, a message came through from his white employers in Nairobi.

Onyango had finished building his hut in K'obama, but the impoverished countryside of south Nyanza offered little to a restless young man. So he returned to Nairobi, where he began to build a reputation among the white colonialists as a reliable house servant and cook. In this respect Onyango resembled many Africans at this time who were obliged to work for cash to pay their taxes. Besides, rural life was hard in Luoland after the war, and Onyango thought himself better off in Nairobi, learning the white man's ways. Sarah Obama claims that Onyango's many employers during this time included Hugh Cholmondeley, the third Baron Delamere, de facto leader of the white community in Kenya and founding member of what became known as the "Happy Valley" set—a clique of wealthy British colonials whose pleasure-seeking habits involved riotous parties, drug taking, and wife swapping.

Around the time that Hussein Onyango decided to work in Nairobi, his older brother, Ndalo, left Kendu Bay and returned to the ancestral home in K'ogelo, which his great-grandfather Obong'o had left in the 1830s. It was a major change for Ndalo—he had two wives and young children, and all his immediate family were in Kendu Bay. The circumstances surrounding his departure comprise a typical Luo story of squabbling and infighting. His grandson, Charles Oluoch, explained to me what happened:

> There were three sons, but Ndalo and Onyango were similar in character. Oguta—their youngest brother—was somebody very polite. But Ndalo was always aggressive and he was very boastful. He was told [by another Kendu Bay villager] he was *jadak* [a foreigner]—"You are disturbing us!" He was a very proud man. So he took his two wives and his cattle and he walked from here up to Alego [a distance of 80 miles].

Moving onto the land his great-grandfather Obong'o had vacated nearly a hundred years previously, Ndalo cleared the land, planted his crops, and built huts for himself and his two wives. He also took to riding a bull around the village, looking very regal; this earned him the nickname "King George," after the reigning British monarch. Here in K'ogelo at least, nobody could call him *jadak*.

Two years later in 1922 Ndalo's senior wife, Odero, gave birth to their second son, Peter Oluoch, who became father to Charles and his older brother, Wilson. When Peter was three, Ndalo and his two wives died unexpectedly, leaving Peter and his two siblings orphaned. People say that the three adults died very suddenly, within a couple of days of becoming ill, and K'ogelo villagers were convinced that a curse had been placed on the family and their homestead. In reality, the cause of their deaths was almost certainly smallpox. The disfigurement and pustules that form on the body of smallpox victims could only have added to the horror their neighbors felt at such a shocking family catastrophe, reinforcing the belief that witchcraft was the cause. A second tragedy was about to befall the family within days of their deaths, as Charles Oluoch explained: "When they died, my father was three years old, so it was around 1925. When people were wailing [at the funeral], he fell into the fire and he was burnt. And it was my aunt, who was called Drusilla, who was the one who rescued him from that fire. At the time he could not walk fully." Peter Oluoch was scarred for the rest of his life.

After the funeral, distant relatives of Ndalo offered to take care of the three young children, as is the Luo custom. But Hussein Onyango would have none of it, and despite not being married, he insisted on taking his two nephews and his niece with him back to Kendu Bay:

> Onyango took them and brought them back here [to Kendu Bay], to their grandmothers. When my father [Peter] was at school age, Onyango adopted him. So where he worked, all these whites, they knew him as the son of Onyango. . . . He also converted him to be a Muslim. Even these Muslims in Kendu Bay, they thought my father was the first son of Onyango.
>
> Odero [the eldest boy] stayed with his grandmother, but Onyango took my father. There was something he admired about him. You know, Onyango was a very harsh person—he'd call you and he'd like you to run. I think my father knew how to work Onyango.

Onyango decided that Peter Oluoch should join him in Nairobi, where he would receive a better education than in Kendu Bay. However, the rest of the family were unanimously against the idea. After all, Onyango was considered to be a madman—or at best, very odd. How could he possibly look after a young boy when he didn't even have a wife? But Hussein Onyango had made up his mind, and together they left to take the ferry from Kendu Bay to Kisumu. Distraught, the women of K'obama followed them down to the jetty, and one—who was more hysterical than most—threw herself into the waters of Winam Gulf as the boat left for Kisumu, in a last-minute attempt to rescue Peter.

The early 1920s saw the beginnings of a grassroots rebellion against the colonial government, both in Nyanza and in the Kikuyu lands. In 1921 Harry Thuku founded the Young Kikuyu Association to protest against unreasonable taxation and the much reviled *kipande* system. *Kipande,* which literally translates to "a piece," referred to a small steel cylinder containing identity papers that every African laborer had to wear constantly if he hoped to find employment. The following year, Thuku founded the East African Association, which campaigned against the forced labor of women and girls. But both efforts were short lived. Thuku was arrested for his political activities on March 14, 1922, and exiled, without charge, to the remote Northern Frontier province. He remained there for the next nine years.

In Nyanza province, the more politicized Luo convened a secret meeting to decide how they should protest against direct governance. The main protagonists were the young "mission boys"—the first generation of Luo boys who had been educated by the missionaries. The mission boys decided to organize a strike and a boycott of classes at Maseno school—the top mission school outside of Kisumu (and later the alma mater of President Obama's father). The missionaries at Maseno were generally sympathetic to the principles of the boycott, having also lost some of their autonomy under the new colonial regulations. Next, Luo

leaders organized a public meeting to call for the Kenya protectorate to become a colony. Nine thousand people attended the meeting
on December 23, 1921, at Luanda in Gem (northwest of Kisumu)—a
remarkable number at a time when the ordinary African had no access
to the telegraph, telephones, or any mechanized transport. The main
demand of the meeting was local autonomy for the Luo under an elected
president—a *ker*. Following the lead of Harry Thuku, the people also
voted to form a new association. The Young Kavirondo Association was
the first attempt to mobilize the people of Nyanza into a militant political force. It was not particularly long lived: in 1923, in order to avoid
being banned by the British, the Young Kavirondo Association rewrote
its constitution and changed its name to the Kavirondo Taxpayers' Welfare Association. Nevertheless, the Young Kavirondo Association was
one of the first African-led political movements in Kenya, and not only
did it challenge British colonial rule, but it also laid the foundation for
Luo tribal politics in an independent Kenya more than forty years later.

Hussein Onyango, however, was not really interested in politics. By
the mid-1920s he was an accomplished and successful cook, working
for the British in Nairobi and the Rift Valley. Onyango had come to
admire the British, especially their discipline and organization. In this
respect, Onyango was not alone among the Luo. The Kikuyu had lost
huge areas of their land to the white farmers and been forced onto
tribal reserves with poor farming land, but the Luo were spared such
draconian measures. It suited the British to "divide and rule" the different Kenyan tribes, and many Luo found well-paid jobs working for
white families or for the colonial administration. Recognizing that the
Luo had a reputation for intelligence (something the Luo put down to
their high-protein diet of fish and meat), the British had encouraged

the education of the young mission boys, hoping they would form the foundation of an Africanized administration in East Africa.

By African standards, Onyango prospered; the good money he was earning in Nairobi allowed him to acquire more cattle back in Kendu Bay, and his hut was always spotlessly clean. But his family and neighbors in Kendu Bay still thought he was odd, for Onyango lived like a white man, even when he was home in Luoland. He ate at a wooden table with a knife and fork, and he wore European clothes, which were always scrupulously neat and tidy. He insisted that people take off their shoes and wash their feet before entering. Inevitably, Onyango became the focus of village gossip, especially as he had still not married. According to President Obama's memoir, Onyango married three women. However, several elders in Kendu Bay indicated that the reality was much more complicated than that. Charles Oluoch had his own theory about his uncle's complex relationships with women:

> Onyango was his own man, and he knew how to find women. He had so many friends, and if they liked him, they would say, "I have a sister here. . . ." He used to travel a lot—Onyango had the spirit of adventure. [And] it took him time to settle, to have his own family, whilst his other brothers overtook him [with a family] when they were younger.

One of his brothers-in-law, Abdo Omar Okech, also knew all about Onyango's reputation as a ladies' man, and he explained why he thought Onyango was so successful with women:

> Onyango was a medicine man and he knew a lot about herbs which could cure people. Because of this, many women liked him.
>
> Most of these ladies were not married, but when they looked at him, I think because of his build, they just loved him. They just fell for him. He must have been a very attractive man because of all these women. A woman would come and stay with him for a month or two, then he would kick them out and take another one.

John Ndalo, who lived close to Onyango's compound in Kendu Bay, recalled the women he finally married:

> There was a lady from Kawango in Mumias [in central Nyanza], and he even took cattle to Mumias and paid a bride price. Then there was Halima, and then Sofia Odera from Karungu, beyond Homa Bay in South Nyanza. Then Habiba Akumu, then Sarah.

Onyango was already up to his Islamic limit of five wives, and they were only the ones he had actually married, but John Ndalo tried to clarify the situation:

> In Africa, if you don't have a child with your wife, it is very easy to marry another one. In our culture, we only recognize somebody as your wife if you take the cattle. But we cannot rule out if there were some who were "good friends," because you can stay with them for one or two years, but we do not recognize them [as a wife], because you have not taken the cattle.

Nobody can remember the name of Onyango's first wife from Kawango, but they do remember that he paid her family twenty head of cattle as a bride-price. When she did not produce a child, Onyango divorced her, but out of pride he never went back for his cows, which was unusual for a Luo.

Onyango had very high standards of cleanliness and behavior, and he also had a violent temper. Even by the harsh standards of Luo husbands in those days, Onyango was cruel toward his women. John Ndalo said, "Onyango loved to welcome visitors. If his women did not behave well in front of them, then he would beat them there, right in front of the visitors. He would not wait."

By the late 1920s, Onyango found a respectful and gentle woman who tolerated his outbursts and beatings. Halima came from Ugenya, a region in central Nyanza, north of Siaya, and he met her when he was working for a white man in the area. Onyango was now in his early thirties, and like any Luo husband in that situation, he looked forward to his new wife producing a son and heir quickly. Unfortunately, their union was not blessed with children. Clearly Onyango was not infertile, as he went on to father eight children with his later wives, but a married man without children soon becomes a subject of gossip in Kenya.

Sarah Obama tells the story of Onyango visiting a Nairobi dance hall one night, whereupon he was confronted by a drunk: "Onyango, you are already an older man [he was in his mid-thirties at the time]. You have cattle, and you have a wife, and yet you have no children. Tell me, is something the matter between your legs?"[21] Onyango was furious, but the cruel words found their mark, and he returned home to Kendu Bay determined to find another wife who could give him children.

So Onyango married again, this time a young girl called Sofia Odera from Homa Bay, a fishing village about twelve miles west of Kendu Bay. John Ndalo recalls that Onyango paid fifteen head of cattle this time as the bride-price, but when Sofia and Onyango parted company, childless, Onyango again was too proud to reclaim his cows.

Onyango's father, Obama, died around 1930. Although they had been estranged when Onyango was young, father and son had since reconciled and Obama had contributed cattle to Onyango's bride-prices. A successful, traditional Luo tribesman, Obama left five widows— Nyaoke (the mother of Onyango and great-grandmother to the president), Auma, Mwanda, Odera, and Augo. Between them they bore him eight sons and several daughters. However after his death, Obama's hut was not destroyed in the Luo tradition; instead, his wives continued to live there, although they were inherited by other men.

In the small village of Kanyadhiang I met a close relative of Onyango called Laban Opiyo. His father's sister was Nyaoke, Obama's first wife, making Laban a first cousin to Onyango and great-uncle to President Obama. A small, thin, frail man who has spent his whole life working in the sun, Laban looked every one of his eighty-seven years.

Born in 1922, Laban was only about eight when Onyango's father died, but he still remembers the event clearly:

> I knew him very well. Obama was a tall man, a huge man, and well built. He married three girls just from our village here. There was Nyaoke and Mwanda, and then Auma, all from the same clan. But Nyaoke and Auma were real sisters. He kept working until he was very old—he loved farming. He didn't go to school. When he was an old man, he went to his *simba,* his hut, to attend to his garden, and he sat there on a small stool, gardening. I know he was very, very old when he died.
>
> Onyango was in Nairobi [at the time]. He brought a gun—a rifle. He said that by 9 p.m., everyone had to be at his father's home. When he reached the compound, he fired into the air. At the first gunshot, everybody ran into the houses because they had never heard anything like this before. I counted six gunshots. . . . I kept asking him, "What is this that is sending fire into heaven?" And we were very much afraid, because we had never heard a gun before, never. That is one thing that I can really remember about Hussein Onyango. He used that gun to send off his father in a dignified way.
>
> Obama had a traditional burial. Before he died, he slaughtered his biggest bull and its skin was used as his shroud. He was buried the next day—his body could not be preserved like today. He was probably in his seventies when he died. When they buried him, they had a ceremony called *tero buru*—it is "taking the dust"—to scare away the dead spirits. They used to run here and there, sing songs and had mock fights. They also slaughtered a big cockerel.

By 1926, twenty-two thousand Africans in the protectorate were working in domestic service—about one in every seven gainfully employed men.[22] In an attempt to monitor this sector, the colonial authorities introduced a system of worker registration after the Great War, issuing to Onyango and others like him a small red book. On its cover was the title Domestic Servant's Pocket Register, followed in smaller type by: Issued under the Authority of the Registration of Domestic Servant's Ordinance, 1928, Colony and Protectorate of Kenya. During his first visit to Kenya in 1987, Barack Obama junior's half sister Auma showed him Onyango's registration document, which Sarah keeps in her hut in K'ogelo.[23] Onyango's booklet is faded now and the spine is broken, but the contents provide a fascinating glimpse of Onyango's life at the time.

Inside the cover are Onyango's two thumbprints—a standard identification mark at the time, even though Onyango could sign his own name as well as read and write English proficiently. The introduction inside the document explains its purpose:

> The object of this Ordinance is to provide every person employed in a domestic capacity with a record of such employment, and to safeguard his or her interests as well as to protect employers against the employment of persons who have rendered themselves unsuitable for such work.

The term *servant* was defined as "cook, house servant, waiter, butler, nurse, valet, bar boy, footman, or chauffeur, or washermen."

The British took their official documents very seriously, and anyone found defacing the booklet was "liable to a fine not exceeding one hundred shillings or imprisonment not exceeding six months or both." The fine was more than a month's earnings for a Kenyan house servant.

Further into the book are Onyango's full registration details:

Name . . . . Hussein Onyango
Native Registration Ordnance No. . . . . . RWL A NBI 0976717
Race or Tribe . . . . Ja'Luo
Usual Place of Residence When Not
    Employed. . . . . Kisumu
Sex . . . . M
Age 35

Height and Build . . . . 6'0" Medium
Complexion . . . . Dark
Nose . . . . Flat
Mouth . . . . Large
Hair . . . . Curly
Teeth . . . . Six Missing
Scars, Tribal Marks, or Other
   Peculiarities . . . . None

The back of the book is reserved for notes, mainly references from previous employers, which explains why the authorities took any defacement or alteration of the booklet so seriously. From the citations, Onyango was clearly highly respected by most of his white employers; Captain C. Harford, who gives his address as Government House in Nairobi, wrote that Onyango "performed his duties as personal boy with admirable diligence." Mr. A. G. Dickson noted that "he can read and write English and follows any recipes . . . apart from other things his pastries are excellent." Dr. H. H. Sherry was equally flattering and commented that Onyango "is a capable cook but the job is not big enough for him."

However, Onyango was not always the model employee, and a certain Mr. Arthur Cole of the East Africa Survey Group noted that after a week on the job, Onyango was "found to be unsuitable and certainly not worth 60 shillings per month." (Introduced in 1921, the East African shilling was equivalent to one shilling sterling; Onyango's monthly wage would now be worth about $220, much the same as what a Kenyan would earn in a similar position today.) The registration book also documents the tenuous nature and short term of Onyango's employment during this period. Mr. Dickson no longer required Onyango's services because, he wrote: "I am no longer on Safari." Nor is it likely that Onyango would have stayed with Arthur Cole for much longer either, after such a poor evaluation.

By 1933, Onyango was a wealthy man by Luo standards, but still he had no children. That year he was back in Kendu Bay on one of his regular visits when he saw a beautiful young girl walking along the road to market. She would eventually become the paternal grandmother of the president of the United States of America, and the circumstances surrounding their meeting and elopement were extraordinary.

Akumu was from the village of Simbi Kolonde, just a short distance outside Kendu Bay. She was tall, young, and striking, and Onyango was instantly smitten. Akumu's youngest daughter, Auma (aunt to President Obama), explained how they met: "My mother was taking fish into the market and she was carrying one of the traditional baskets [on her head]. And when my father saw my mother, she was very beautiful. My father forced my mother to leave the fish and then grabbed her and put her into the car and sped off."

Akumu's family claim that she was abducted in broad daylight. Nobody knew where Onyango had hidden the young girl, and her family was distraught by his foolish and impulsive action. Auma continued the story:

> My father had taken my mother forcefully, and he was cautioned by the local leadership . . . he was questioned and they arrested him.
>
> Now this is what my father said: "I can't leave this woman because I love her and I did not rape her. I want her and I love her and I will pay everything that the people want." My father went and untied thirty-five cattle just to come and pay for this girl . . . because he loved her so much.
>
> Having paid this, the authorities allowed him to take Akumu back to Nairobi. At first, my mother did not like my father, because she had not known him at all. This was a forceful marriage. But now, having taken her, he showed her a lot of respect and love, then she loved him and she agreed to stay with Onyango.

Onyango was nearly forty and Akumu was only sixteen or seventeen years old, but such an age difference was not unusual in African marriages at the time. (When Onyango married for the fifth time several years later, Sarah too was in her teens.) Akumu came from a Christian family—indeed, she was the only Christian woman Onyango ever married—but Hussein Onyango insisted that she convert to Islam, and she took the Muslim name Habiba. Their union quickly brought the long-desired result of a child for Onyango, and Sarah Nyaoke was born in 1934, followed by Barack senior (father to the president) two years later. Their third child, Hawa Auma, was born in 1942, and a fourth child, Rashidi, was born in 1944; Rashidi died from a fever when he was about ten. All of Hussein Onyango's children were raised as Muslims.

In a pattern of married life that is still common in Kenya even today, Onyango continued to work in Nairobi as a cook while Akumu and her young children lived more than two hundred miles away in Kendu Bay. But after several years of married life, passion began to wane and Akumu and Onyango began having heated arguments. By all accounts the president's grandmother was a strong and determined woman, and she was not prepared to tolerate what she saw as Onyango's unrealistic expectations of discipline and cleanliness around the compound.

As the marriage began to fade, Onyango took a fifth wife. Sarah Ogwel was born into a Muslim family in Kendu Bay in 1922, and she told me that she married in 1941, when Onyango was forty-six. Her youngest brother, Abdo Omar Okech, is seventy-six and he still lives in the Muslim quarter of Kendu Bay, a stone's throw from where he was born. He explained that his father, Omar Okech, had been a good friend of Onyango's for years:

> At that time I was only a small kid, but I overheard that my sister Sarah was to be given to Hussein. They were very good friends and my father said, "Will you marry my daughter?" According to our African customs, Sarah could not go against my father's will.
>
> It is possible that she would even have been given freely, but

because Onyango loved my father, Hussein gave many cows to my family for her bride price.

Sarah remained married to Onyango for more years than all his other wives combined, and her brother explained Sarah's secret:

The difference between Mama Sarah and these other women was that Sarah would not talk back to him. He loved Sarah because whatever he said, Sarah complied.

Sarah and Onyango married after Onyango returned from a brief spell of service in the King's African Rifles during the Second World War, and they spent their first years of married life living together in Nairobi, while Akumu tended the farm back in Kendu Bay and brought up her young children.

Although Onyango had a reputation as a strict disciplinarian with a fiery temper, he was also generous with his family. The Luo have a saying, *pand nyaluo dhoge ariyo*—an old knife has two edges—and this certainly applied to Onyango; he could be violent and cruel, but also generous and supportive. As a young man, John Ndalo knew Onyango well:

I have known Onyango since I was very young. He was a very interesting man. He did not want any friends—everybody had to be under him, not above him. He had a very strict set of rules about where you would sit. He would even whip you—friends and visitors—if you did not do what he said. He had a lot of influence. He was well known all around the area—he was known even fifty miles away!

I have lived here [in Kendu Bay] all my life, but I worked in Nairobi for the whites in big hotels, and also at the airport. Hussein Onyango taught us how to work . . . he moved me to Nairobi in 1941 and found me a job. He did not want us to be lazy. He always said, "If you do a good job for the white man, then he will always pay you well." Many whites loved him because he was a good worker.

By the end of the 1930s Hussein Onyango was a committed Anglophile: he dressed like a white man, he behaved like a white man, and he even had dentures fitted to replace the six teeth that had been removed during his initiation into Luo adulthood. From his time in Nairobi, he had developed a deep respect for the British, although it was more a reverence for the power, organization, and discipline that they brought to Africa than any real emotional attachment. Charles Oluoch adamantly denied that Hussein Onyango, deep down inside, might have wanted to be British:

> No! He was proud to be a black man. But he admired the British because of their openness, and that is why he did their things. Onyango never liked somebody who lies. He liked people who were truthful to him, and that is why he was very close to my father, because my father would always tell him the truth. If he asks you, "Where have you been?" you tell him exactly where you were. The British liked people who were truthful, and if you were truthful, then they would promote you and give you things. So Onyango admired them.

But Onyango's unpredictable nature eventually led to an acrimonious split with Charles Oluoch's father, Peter. Onyango had adopted Peter when he was young and wanted him to have the best education he could find. So he enrolled Peter in a top school in Kisii, where Onyango was working at the time. Peter was twelve or fourteen, so this must have been in the mid-1930s. One day Peter was sent out on an errand, but he dropped the coins Onyango had given him. When he got home, rather than lie and tell Onyango that the money had been stolen, Peter admitted that he had lost the coins somewhere. Onyango was furious and beat Peter until his back bled. Peter was shocked at the injustice—after all, he had owned up to a small mistake, so why was he being beaten? Disillusioned, Peter ran away back to Kendu Bay. Onyango followed him to bring him back, but by the time he arrived at the family compound, Peter had already left for Kisumu and would have nothing more to do with Onyango.

September 1, 1939, marked the beginning of another global conflict. More than 100 million military personnel were mobilized around the world, and in East Africa, the British conscripted 323,483 African troops into the King's African Rifles. This time, instead of fighting in East Africa, the KAR saw action against Italian forces in Ethiopia and against the Japanese in Burma.[24] Even though he was now in his mid-forties, Hussein Onyango joined the KAR for a second time in 1940. According to Sarah, he saw service in both theaters:

> The white man he was working for was called Major Batson. . . . They went to Addis Ababa, they went to India and Burma and everywhere. He was old, but he was a man who could cook very well and they liked him. He was a cook, but when the enemies came, he had to put on all the uniform and he was ready for combat.

When Onyango was on active service in Burma, he claimed to have met and married another wife. Onyango might have had a rather casual attitude about what exactly constituted a marriage, but he returned from overseas with a framed photograph of the woman, which Sarah Obama still keeps in her hut in K'ogelo.

This second European conflict was another turning point for the Africans. When they went to war for the British, they were told that they were fighting for liberty and freedom from repression. After hostilities ended, they came home with high expectations. They looked forward to being granted freedom in their own country, and to the end of British rule. But Hussein Onyango, Peter Oluoch, and hundreds of thousands of other Kenyan soldiers returned to a country that offered little hope and even less opportunity. They had saved their army wages, but their attempts to start small businesses were thwarted by the imposition of petty colonial rules and regulations. The ex-soldiers became disillusioned, and that made them dangerous.

For the British, the war marked the end of empire and the beginning of the end of colonial rule in Kenya. But disengagement would take another eighteen years, and once again Onyango Obama would be drawn into a conflict of interests between the white men he admired and his own people.

Onyango returned from the war early, in 1941, and that year he married Sarah. Shortly after, Onyango moved his family back across the Winam Gulf to his family's ancestral home in K'ogelo. Onyango's great-grandfather Obong'o had left K'ogelo around 1830 and moved south to Kendu Bay because of overpopulation and constant fighting between the subclans; Onyango's older brother, Ndalo, returned to K'ogelo after the Great War, only to die along with his wives from smallpox, leaving three young children orphaned (including Peter Oluoch). But in the early 1940s, Onyango had no close relatives living in K'ogelo, so it was no small matter for him to leave Kendu Bay and return to his ancestral village with his two wives and young children. Once again, the reason for this family upheaval was Onyango being his usual hotheaded self.

By 1943 Hussein Onyango was nearly fifty years old, a wealthy middle-aged man, well respected within the community by all accounts, with two wives, three young children, and his extended family living around him. The problem started, apparently, with a football trophy. At the time, Onyango was working for the local British district commissioner, a man called William. (Nobody can remember his last name.) William knew that the local boys were passionate about playing soccer, so he gave Onyango a trophy—really more of a bell than a cup—and suggested that Onyango should organize the local soccer teams to play in a tournament, presenting the winning side with the trophy.

John Ndalo explained how things suddenly went so terribly wrong: "Onyango was very proud of the trophy and he wanted to call it the 'Onyango Cup.' The local chief, Paul Mboya, did not like this and he insisted on renaming it the 'Karachuonyo Cup,' after the name of the local district. Onyango was furious—he could not be told what to do by another African. He thought he was better than other Africans."

Onyango and Mboya had crossed swords several times before, including over the recruitment of forced labor in the 1930s, and also over the abduction of Akumu—it was Mboya who had had him arrested over that episode. Now Onyango was challenging the chief's position again, and insults were exchanged between Mboya, who was trying to impose his authority on the situation, and the fiercely proud and argumentative Hussein Onyango. They must have been like two old bulls fighting in a field—and neither one of them was prepared to back down:

> Mboya became very angry and he accused Onyango of being *jadak*—a settler [because his family had moved to the area three generations previously]. Onyango was furious! "I know my roots," he said, and he immediately went back home and told his family that they were leaving. Samuel Dola was one of Onyango's best friends—he was the previous chief before Mboya—and when Dola heard what had happened, he ran to Onyango's house and beseeched him to stay. But Onyango had made up his mind and he would not change it, so he packed up and left. He gave away all his possessions and left the village and went back to K'ogelo.

It was exactly the same insult that Onyango's brother Ndalo had heard more than twenty years previously—and Onyango's response was the same. Not surprisingly, neither of Onyango's wives wanted to leave Kendu Bay, especially not because of a ridiculous argument about the name of a football trophy. Sarah claims she was young and adaptable and was prepared to move—one family friend indelicately explained there was "hot love" there—and Onyango had little trouble persuading her to go. However, Akumu strongly opposed the idea of moving, and this only made her frequent arguments with Onyango worse. Her family intervened and eventually prevailed upon her to go for the sake of her children: they needed their mother, and Onyango was going to take them to K'ogelo whether Akumu went or not. Onyango's move to K'ogelo created a division in the Obama family that still exists today, intensified by the fact that the family in K'ogelo are all Muslim, like Onyango, while the Obamas who stayed behind in Kendu Bay remain Seventh-Day Adventists. And that is why Onyango lived out the last of his days in K'ogelo, and why both he and Barack senior are buried there today, instead of in Kendu Bay.

Nobody is quite sure exactly when Onyango moved to K'ogelo with Akumu and Sarah, but Paul Mboya stepped down in 1946, so the argument over the trophy must have happened before then. Sarah gave birth to her first child, Omar, in K'ogelo in June 1944, so the family probably moved in late 1943, a couple of years after the birth of Hawa Auma. The first thing that Onyango did when he arrived in K'ogelo was to claim his brother's old compound, which had sat empty for over twenty years. Even though Ndalo and his two wives had died there in 1925, the local people still thought the homestead was bewitched and they would have nothing to do with it. Their superstitions did not deter Onyango; perhaps he even relished the chance to prove everybody wrong and show that he was stronger than the curse of any local witch doctor.

With his difficult temperament, Onyango soon made his mark in this tightly knit community. Word spread quickly that the family were living in Ndalo's blighted compound with no adverse effects. This was seen as a bad omen and a threat to the well-being of the village, and the local people summoned their local witch doctor—the *uyoma*—to finish him off. The locals seem to have genuinely believed that their *uyoma* had caused the deaths of Ndalo and his two wives and was not a man to be crossed. The *uyoma,* for his part, probably boasted of his part in the death of these three adults, making the most of his "success" for years. The stage was set for a confrontation between the most powerful witch doctor in the community and a headstrong disbeliever.

The *uyoma* arrived with his supernatural paraphernalia and cast his spells over the family compound while Onyango looked on, unimpressed. When the *uyoma* had finished, Onyango walked up to him, took away his magical tools, beat him up, and threw him out of his compound. The neighbors, appalled at Onyango's audacity, waited patiently for the most horrible curse to befall the family. But nothing happened, and Onyango's reputation went from strength to strength.

Nor was this the only confrontation Onyango had with a *uyoma.* On another occasion a local witch doctor was sent from outside the area to kill one of the neighbors in K'ogelo following a dispute over a girl. Onyango's reputation was now rock solid in the community, and he was asked to intervene. Picking up his whip and his *panga*—a broad-bladed machete—he waited on the roadside for the *uyoma* to arrive.

Sarah Obama recalls that Onyango confronted the *uyoma:* "If you are as powerful as you claim, you must strike me now with lightning. If not, you should run, for unless you leave this village now, I will have to beat you."[25] No lightning strike was forthcoming, so Onyango did as he threatened and beat up the *uyoma,* then took away his case of medicines. The *uyoma* had never been confronted like this before, and he was taken by surprise. He turned to the elders and threatened to bring a curse down on the whole village unless his medicine case was returned. But Onyango stood his ground, repeating: "If this man has strong magic, let him curse me now and strike me dead."

Once again, nothing happened and the neighbor kept his girl. But this time Onyango made a very clever move: he befriended the *uyoma* and took him back to his hut, where Sarah fed him boiled chicken. Before sending him on his way, he insisted that the *uyoma* explain to him how all his potions worked. Onyango, already an experienced herbalist, wanted to learn new techniques from another expert. He had befriended the British, learned how they worked, and used the knowledge to his own advantage; now he did the same with his own people, learning new things about the properties and powers of plants.

One other story about Onyango says much about his temperament. Barack Obama junior heard the family anecdote from his step-aunt Zeituni on his first visit to Kenya in 1987.[26] According to Zeituni (who was a young girl at the time), a neighbor started to walk across Onyango's land with his goat on a leash; it was a shortcut that he frequently took. Onyango stopped the man and said: "When you're alone, you are always free to pass through my land. But today you can't pass, because your goat will eat my plants." The man insisted that because his goat was on a leash, he could control it and not allow it to eat any vegetation. The two men argued, and Onyango called Zeituni to bring "Alego"—his pet name for one of his *pangas*. "I will make a bargain with you. You can pass with your goat. But if even one leaf is harmed—if even *one half* of one leaf of my plants is harmed—then I will cut down your goat also."

The man decided to take a chance and he walked across Onyango's land, closely followed by the old man and his young daughter. Zeituni recalls that they had taken barely twenty steps before the inevitable happened and the goat started to nibble a plant. With one swift stroke, Onyango decapitated the goat: "If I say I will do something, I must do it," said Onyango, "otherwise how will people know that my word is true?" The neighbor was furious, and he took his complaint to the village elders to arbitrate. Although they were sympathetic to the owner of the goat, they had to agree that Onyango was in the right, because the neighbor had been warned about the consequences of allowing his goat to eat the vegetation.

The story said a lot about the simple, black-and-white way in which Onyango saw things. I related the tale to John Ndalo and asked him if he thought it was true. He looked at me slightly bewildered at first before shrugging and saying, "That sort of thing happened all the time with Onyango!"

7

A STATE OF EMERGENCY

KUDHO CHUOYO NG'AMA ONYONE

A thorn only pricks the one who steps on it

THE TOWNSHIP of Oyugis lies to the south of Kendu Bay and straddles the primary trucking route from Kisumu to Kisii. To the first-time visitor, this typical ramshackle Kenyan town is total chaos. Dangerously overloaded minibuses—the ubiquitous matatus—screech to a halt every few minutes to squeeze even more passengers inside; pedestrians risk life and limb every time they cross the road, first dodging a fuel tanker from one direction, then a pair of speeding matatus jostling for position from the other. You can buy almost anything on the main street: beautiful ripe fruit, a secondhand T-shirt, a bottle of warm beer, or a woman for the afternoon. Oyugis has a reputation for having one of the highest HIV/AIDS mortality rates in East Africa. It is also well known as the home of some of the best coffin makers in western Kenya.

Down the side streets leading off the main road, life is a little safer, as the potholed dirt roads force even the most reckless drivers to slow down. Here you find the smaller businesses—dressmakers, food stalls, and corner shops selling telephone credit. On most days an old woman sits here selling charcoal by the side of the road; on a good day, she makes $2 profit. Her name is Hawa Auma Hussein Onyango, wife of the late David Magak, and she is the closest living blood relative to the president of the United States:

> I am the daughter of Hussein Onyango Obama and the sister of Barack Obama senior and the aunt of the president. His first child was Sarah Nyaoke, the second was Barack, and the third is me. I was born in 1942 in the Kendu Bay area. We migrated to K'ogelo when I was still young. I was still being fed on the breast.

I first met Auma at the Obama inauguration party in Kendu Bay, when she introduced herself in a torrent of incomprehensible Dholuo. She told me in no uncertain terms that it was my duty to write about the forgotten Obamas of Kendu Bay. She has one of the biggest toothless smiles in the world, and she instantly became one of my favorite Kenyan "aunts." The day after the inauguration party, I went to see her in her small hut, a half-hour walk from the center of Oyugis. She told me that she was too young to remember living in Kendu Bay, but she remembers life in the family compound in K'ogelo, with her father, his two wives, and her two older siblings:

> When my father left the army [in 1941], he came back and became a professional cook. He used to work for the whites in Nairobi until he came back to K'ogelo to retire. My father was a friend toward the British, and they would come and visit us on motorcycles and using cars. They were very good friends. He loved all the whites and they loved him.
>
> We had a very big home, a typical African home, with all the family there. There used to be so many. Many cousins have since died, which has reduced the number. There were five houses there, five huts, for the first mother, the second mother, the girls, Barack's house, and Baba's [Father's].

In those days there was no water in the compound as there is today. We had to fetch water down by the river. We would have to walk about two miles for the water. There were *crocuta* [spotted hyena]—these were very common. Even if you went out with two or three others, they would come and attack you. They always went for your buttocks. So we could not go out by ourselves.

At the time there were also lots of leopards. Baba also had a lot of poultry—he had all the chickens and all the turkeys and other small animals in our home. But then the leopards would come and eat them. One day I was sitting next to our cat—a big fat cat, our family pet. A leopard came and took the cat. I cried so much. I was very little.

Soon after moving to their new home in K'ogelo, Sarah Obama gave birth to her first child, Omar, in June 1944. Hussein Onyango went on to father three more children with Sarah: Zeituni Onyango Obama in 1952, and two more sons, Yusuf and Sayid. For much of the time, Onyango was still working as a cook in Nairobi, but when he came back to K'ogelo he worked hard on his smallholding. The land had been left derelict since his brother Ndalo died in the early 1920s and bush had taken over. Yet within a year Onyango had cleared the undergrowth and started to apply modern farming ideas, which he had learned from people in Nairobi. Soon he had enough of a surplus to sell at the local market.

Today his wife Sarah holds court in K'ogelo, sitting under one of the mango trees that Onyango planted soon after he moved to the village. On one of my visits there, Sarah waved her arm across the compound: "Look at all these fruit trees that he left here—he planted these. He wanted all this to be beautiful. He had lots of paw-paw plants, and oranges, all these mangoes, everything here."

Life in K'ogelo, however, was not a bed of roses. Onyango's fourth wife, Habiba Akumu, had never wanted to leave Kendu Bay, doing so only because her parents pressured her into going with her children. Now life was as she had feared: she was lonely, she was away from her family, and she had been displaced by Sarah as her husband's favorite wife. According to Hawa Auma, Akumu and Sarah did not get along well, and this only exacerbated Akumu's loneliness. But Akumu was proud and stubborn, and she continued to stand up to Onyango's excessive demands for cleanliness and obedience. Their arguments became more frequent and more violent.

Auma told me that one day Onyango had a furious row with Akumu, and things came to a head: "My father then went out to dig a very big grave, to go and kill my mother." After Auma's unexpected revelation, she told me that she did not want to talk anymore; she was tired from sitting in the hot sun selling charcoal all day, and thinking of her mother upset her too much.

As a farmer, Onyango must have spent a lot of time in those early days in K'ogelo turning over the soil; Auma could only have been a very young girl at the time, so perhaps she had misunderstood the situation. Still, the story was too intriguing to pass up. Knowing that Akumu came from a village close to Kendu Bay, I decided to try my luck at tracing her family. Like many of the small villages in the area, Simbi Kolonde lies some distance off the main thoroughfare along a bone-rattling dirt road. The track runs around the edge of Simbi Lake—a deep volcanic lake that is steeped in myth. One story claims that when an old woman visited the village many years previously, no one had offered the hospitality that was expected under the circumstances. In a fit of anger, the old woman created a massive flood that swamped the village and drowned all the people, leaving the magnificent lake. Fortunately, my own experience was the exact opposite, and not for the first time during my research I arrived unannounced at a home, only to be welcomed with warmth and kindness. Here I found Charles Odonei Ojuka and Joseph Nyabondo, both brothers of Akumu. We spent a couple of hours or so chatting about life in the past, then I casually asked Charles if he knew why Akumu left Onyango:

> Onyango used to love cleanliness, and he being a clean man, he
> never wanted his face to be touched by dirt. He didn't like anything

that is called dirt to be around him. So that is the number one cause which brought the disagreement with Akumu. There was a fight between Akumu and Onyango in K'ogelo—a quarrel. He dug a grave and he was going to cut her up and bury her there. An old man [a neighbor] came and helped Akumu, otherwise she would have been killed.

The old man came and wrestled with Onyango, then Akumu escaped and walked all the way to Kisumu by foot [forty miles]. I think there was some problem because having married the other wife Sarah, it might have put a lot of pressure on Akumu. When Akumu came back [to Kendu Bay], Onyango never followed her, to look for her or to be reconciled with her. He just left her.

When Akumu came over to this side [of the gulf], the man who came to marry Akumu was called Salmon Orinda, and she gave birth to another five children. She was buried here when she died in 2006.

In her desperation to get away from Onyango, Akumu had abandoned her children, leaving Sarah Obama to raise President Obama's father. Sarah said that Barack senior was nine years old when Akumu left, so this must have happened in late 1944 or early 1945, shortly after the family moved to K'ogelo.

Akumu's three children—Sarah Nyaoke, Barack, and young Auma—were not happy in K'ogelo either. Auma claims they were not looked after, and often went hungry:

Sarah was very bad to us and she really inflicted a lot of pain on us. She never wanted us in any way when we were young children . . . she mistreated us because she didn't want us to have food. Then every time and again she kept on beating us. She forced Sarah Nyaoke and Barack to work on the farm. If they could not work when they were very young, then nobody would eat, so [sometimes] we did not eat for many days.

Akumu's three young children decided to run away. Sarah Nyaoke was only eleven at the time, Barack senior was nine, and Auma was still a toddler. Together, they set out on the seventy-five-mile trek back to their mother in Kendu Bay. Little Auma was too young to walk far, and her brother and sister tried to carry her, but she became too much of a burden:

> They were walking all the way to Lake Victoria, and this was very difficult for them. They left me behind. You need to know this, that Barack and Sarah left me because I was heavy, and they could not carry me. I was left alone, crying by the sisal plantation.
>
> Now, there were leopards near me, looking at me. I think they were sympathetic toward me. They never wanted to interfere with me. Then women from the community came and picked me up and took me home. I was still very young, but I can't remember how old. I was still a toddler.

In fact, Auma must have been three years old at the time. Sarah Nyaoke and Barack wandered for several days before a local chief found them walking near the lake at a village called Nyakach—seventy miles from K'ogelo. The two children had managed to walk almost all the way back to Kendu Bay before being returned to Onyango and Sarah in K'ogelo.

Not surprisingly, Sarah Obama has a very different recollection of these dramatic events back in 1945. When first asked about Akumu, Sarah replied dismissively, "Who is Akumu?" But her memory soon returned: "She left when the father of the president was nine years old. And by that time, he had never started schooling [in K'ogelo]. So it was me—Mama Sarah—who protected and took care of them!"

I asked Sarah why she thought Akumu left K'ogelo. "She never liked this place, saying that people would kill her here," she told me. "So she went, and left me to take care of Barack senior."

Once Akumu's three children had been returned to K'ogelo, life for everybody began to get back to normal. Hussein Onyango had always made education a high priority; he had enrolled Peter Oluoch in the Kisii high school in the 1930s, and now it was time for his own son to go to school. Barack senior started at the Gendia SDA primary school near Kendu Bay, but Sarah recalls that he found the schooling to be too easy: "He came back after the first day and told his father that he could not study there because his class was taught by a woman and he knew everything she had to teach him. This attitude he had learned from his father, so Onyango could say nothing."[1]

Once they were settled into their new homestead in K'ogelo, Barack went to another school in the nearby village of Ng'iya, a five-mile walk from his new home.

Barack's primary school teacher from Ng'iya, Samson Chilo Were, lives in retirement in a small settlement called Malumboa. The village is in a very remote part of western Kenya, close to Got Ramogi, where the first Luo settled in Kenya five hundred years ago. I visited him during the rainy season, and even a four-wheel-drive vehicle could not make it all the way to Samson's house, so we went the last half mile on foot, wading ankle deep in mud and water. Samson was delighted to have unexpected visitors. He said he was born in April 1922, which made him eighty-seven years old, and apart from a slight deafness he showed little evidence of his advanced years—certainly his memory seemed as good as ever:

> I taught [Barack] Obama in standard five when I was teaching in Ng'iya primary school for boys. He was a smart boy, very clever in class. Very keen at hearing what we were telling him. Every time he learned well—English, Swahili—he did it properly. He liked sports and he liked singing as well. He was a very good singer and a very good dancer.
>
> We started before eight in the morning and school finished after games around 5 p.m. There were only six classrooms, just mud huts—there were no permanent huts then. We used to make iron sheets out of old oil drums for the roof.
>
> At that time, the whole school was about two hundred [students], because many parents didn't like school. They thought it was a waste of time. The parents liked their children to look after

their cows. School was a white man's thing. The school fees were three [Kenyan] shillings [a few dollars at today's prices] a year, at most. His father used to pay for his uniform—it was a white shirt and brown shorts. Even at secondary school there were no long trousers at that time. They were all walking barefoot.

Samson also knew Hussein Onyango, who often invited the schoolteacher to his compound for a meal. Like everybody else I had met, Samson stressed Onyango's priority on education and obedience:

> Onyango used to prepare a meal for me at [his] home. He was very keen on education, on [Barack] Obama getting an education. Onyango was keen like a white man; he knew how to be organized like a white man.
>
> He was a very harsh man as well. He would not allow Obama to joke with school. He wanted Obama to study and become a good man in the future. Sometimes Obama would hang around because he didn't want to go to school, so Onyango would bang everything! "You've not gone to school yet and you are still here! Wake up and go to school." And he would chase him to school.

In 1948 Onyango donated land adjacent to his compound to build the first primary school in K'ogelo, and twenty years later a secondary school was constructed with money partly donated by Barack senior. But even though Hussein Onyango stressed the importance of education for his sons, he was a traditional African at heart and he put less emphasis on the education of girls. After all, the reasoning went, why spend good money to educate your daughters if they were only going to leave home and become part of another family? So neither Sarah Nyaoke nor Hawa Auma went to school, and to this day Auma cannot read or write.

Some African families were more progressive about schooling girls, giving their daughters the benefit of at least a primary education. One such local girl was Magdalene Otin, who went to school with Barack Obama. Magdalene still lives in a traditional Luo roundhouse, which is something of a rarity in Kenya today: their fragile construction means that they seldom last more than thirty years, and most "modern" huts are now built square with a roof of corrugated iron. After many inquiries in and around K'ogelo, I was eventually directed to Magdalene's hut, which was a short walk from the dirt road that led into the village. After some searching, I found her house hidden among trees and fields of tall maize.

Magdalene couldn't remember how long she had lived there, but she told me it was "a very long time"; her hut must have been at least fifty years old. A thick mud wall ran around the inside like a doughnut, and she entertained her guests in the center of the hut—the "hole" in the doughnut—where there was a small table and several chairs. Between the inner and outer walls was a small, private space that provided a tiny sleeping area, plus dry storage for grain and a place for her chickens. The birds obviously felt at home, wandering in and out all the time in search of something to peck. Even with the birds, Magdalene's home was spotless. She had few other personal possessions, except for a dozen framed family portraits—her husband was long dead, as were seven of her eight children.

Magdalene was tiny, frail, and shy. She didn't know how old she was, but she did remember when Barack Obama senior went to school in Ng'iya, so she was probably in her mid-seventies, although a lifetime in the fields had made her look much older. The first three times I visited Magdalene she seemed overwhelmed by the attention of a *mzungu* and unsure of herself, not wanting to speak out of turn or inappropriately. On my second visit she insisted on preparing a meal of boiled chicken and *ugali,* the traditional dish of maize flour cooked to a thick dough. In the traditional way of Luo women, Magdalene served her guests (all of them men), but she did not eat. Instead she gently berated us for not eating enough, and kept piling more food on our plates; she then sat opposite with the other womenfolk from the compound, and watched us eat.

On my fourth visit to see Magdalene, she finally opened up and started to talk about her past:

> I grew up with Obama. Barack loved school—he attended school regularly, and this was because his father was very strict and would not allow him to stay at home. Obama liked football—most African children like football. But he would come home early, not like the other children. He had to put the cows back in the pen—they couldn't be left out late. If they are rained on badly they get sick, and we didn't have the drugs for them that we have today.

I asked her what life was like in K'ogelo back in the late 1940s:

> In those days the population was very small, and the trees were very tall and bushy. We had to meander through the trees to go anywhere. There were leopards and hyenas and all the other animals you talk about. And many snakes. I was very much afraid of the hyenas in those days. They are gluttons—I think they're worse than leopards. We could only fetch water in the mornings because they chased us later in the day. They go for the buttocks of humans, as this is the bit that's fat and soft.

I asked her if the animals were still dangerous today:

> It's the leopards which have killed most of our children. They took two children here just a couple of years ago. They go up in trees, and jump on them when they're going to school. They twist your neck and you're dead. If the hyenas kill you, they will eat you right there, but the leopards will always drag you away to a safe distance.

After his primary schooling in Ng'iya, in 1950 Barack senior sat for what was then called the Kenya African Preliminary Examination. This selection exam, based on the British education system, was designed to identify the brightest African students for admission to secondary school. Barack senior easily exceeded the standard required to gain admission to the prestigious Maseno high school, which was, and still is, one of the top boarding schools in Kenya. The Maseno school lies almost equidistant between K'ogelo and the main town, Kisumu; established in 1906 by the Church Mission Society (CMS), it is the second oldest secondary school in Kenya. Presumably Onyango had no religious objection to sending Barack to a Christian school, even though he was raising his son as a Muslim. Maseno was founded as part of the British initiative to tutor the sons of local chiefs, thereby creating an educated elite to work for the colonial administration. Today, the school looks much like any provincial English boarding school from the 1930s, except for the *tumbili* (vervet monkeys) playing around the roofs of the classrooms, and the simple black-and-white painted sign on the main driveway telling visitors that they are about to cross the equator from the Southern Hemisphere to the Northern.

Maseno was substantially more expensive than Ng'iya primary school, and like parents the world over, Onyango and Sarah struggled to find the money for their son's school fees. Despite being a practicing Muslim, Sarah decided the best way to earn some much-needed extra cash was to brew *chang'aa* to sell to the neighbors. Sarah earned a useful income from her brewing until Onyango came home one afternoon and discovered her fermentation vats. He was furious, tipping them over and refusing to allow Sarah to continue her home brewing. Instead, she resorted to a less profitable trade in homemade chapatis.

In 1951, Barack's second year at Maseno, a new headmaster arrived. B. L. Bowers, who stayed at the school until 1969, was the longest-serving principal in the history of Maseno. Even by the standards of the early 1950s, Bowers—a white Anglican missionary from the United Kingdom—had a reputation for strictness, and he would ultimately prove to be the young Barack's nemesis. But for the first couple of years at least, Barack excelled. One of his old friends and drinking companions, the journalist Leo Odera, recalled the elder Barack's achievements at school:

Barack Obama at his family's home in the Kenyan homestead of Alego, with his grandmother, Sarah; sister, Auma; and stepmother, Kezia.
© *INS News Agency Ltd/Rex Features*

Dudi, home of William Onyango and his family, lies a few miles from the Kenya-Uganda border. In the background is the densely wooded ridge of Got Ramogi, the sixteenth-century hill fortress of the great Luo leader Ramogi Ajwang' and a sacred site for Luo people. © *Peter Firstbrook*

A Luo man heavily adorned with a necklace of cowrie shells (*gaagi*) and other ornaments; he is described as Ukeri, a professional buffoon from the Ugenya clan in Nyanza, c. 1902.

© Pitt Rivers Museum, University of Oxford PRM 1998.209.43.1

A portrait of a Luo father and son from 1902; they are wearing large metal arm and leg rings (*minyonge*) as well as elaborate necklaces of cowrie shells.

© Pitt Rivers Museum, University of Oxford PRM 1998.206.4.4

Henry Morton Stanley with his trusted African gun bearer and servant, Kalulu, a Swahili word for an antelope. Kalulu was originally a young slave who was given to Stanley by an Arab merchant during his first visit to Africa.

© Hulton-Deutsch Collection/Corbis

An African soldier from the King's African Rifles. During the first twelve months of World War I, 4,572 Africans were recruited into the KAR from central Nyanza alone.

© from the Winterton Collection of East African photographs, Melville J. Herskovits Library of African Studies, Northwestern University

This photo of Barack Obama senior with his ten-year-old son was probably taken at Honolulu airport in December 1971.

© *Obama for America/Handout/Reuters/Corbis*

Hawa Auma is aunt
to President Obama
and his closest living
relative; on a good
day, she can earn
$2 selling charcoal
at the roadside in
Oyugis.
© *Peter Firstbrook*

Sarah Obama is Hussein Onyango's
fifth wife and step-grandmother to
President Obama; she raised the
president's father from a young age.
© *David Firstbrook*

This portrait of Barack Obama senior hangs in Sarah Obama's family house in K'ogelo.

Left: Habiba Akumu, paternal grandmother to President Obama, grieving by the coffin of her son, Barack Obama senior, K'ogelo, November 1982.
© *Hawa Auma*

Below: The graves of Hussein Onyango (above) and Barack Obama senior in Sarah Obama's compound in K'ogelo.
© *Peter Firstbrook*

Many residents of Kisumu, in the heartland of the Luo tribe, celebrated the election of Obama in November 2008.
© *epa/Corbis*

The forty-fourth President of the United States takes the oath of office from Supreme Court Chief Justice John Roberts on January 20, 2009. Michelle Obama holds the Bible used by President Abraham Lincoln at his inauguration in 1861. © *Brooks Kraft/Corbis*

Barack had a very excellent record in form one, form two, and form three. He was top in mathematics, English, and almost every subject. But his personal conduct from the end of form three was not so excellent; academically he was okay, but became difficult.

The student records at Maseno go back to 1906, and the administrators retain the reports of every boy who has passed through the school since it opened. Barack Obama senior's records are kept securely in a safe in the principal's office, rather than in the school archives. The documents are concise to the point of pithiness. Obama senior's fading brown card, index number 3422, explains that Barack was a bright boy and had been promoted from Class B to A. In graceful handwriting, Bowers notes that the young Obama was "very keen, steady, trustworthy and friendly. Concentrates, reliable and out-going." It was a good report, but things started to go downhill soon after that.

By the time Obama reached form three at Maseno, he was seventeen years old and his attitude toward the staff and discipline at the school began to change. Sarah Obama recalls that he was rebellious—he would sneak girls into the dormitories or raid the nearby farms with his friends, stealing chickens and yams because the school food was not very appetizing. However, Leo Odera tells a much more complicated story about what happened in Barack senior's final year at the school, which ultimately led to his downfall:

As he was moving to senior classes, he became rude and arrogant. He did not like to do the manual work, like when the boys were clearing the bush or working the plow. . . . This developed friction between him and the principal, because at the school, the work was done communally and collectively. The teacher may assign you [the task] to go and clear an area of the school where grass was overgrown, but Barack didn't like doing these things.

At Maseno, when Obama senior was in form three and progressing well as one of the top students, something strange happened. Some of the senior boys wrote a nasty letter, accusing and outlining some serious grievances the students had about the school administration. The letter was anonymous and unsigned. But because Barack Obama senior had been identified as the cleverest boy and politically minded, he became the prime suspect.

The principal was furious, and so was the board of governors. The school authority then threatened to invite the dreaded Special Branch Police [the directorate of security intelligence].

Obama senior got wind that he was to be investigated, and that handwriting experts had been summoned to the school to come and examine the offensive letter. So Obama left the school voluntarily. He was never expelled as such, but opted out of his own volition, leaving behind the belief by the other students that he'd had a hand in the authorship of the offending letter.

Barack would have been wise to have heeded the Luo proverb *kudho chwoyo ng'ama onyone*—"a thorn only pricks the one who steps on it."

Hussein Onyango was furious with his son; after all, he and Sarah had saved every penny they had to give him the best education that was available to a black student in Kenya at the time, and Barack had thrown the opportunity away. Onyango's response was predictable: he beat Barack with a stick until his back bled. Then, still angry, he effectively threw him out by sending him to work in Mombasa with the parting words "I will see how you enjoy yourself, earning your own meals."[2] Barack had no choice but to obey his father, and he left for Mombasa immediately.

Meanwhile, political and civil unrest had been brewing across the protectorate for several years, and Kenya was about to suffer one of the most deeply shocking and violent decades experienced by any British colony. The 1950s were dominated by the Mau Mau insurgency—a brutal and violent grassroots rebellion by Africans against white colonial rule. Like many such revolts in history, it started slowly. Ever since the 1920s the indigenous Africans had grown increasingly resentful over the way the white settlers had reduced their wages, and over the much reviled *kipande*—the identity card that was introduced after the First World War, without which no African could gain employment. (The white settlers frequently punished badly behaved workers by tearing up their *kipande,* making it impossible for them to find work elsewhere.)

The early 1920s had also seen the emergence of African political groups such as the Young Kikuyu Association, led by Harry Thuku, and the Young Kavirondo Association, founded by the Luo of Nyanza. However, the colonial government soon became concerned about what they considered to be "seditious" activities by the leaders of these organizations. On March 14, 1922, Harry Thuku was arrested in Nairobi and exiled for eight years, without charge or trial. Within two days of Thuku's arrest, between seven thousand and eight thousand of his supporters protested outside the police station in Nairobi where he was detained. The police, armed with rifles and fixed bayonets, attempted to control the crowd; stones were thrown, shots were fired, and the crowd panicked. The official report into the incident claimed that twenty-one Africans were killed, including four women. Unofficial reports from staff at the mortuary claim that fifty-six bodies were brought in. The riot was the first violent political protest in Kenya's history, but worse confrontations were to come, and the killings only added to the growing resentment among Africans that they had no hand in the governance of their own country.

In Luoland, a young teacher called Jonathan Okwiri established the Young Kavirondo Association in the same year as Thuku's arrest. Among other things, the group also called for the abolition of the infamous *kipande,* a reduction in hut and poll tax, an increase in wages, and the abolition of forced labor.[3] This time the colonial administration used less confrontational means to control the movement. They persuaded the Young Kavirondo Association to make W. E. Owen, the Anglican archdeacon of Kavirondo, their president; the authorities claimed that he would make an excellent intermediary to negotiate with

the colonial government. Instead, Owen subverted their political ini-
tiatives and persuaded the group to focus on nonpolitical issues such
as better housing, food, and hygiene. In a master stroke, he even convinced the group to change its name to the Kavirondo Taxpayers' Welfare Association, rendering what might have been a grassroots activist
movement utterly impotent.

In the 1930s the issue of land ownership became the focus of even
greater political dissent—perhaps even *the* crucial political grievance
in Kenya, according to the historian David Anderson.[4] This resentment had first taken root in 1902, when the first white settlers claimed
the most fertile hills around Nairobi. Within three decades the settler
farms had grown in size and fences were beginning to enclose them,
which worsened the land shortage problem for the Africans, especially
for the Kikuyu of central Kenya. What Anderson calls "the tyranny of
property" only fueled the Africans' sense of injustice, but the government continued to thwart Kikuyu attempts at political organization. A
new group called the Kikuyu Central Association replaced the banned
Young Kikuyu Association, but this too was outlawed in 1941 when the
colonial government clamped down on African dissent during the Second World War.

Between 1939 and 1945 the colony was put on a war footing as
Italian troops massed on Kenya's northern border with Ethiopia and
Somaliland. The British responded to this threat by sending the KAR
north, and Hussein Onyango went with the force to Addis Ababa. But
as the war came to a close, the colonial government turned its attention at last to improving political representation for Africans. In 1944
Kenya became the first East African territory to include an African
on its Legislative Council. The government progressively increased
the number of local representatives to eight by 1951, although none of
them was elected; instead, they were appointed by the governor from a
list of names submitted by the local authorities. Not surprisingly, this
did not satisfy African demands for either political equality or democracy. Nor was the injustice of land ownership being addressed: in 1948,

1.25 million Kikuyu were restricted to living on just two thousand square miles of farmland, whereas thirty thousand white settlers occupied six times as much space.[5] Inevitably, the most fertile land was almost entirely in the hands of the colonists.

The Kikuyu were led by Jomo Kenyatta. Kenyatta had lived in Britain throughout most of the 1930s, studying anthropology at London University and also traveling to other European countries as well as the Soviet Union. During his time abroad, he married an Englishwoman called Edna Clarke, who became his second wife. Shortly after returning to Kenya in September 1946, he became president of the newly formed Kenya African Union (KAU) and the leading advocate for a peaceful transition to African majority rule. The KAU, which had been established in 1944 to articulate local grievances against the colonial administration, attempted to be more politically inclusive than the banned Kikuyu Central Association (KCA) by avoiding tribal politics. However, the KAU progressively fell under Kikuyu domination until it was generally regarded as little more than a reincarnation of the KCA. Kenyatta's powerful, domineering personality was resented by some of the political leaders, and especially by the Luo.[6] This tension between the Kikuyu and the Luo was just the beginning of the deep-rooted problem of tribalism in Kenyan politics, a conflict that would eventually plunge the country into turmoil.

Some critics, especially among the Kikuyu, thought that Kenyatta's approach was not producing results quickly enough. The land issue had caused thousands of Kikuyu to migrate into towns and cities in search of work; as a consequence, Nairobi's population doubled between 1938 and 1952. Increasing poverty, rising unemployment, and growing urban overpopulation plagued the colony.

During the late 1940s the general council of the banned KCA began a campaign of civil disobedience to protest the land issue. Members took what were said to be traditional Kikuyu ritual oaths to strengthen their commitment to the secret group; the militants believed that if they broke their oaths, they would be killed by supernatural forces. These oathing rituals often included the sacrifice of animals or the drinking of animal blood. By 1950, what had begun as a peaceful movement to organize civil disobedience was getting out of hand. Rumors circulated among the British that members of the group indulged in cannibalism, bestiality with goats, and wild orgies, and that the ritual oaths included a commitment to kill, dismember, and burn white settlers. Although mostly either untrue or greatly exaggerated, these stories would help convince the British government to send troops out to Kenya in 1952 to support the colonists.

After the Second World War, Nairobi had become a fertile recruiting ground for the militants. The genteel colonial city of whitewashed government offices and luxury hotels was gradually becoming surrounded by squalid shanties and seedy slums, as more and more landless Africans moved into the city. With few jobs and fewer opportunities, many could not resist the temptation to drift into petty crime; in the absence of an effective police force, criminal gangs began to control the poor areas, and street crime, robbery, smuggling, and protection rackets increased alarmingly. As is so often the case, though, impoverished Africans, rather than wealthy white colonials, suffered most from the violence and crime. The Kikuyu gangs controlled the slums, and by early 1950 the Nairobi-based urban militants known as the Muhimu started to organize mass oathings throughout central Kenya. Guns and ammunition were plentiful throughout the colony, brought back by the seventy-five thousand Africans who had served in the King's African Rifles during the war, and the Muhimu set about collecting whatever weapons they could find, in preparation for what they saw as an inevitable armed struggle to free themselves from colonial rule.

Nobody is really quite sure how the name Mau Mau came to be used for the insurgents who set themselves on a course of violence to achieve independence from the British. The Kikuyu never used the name to describe themselves, and some argue that the white settlers invented the name to ridicule the rebellion. Others maintain that the name refers to the mountains in the Rift Valley, where the rebellious Kikuyu took refuge during the hostilities; or it might have been a corruption of Muhimu. Still others claim it is an acronym for *Mzungu aende ulaya—mwafrica apate uhuru,* which, loosely translated from Swahili, means "The white man should return to Europe—the African should gain freedom."[7]

As the Kikuyu had suffered most from the confiscation of their land by the white settlers, most of the violence during the Mau Mau period occurred in the White Highlands and the Rift Valley—the traditional home of the Kikuyu. However, the general state of unrest in the late 1940s and early 1950s had an unsettling effect throughout the colony, and in Nyanza the repercussions of the violence involved even Hussein Onyango.

In *Dreams from My Father,* President Obama relates the story told to him by his stepgrandmother Sarah of how her husband was arrested in 1949, during the very early years of the Mau Mau insurrection. Like many Luo in Nyanza, Onyango went to political meetings where there was much talk of independence. Although he believed in principle that independence was a good thing for the colony, he was skeptical whether it was really possible. Onyango warned his son Barack senior that it was unlikely that anything would come of the initiative:

> "How can the African defeat the white man when he cannot even make his own bicycle?" he would say to Barack. "The white man alone is like an ant. He can easily be crushed. But like an ant, the white man works together. His nation, his business—these things are more important to him than himself. He will follow the leadership and not question orders. Black men are not like this. Even the most foolish black man thinks he knows better than the wise man. That is why the black man will always lose."[8]

Onyango was not particularly politically minded, and in many ways he greatly admired the British. Yet despite his loyalty and long service to the British going back thirty years, he was arrested and interned during the early years of the troubles. In 1949 Onyango was accused of being a subversive by an African who harbored a long-standing grudge against him.

Mau Mau was not yet a serious threat to the colonial government, but the first rumblings of dissent were emerging from underground groups. Onyango's accuser, so Sarah Obama claims, had been cheating people by charging them excessive taxes and then pocketing the surplus. This practice was far from unusual, as the local chiefs selected by the British wielded wide-ranging powers. According to Sarah, Onyango had challenged the man over his embezzlement, and the chief waited for a chance to take his revenge. He accused Onyango of being a supporter of the rebels, and her husband was arrested and taken away to a detention camp. The penal regime set up in the camps to deal with suspected Mau Mau supporters was brutal, and Sarah claims that Onyango sustained regular beatings at the hands of his keepers:

> The African warders were instructed by the white soldiers to whip him every morning and evening until he confessed. . . . He said they would sometimes squeeze his testicles with parallel metallic rods. They also pierced his nails and buttocks with a sharp pin, with his hands and legs tied together with his head facing down. . . . That was the time we realised that the British were actually not friends but, instead, enemies. My husband had worked so diligently for them, only to be arrested and detained.[9]

Nobody can be absolutely sure who it was that accused Hussein Onyango of supporting the Mau Mau, and Sarah Obama does not name him. However, one serious contender is Paul Mboya from Kendu Bay. Onyango had been at loggerheads with Mboya ever since Mboya had been appointed chief in central Karachuonyo around 1935, and Obama had later taken him to task over recruiting forced labor. Even though he had stepped down by 1946, Mboya still wielded considerable influence with the colonial authorities. Perhaps Mboya thought that he had at last extracted his revenge on Onyango for constantly challenging his authority in Kendu Bay.

Whoever was responsible, it was a traumatic period for Onyango. The old man remained in custody for over six months, and he certainly would have been interrogated by the Special Branch—in those early years of the Mau Mau uprising, the British were desperate to find out as much as they could about the emerging movement and any arrest was taken seriously. He was ultimately cleared of all charges and released, returning home a broken man—thin, dirty, with a head full of lice, and permanently scarred from his beatings in the detention center. From that day, Sarah Obama claims, Onyango became an old man.

By the middle of 1951 rumors of secret Mau Mau meetings in the forests outside Nairobi were beginning to filter back to the colonial government. In early 1952 there were arson attacks against white farmers in Nanyuki and also against government chiefs in Nyeri, both important towns in the White Highlands. However, attacks on the white settlers were rare, and the main violence was directed against other Africans who were seen as being "loyal" to the whites. In this respect, the Mau Mau insurrection was as much an internal conflict—a civil war where African turned on his fellow African—as it was a struggle for independence against the colonial powers. Certainly, black Africans suffered infinitely more than the white colonials.

One typical victim of the Mau Mau was Mutuaro Onsoti, a Luo from the Kisii area of south Nyanza.[10] Onsoti had been employed by a white farmer, James Kean, to help control the disruption caused on his farm by his Kikuyu squatter laborers. In May 1952, Onsoti told his employer that he suspected that Mau Mau activists were plotting to take over his farm. Kean was concerned about the safety of his foreman after this revelation, but was unable to prevent a brutal attack on

Onsoti by four Kikuyu squatters on August 25. His decapitated body was recovered from the woods on the following day, but his head was never found.

In October 1952 Governor-General Sir Evelyn Baring cabled London to request that a state of emergency be declared in the colony. This would allow the governor special powers to detain suspects, deploy the military, and impose other laws without further reference to London. The Colonial Office was loath to devolve such power to the Kenyan government, which had a reputation for being reactionary and unpredictable. However, Whitehall reluctantly granted his request on October 14, and Baring began rounding up KAU activists and suspected Mau Mau leaders in an offensive code-named Operation Jock Scott. Many senior officials in the KAU had no association with Mau Mau at all, but Baring was convinced the tactic would stop the insurrection in its tracks.

Not everybody was quite so confident that Baring's plan to screen and inter suspected Mau Mau sympathizers would be successful. One of the more thoughtful and insightful white highlanders drafted a memorandum to the governor:

> It is obviously illogical that any person of European extraction could, by looking at an African and examining his papers, know whether or not he has Mau Mau inclinations. . . . The methods adopted so far usually culminate in a parade of Kikuyu, and any that can produce a current hut-tax receipt and an employment card, or appear to be unaggressive, are released. Others who cannot produce these documents are frequently detained, and more often than not a proportion of these quite decent people are forced into close association with criminals and taken off to some detention camp. These decent people, or any of them who are in a state of indecision, immediately build up the utmost contempt for the methods of law

and order, and are ripe for Mau Mau allegiance, either now or when released from detention.[11]

A week after the declaration of a state of emergency, the Lancashire Fusiliers flew in from Egypt to supplement three battalions of the King's African Rifles who were recalled from abroad. The authorities still lacked good-quality intelligence when hostilities began in earnest in late 1952, so the colonial forces struck out blindly to suppress the violence. The brutal period of repression that followed would permanently change the image of Kenya as a paradise for the white colonials. In the words of the historian David Anderson:

> Before Mau Mau, Kenya had an entirely different image. In the iconography of the British imperial endeavour, it was the land of sunshine, gin slings and smiling, obedient servants, where the industrious white colonizer could enjoy a temperate life of peace and plenty in a tropical land. This was "white man's country," with its rolling, fertile highlands. Sturdy settler farmers had made their homes here, building a little piece of England in a foreign field. . . . Mau Mau shattered this patronizing pretence in the most poignant, disturbing manner, as trusted servants turned on their masters and slaughtered them.[12]

News of the intended arrests under the emergency powers leaked out, allowing the real revolutionaries to flee to their forest refuges in the Aberdare Mountains, while the moderates stayed put and awaited their fate. Many Africans considered Jomo Kenyatta to be a moderate leader, but he failed to unambiguously denounce Mau Mau violence to the satisfaction of the colonial government. Kenyatta knew exactly what to expect: he was arrested on November 18, 1952, and flown to a remote district station in Kapenguria, which reportedly had no telephone or rail communications with the rest of Kenya. He was charged, together with five other Kikuyu leaders, with "managing and being a member" of Mau Mau. They became known as the "Kapenguria Six," and their trial lasted for fifty-nine days—the longest and most sensational trial in British colonial history. The main prosecution witness, a Kikuyu called Rawson Mbugua Macharia, claimed that he had taken a Mau Mau oath in the presence of Kenyatta. (Macharia was the only witness at the trial to give evidence that linked Kenyatta with Mau Mau directly, yet six years later he swore an affidavit that he and six others had perjured themselves, and that some of them had been rewarded with land for their testimony.) For security reasons the trial was held without a jury, and the British judge received £20,000 (nearly $1.1 million adjusted for 2010 prices) to travel to Africa to put Kenyatta behind bars. (Many claim this fee was a bribe to gain Kenyatta's conviction.) In April 1953 Kenyatta was found guilty and sentenced to seven years' imprisonment with hard labor, and indefinite restriction thereafter; the British Privy Council refused his appeal the following year.

For the ordinary Kikuyu, the emergency brought terror and privation. Large bands of Mau Mau fighters moved freely around the highland forests of the Aberdare Mountains and Mount Kenya, attacking isolated police posts and terrorizing and killing Africans loyal to the white settlers. A typical group of insurgents numbered about a hundred; they operated mainly at night and took refuge in the forest during the days. Some of them had learned the techniques of guerrilla fighting during the war, when they assisted the British army against the Japanese in the Burmese jungle.

On January 24, 1953, two British settlers, Roger and Esme Ruck, together with their six-year-old son, Michael, were hacked to death by Mau Mau fighters on their isolated farm in Kinangop, together with one of their farmworkers who came to their assistance. The Rucks were a hardworking and respected farming couple in their early thirties, and they played an active role in the community. Esme Ruck ran a clinic on their farm, where she treated squatters in the area free of charge; her husband was a member of the Kenya Police Reserve. They were the embodiment of everything that white settlers held dear in postwar Kenya.

Panic immediately spread among the white community, and the Rucks' murder became a turning point in the war for the colonials, who demanded that the government toughen its response to the crisis. The day after the murders, white Kenyans massed outside Government House in Nairobi, calling for the cordon of "nigger police" who were holding the crowd at bay to be taken away. Some demonstrators even stubbed their cigarettes out on the arms of the black constables in an attempt to break through the police line. Sir Michael Blundell, the acknowledged leader of the settler community in Kenya at the time, was in a crisis meeting inside Government House with the governor-general. When he came out to try to pacify the crowd, he was shocked by their mood:

> This was my first experience of men and women who had momentarily lost all control of themselves and had become merged together as an insensate unthinking mass. I can see now individual pictures of the scene—a man with a beard and a strong foreign accent clutching his pistol as he shouted and raved; another with a quiet scholarly intellectual face, whom I knew to be a musician and a scientist, was crouched down by the terrace, twitching all over and swirling with a cascade of remarkable and blistering words, while an occasional fleck of foam came from his mouth.[13]

A few days after the Rucks' murder, it became clear that their killers had been employed by them for several years—loyal workers who had suddenly turned and butchered them without warning. As a consequence, long-standing relationships and friendships between black and white could no longer be trusted. White settlers, including women, armed themselves with any weapon they could lay their hands on, and they fortified their farms as best as they could. Some of the farmers dismissed their Kikuyu staff because nobody could tell Mau Mau sympathizers from loyal servants.

Only a week before the brutal murders in Kinangop, Governor-General Sir Evelyn Baring had sanctioned the death penalty for anyone caught administering the Mau Mau oath. (The oath was often forced upon Kikuyu tribesmen at the point of a knife, and they were threatened with death if they failed to kill a European farmer when ordered.) Now, in the first few months of 1953, the authorities mounted a new offensive against Mau Mau, killing hundreds of suspects and arresting thousands more on suspicion of being members of the insurgency. At the height of the crisis more than 70,000 suspected Mau Mau supporters were held in British detention camps, and throughout the eight years of conflict at least 150,000 Africans spent some time in detention, including Hussein Onyango and his son Barack senior. (In her controversial book on the Mau Mau, historian Caroline Elkins claims the number of Africans detained was much greater than the official British figures, anywhere between 160,000 and 320,000.)[14]

On March 26, 1953, the Mau Mau demonstrated that they could organize a large-scale attack with impunity. In response to the declaration of emergency and the mass roundup of KAU officials and Mau Mau suspects, the insurgents sought revenge—not on the whites but on fellow Kikuyus. That evening, a patrol in the town of Lari was called to investigate a body. They found nailed to a tree the mutilated remains of a local man known to be loyal to the British. It was a trap; his body had obviously been left there so that its inevitable discovery would lure the Home Guard away from the town. When they returned, they found that nearly a thousand Mau Mau fighters had attacked the settlement.

The Mau Mau assault on Lari was carefully planned, with the insurgents organized into four or five gangs numbering more than a hundred men each. The gangs had systematically moved through the unprotected homesteads of Lari, killing and mutilating as they went. They tied ropes around the huts to prevent the occupants from opening their doors, then set fire to the thatched roofs. As the occupants struggled to escape through the windows, they were butchered from outside. The Home Guard patrol reached Lari at 10:00 p.m., just as the attackers had finished their gruesome work; more than 120 people, mostly women and children, were killed or seriously injured. No other attack by the Mau Mau during the emergency had the same terrifying impact on public opinion.

At first the killings were thought to be random, but as the true horror of the night began to unfold, the real target of the raid became clear. The heads of those households that were attacked were loyal to the British—members of the Home Guard, local chiefs, councilors, and outspoken critics of the Mau Mau. The following night a police outpost near Naivasha in the Rift Valley was also attacked; three black policemen were killed, and the Mau Mau rebels released 173 suspects being held by the police. They also captured fifty rifles and twenty-five machine guns, together with a large quantity of ammunition. The attacks changed the way Africans viewed the conflict, and the ordinary Kikuyu began to realize that they were now embroiled in a civil war as the Mau Mau inflicted a reign of terror on their own people.

As with the murder of Mutuaro Onsoti, the foreman from Kisii, these murders of other Africans were often particularly brutal, and intended to terrorize the population. One district officer reported: "There was one murder of an old man at Ruathia; he was chopped in two halves because he has given evidence against the Mau Mau in court . . . and down by the river below Gituge we found the corpse of an African Court Process Server who had likewise been strangled for informing against the Mau Mau."[15] Many Christian Kikuyu refused to take the Mau Mau oath because they believed that taking the blood of a goat was blasphemous; this left them vulnerable to attack. One Mau Mau fighter recalled, "We generally left the Christians alone. But if they informed on us, we would kill them and sometimes cut out their tongue. We had no choice."[16]

More than eighteen hundred Kenyan civilians are known to have been murdered by the Mau Mau during the emergency; hundreds more disappeared and their bodies were never found.[17]

The British authorities were also guilty of carnage, especially during the "screening" process that was designed to isolate the hard-core Mau Mau supporters from innocent Kikuyus rounded up in error. The interrogation process was designed to terrorize the Mau Mau supporters, first by breaking the spirit of the detainees, and then by making them confess. Onyango had endured a similar procedure when he was arrested in 1949, but the techniques now used by some of the colonial authorities were much more brutal. In her book on the insurrection, historian Caroline Elkins assembled damning evidence of extensive human rights abuses:

> Teams made up of settlers, British district officers, members of the Kenya police force, African loyalists, and even soldiers from the British military forces demanded confessions and intelligence, and used torture to get them . . . electric shock was widely used, as well as cigarettes and fire. Bottles (often broken), gun barrels, knives, snakes, vermin and hot eggs were thrust up men's rectums and women's vaginas. The screening teams whipped, shot, burned and mutilated Mau Mau suspects, ostensibly to gather intelligence for military operations and as court evidence.[18]

At least one detainee had his testicles cut off and was then made to eat them. "Things got a little out of hand," one witness told Elkins when referring to another incident. "By the time we cut his balls off he had no ears, and his eyeball, the right one, I think, was hanging out of its socket. Too bad, he died before we got much out of him." Another British officer described, with remarkable openness, his exasperation with an uncooperative suspect during an interrogation:

> They wouldn't say a thing, of course, and one of them, a tall coal-black bastard, kept grinning at me, real insolent. I slapped him hard, but he kept right on grinning at me, so I kicked him in the balls as hard as I could. He went down in a heap but when he finally got up on his feet he grinned at me again and I snapped, I really did. I

stuck my revolver right in his grinning mouth and I said something, I don't remember what, and I pulled the trigger. His brains went all over the side of the police station. The other two Mickeys [Mau Mau] were standing there looking blank. I said to them that if they didn't tell me where to find the rest of the gang I'd kill them too. They didn't say a word so I shot them both. One wasn't dead so I shot him in the ear. When the sub-inspector drove up, I told him that the Mickeys tried to escape. He didn't believe me but all he said was, "Bury them and see the wall is cleared up."[19]

In the early hours of the morning of October 21, 1956, four years to the day after Kenya entered a state of emergency, a tribal policeman shot and captured the insurgent leader Dedan Kimathi as he tried to break out of his forest hideout near the town of Nyeri—a Mau Mau hotspot. Kimathi's capture and subsequent execution by hanging marked the end of the forest war against the Mau Mau.

The official number of casualties among the European settlers during Mau Mau was 32 dead and 26 wounded, and British records claim that 11,503 Kenyans were killed. David Anderson maintains the real figure was nearer 20,000, and Caroline Elkins has controversially estimated that at least 70,000 Kikuyu died, possibly hundreds of thousands.* The demographer John Blacker has recently estimated the total number of African deaths to be about 50,000, half of whom were children under the age of ten.[20] The real figure will never be known with any certainty, but it must surely run into tens of thousands of Kenyans—most of them innocent civilians.

There is little doubt that the very worst of the atrocities committed by the British and white Kenyans were limited to a small number of people, as indeed was the case within the Kikuyu population. For the most part, the white community struggled to maintain law and order

---

*Caroline Elkins' highest figures have been challenged on the grounds of unsound statistics.

during a very difficult, violent, and uncertain period in Kenya's history. Nevertheless, many people in a position of power were guilty of overlooking the many acts of violence by members of the white community against black Kenyans during the Mau Mau rebellion, making the decade one of the most shameful and inglorious episodes in British colonial history.

8

MR. "DOUBLE-DOUBLE"

KAPOD IN EPI TO KIK IYANY NYANG'

Don't abuse the crocodile when you're still in the water

THE WORLD changed in 1953.

On January 7, President Harry S. Truman ushered in the New Year by announcing that the United States had developed a hydrogen bomb. When Dwight D. Eisenhower took office as president later that month, he kept up the pressure on the Soviet Union by making nuclear weapons central to his foreign policy.[1] In June, Julius and Ethel Rosenberg were executed in New York's Sing Sing Correctional Facility, having been found guilty of spying for the USSR. The Cold War was about to get a lot cooler.

In the Soviet Union, Joseph Stalin collapsed and died from a hemorrhagic stroke, and he was replaced as first secretary of the Soviet Communist Party by Nikita Khrushchev. On August 8 Prime Minister Georgy Malenkov announced that the USSR had also developed an H-bomb, and four days later they carried out their first test. Code-named RDS-6, it was thirty times more powerful than the crude atomic bomb dropped by the Americans on Hiroshima.

In the United Kingdom on June 2, Elizabeth walked up the aisle of

Westminster Cathedral a princess and walked out a queen. Britain was, at last, emerging from the penury of the Second World War: a British-led climbing team had reached the summit of Everest, the country was experiencing full employment, and for the first time its citizens enjoyed the benefits of the newly created National Health Service. But the country would never regain its prewar global status, and over the next two decades the United Kingdom had to come to terms with its lost empire as its colonies moved one by one toward independence. Kenya was particularly turbulent by mid-1953, as the government there tried to suppress the Mau Mau rebellion. The rift between the white colonial community in Kenya and the Home Office in London continued to widen, and the growing nationalist movement would inexorably lead to Kenyan independence within a decade.

In this maelstrom of uncertainty both at home and abroad, Barack Obama senior was moving from rebellious adolescence into adulthood. Obama had decided that he needed to leave Maseno school, fearing that he might be linked to the anonymous letter sent to the principal. Furious and disappointed, Hussein Onyango banished his son to make his own way in Mombasa, where he started working for an Arab trader. However, the relationship did not flourish, and Barack left his employer without even asking to be paid. After working briefly as a clerk in another office in Mombasa, Barack moved to Nairobi, where he found a temporary job working for the Kenya Railway. These years were a time of real tension between Barack and his father; Onyango had only recently suffered the indignity and pain of internment, and now he watched as his son seemed to fritter his life away. Onyango, who put such a high priority on education and hard work, thought that Barack was wasting his opportunities and bringing shame to his family.

When Barack arrived in Nairobi in 1955, the Mau Mau emergency was at its height, and Nairobi was a hotbed of political action. Nineteen-year-old Barack began to take an interest in politics, and one evening the following year he was attending a Kenya African Union meeting when it was raided by the police. Using its emergency powers, the colonial government had declared the KAU illegal in 1953, and Barack was among those arrested and charged with violating the meeting law. Onyango was again furious with his son, and refused to pay his bail. According to Obama's friend Leo Odera, the British colonial police briefly detained Barack, but released him after his white employer in Nairobi gave the authorities reassurance that the young man's social and political activities were unconnected with the Mau Mau.

While he was living in Nairobi, Barack Obama senior became a regular visitor to Kendu Bay. With his father angry with him and considering him a failure, it was best not to be around K'ogelo too much. Also, even today, K'ogelo is a quiet and remote village—so in the early 1950s it must have seemed like the end of the world for a restless teenager with an eye for the girls.

Leo Odera recalls how Barack senior met his first wife: "In Nairobi, Barack Obama senior became a frequent visitor to his Kanyadhiang roots, and here is when he came into contact with two young girls, whom he had known while learning at the SDA Gendia Mission [primary school]. One of the girls was called Mical Anyango, daughter of Mr. Joram Osano, a local pastor. The other girl was the seventeen-year-old Kezia Nyandega."

Today, Kezia is a sixty-eight-year-old grandmother living in a modest semidetached house in Bracknell, a commuter town fifteen miles west of central London. She remembers clearly the place and day of her first dance with Obama senior: the local hall in the Obama family compound in Kendu Bay, Christmas Day 1956. "Barack was there on holiday with his family. I went to the dance hall with my cousin William and I saw Barack enter the room. I thought, 'Ohhh, wow!' He was so lovely with his dancing. So handsome and so smart. We danced together and then the next day my cousin came to our house and told me that Barack liked me."[2]

Kezia's older sister, Mwanaisha Atieno Amani, confirmed the story of their meeting. "Barack was a very good dancer. It was at Onyango's [old] home, there was a dance there. . . . He took Kezia dancing, they were number one. Number one!"

What the family will not tell you (but Leo Odera will) is that Kezia and her rival Mical had an argument over the attentions of Barack Obama senior, which soon turned into a bit of a brawl: "Kezia was very young at the time. Kezia fought with the other girlfriend, who gave up after fighting on the dance floor in Onyango's small hall. That is where they fought, and Kezia became the winner."

Even though Kezia and Barack had known each other at primary school in the SDA Gendia mission in Kendu Bay, they had inevitably lost contact after Barack moved to K'ogelo with his family at age nine. Now their attraction was instantaneous, and Barack quickly proved to be just as impetuous as his father when it came to a pretty young girl. Throughout late December and into early January, Barack and Kezia's cousin William stopped by her house to talk to her, to try to convince her to run off to Nairobi with Barack. Kezia's sister still remembers just how persistent Barack senior was in pursuit of Kezia: "Barack came back again and again. And in their meetings, the relationship began, and they informed his father. Then Barack said, 'My dad, Onyango, will go and talk to Nehemia [Kezia's father].'"

When Barack senior went to the railway station in Kisumu to catch the train back to Nairobi in early January 1957, Kezia went with her cousin William to see him off—except that Barack's smooth talking persuaded Kezia to stay with him. The two lovers eloped to Nairobi, where Kezia moved into Barack's apartment in Jericho, a suburb of Nairobi specially created for government employees. She recalls that her father was furious over what had happened: "He did not like Obama. My father and brothers came to Nairobi to bring me back. They said I had to go back to school. When I wouldn't, they said they would never speak to me again."[3]

For his part, Barack was worried about what Hussein Onyango's reaction would be. In the previous four years Barack had left Maseno school under a cloud, walked out of two jobs in Mombasa, and been arrested and jailed by the authorities on suspicion of being a political activist. Now he had eloped with a young girl to Nairobi, where he had only a menial job as a clerk working for the railway company. This was not the life that Hussein Onyango had planned for his fiercely intelligent, capable son.

Nevertheless, according to Kezia's sister Mwanaisha, Onyango agreed to the wedding: "So Hussein met with my father, who told Hussein, 'I want sixteen head of cattle. That is when you can take her as Barack's wife.' Then Onyango said, 'I am willing to pay anything, even if you want twenty of them. This is my eldest son, and if he wants a woman, and that is the woman he wants, I will not stand in his way.'"

Kenya has three different forms of marriage, and all of them are recognized as being legally binding. Today, as in 1957, a couple can choose to have a civil wedding, a church wedding, or a traditional tribal wedding. Civil and church weddings are very similar to ceremonies in Europe and North America, but a tribal wedding is significantly different; in all cases, a bride-price is still paid in the traditional way. In Kezia's case, Onyango paid her family sixteen cows. Barack Obama senior went on to marry another three women (including two Americans), but he never divorced Kezia. In Kenya, polygamy was (and still is) legal, and there is no limit to the number of wives a man can have. Muslims usually consider five wives to be a maximum, but it is not unusual for a Kenyan—Muslim or Christian—to take many more. (Ancentus Akuku is an infamous ninety-year-old Luo living in nearby Homa Bay and known locally as "Akuku Danger"; he has 130 wives, and jokes that "I am still very strong, though I am now worn out.")

While Barack senior was living in Nairobi and becoming more involved in African politics he met Tom Mboya. Mboya (no relation to

Paul Mboya from Kendu Bay) was six years older than Obama senior and a typical Luo: charming, charismatic, intelligent, and ambitious. He was also a leading trade unionist and a rising political star in Kenya, and Barack became his friend and protégé—often referring to Mboya as his "godfather," even though Mboya was not much older. When Jomo Kenyatta was arrested in 1952 during the Mau Mau emergency, Mboya stepped into the political vacuum by accepting the position of treasurer in Kenyatta's party, the KAU. In 1953, with support from the British Labour Party, Mboya brought Kenya's five most prominent labor unions together to form the Kenya Federation of Labour (KFL). When the KAU was banned later that year, the KFL became the largest officially recognized African political organization in Kenya. This made Mboya, at the age of just twenty-three, one of the most powerful and influential Africans in the country. He was seen—both within Kenya and also in the West—to be one of the rising stars in a new generation of moderate, well-informed, democratic African leaders. Mboya organized protests against the detention camps and secret trials of the emergency, while managing to stay free of arrest himself. In 1955 the British Labour Party arranged a year's scholarship for him to study industrial management at Ruskin College in Oxford. By the time he returned to Kenya a year later, the Mau Mau rebellion had been effectively quashed. Mboya, who had become a leading Luo politician and enthusiastic champion of national unity by the late 1950s, turned to campaigning for Kenyatta's liberation. When the Kikuyu leader was released on August 21, 1961, Mboya stepped aside to allow the older and more experienced Kenyatta to take over the leadership of Kenya's struggle for independence.

With visionary foresight, Tom Mboya sought to plan and prepare for Kenya to manage its own affairs once it gained autonomy from Britain. During the 1950s, university education for Africans remained out of reach for all but the highly elite, and Mboya knew that this had to change in preparation for independence. In the middle of 1959 he returned from an extensive tour of the United States to announce that he had secured scores of privately funded scholarships for young

Kenyans to study on American campuses. (Although this was at the height of the Cold War, and despite an alarming number of Kenyan students being offered lucrative scholarships in the Soviet Union, the student airlift to the United States was organized without the support of the U.S. State Department.) Some of Mboya's early supporters in America included the African American baseball legend Jackie Robinson and the actors Harry Belafonte and Sidney Poitier. Mboya's enterprise became known as the "Airlift Africa" project, and in its first year it gave eighty-one Kenyan students the opportunity to study at top universities in the United States. The American scholarships were offered annually through the mid-1960s, by which time more than eight hundred East African students had had the opportunity to study at some of America's most prestigious universities.[4]

Barack Obama senior has often been considered part of this first wave of Kenyan students to come to the United States. President Obama himself implied that his father was part of the airlift that was partially funded by the Kennedys, suggesting in a 2007 campaign speech that his "very existence" was due to the generosity of the Kennedy family. In his March 4, 2007, address to civil rights activists in Selma, Alabama, Senator Obama said:

> What happened in Selma, Alabama, and Birmingham also stirred the conscience of the nation. It worried folks in the White House who said, "You know, we're battling Communism. How are we going to win hearts and minds all across the world? If right here in our own country, John, we're not observing the ideals set forth in our Constitution, we might be accused of being hypocrites." So the Kennedys decided we're going to do an airlift. We're going to go to Africa and start bringing young Africans over to this country and give them scholarships to study so they can learn what a wonderful country America is. This young man named Barack Obama [senior] got one of those tickets and came over to this country.[5]

The "Camelot connection" became part of the mythology surrounding Obama's bid for the nomination, but the Kennedy family was

not, in fact, involved in the first airlift in 1959. (The Kennedy Foundation did contribute $100,000 toward the second airlift in 1960, and a
spokesperson for Senator Obama soon corrected the error.) Neither was
Barack senior on Mboya's first student airlift in 1959. It was a simple
assumption to make, as Obama senior and Mboya were good friends in
Nairobi, but the true story of how Barack senior got to the University of
Hawaii is much more interesting—and very much reflects the "Obama
way" of using his charm.

During his time in Nairobi in the mid-1950s, Obama watched as
his old school friends from Maseno graduated and went on to study at
university in Uganda and even London. Barack considered these students to be less gifted than he was, and he became depressed—Sarah
Obama says even desperate—at the thought of becoming trapped in
a menial administrative job. Sarah claims that two American women
befriended him and helped him take a correspondence course, which
would give him the school certificate he needed to move on to higher
education. For several months Obama used every opportunity to study
for his Cambridge A-level examinations—the recognized British high
school certificate. He took his exams at the U.S. embassy in Nairobi,
and after several months of nervous waiting he finally received word
that he had passed with excellent scores.

In his early twenties John Ndalo had moved to Nairobi and found
work in some of the city's big hotels, with help from Onyango. He was
still living in Nairobi in the late 1950s when Barack senior made his
breakthrough, and recalled:

> At the time, Hussein worked for the U.S. ambassador in Nairobi—
> this was around 1956 or 1957. I remember Onyango got involved
> with these people who got Barack a scholarship abroad. One
> woman at the embassy liked Barack a lot—I can't remember her
> name. Barack loved education, he was hardworking and present-
> able. He caught the eye of these people, and they supported Barack
> going to the U.S. They said, "This young man has the potential to
> become a leader."

One of the women who helped Barack secure his scholarship was Helen Roberts from Palo Alto, California, who was living in Nairobi at the time. Another was Jane Kiano, the American wife of the first Kenyan to gain a U.S. doctorate, Dr. Julius Gikonyo Kiano. A Stanford alumnus, Dr. Kiano played an important political role in the years running up to Kenyan independence, and helped Mboya significantly in organizing the student airlifts to the United States.

In 1958 and 1959, these women helped Obama to apply for scholarships. He applied to more than thirty colleges in the States before being accepted at the University of Hawaii. One hundred forty East African students submitted serious applications for eighty-one places on Mboya's 1959 chartered aircraft, and Obama did not make the final selection. Instead, Roberts and another American woman, Miss Mooney, paid for his flight to Honolulu and gave him a partial scholarship. The records of Barack's move to the United States are incomplete, but it seems that he also received some funding from Jackie Robinson.

In 1959, when the president's father left Nairobi, the long flight to Honolulu took several days. Kezia, three months pregnant with her second child, Auma, came to the airport for a tearful parting. Meanwhile, on the opposite side of the world, Hawaii became the fiftieth state of the Union on August 21 amid an explosion of cannon fire, marching bands, and parades. When Barack arrived at the campus at Manoa in the summer of 1959 he was just twenty-three years old. The campus is spread along the beautiful Manoa Valley outside of Honolulu, and the rich vegetation and subtropical atmosphere must have made Obama feel comfortably at home. As the first black African student at the university, he inevitably became the focus of great curiosity, and within a short period he had gathered a group of supportive friends around him. He had long ago renounced Islam and now declared himself to be an atheist, claiming that all religion was nothing more than superstition. As he started his classes in mathematics and economics in September, he must have reflected how far he had come from a mud hut in K'ogelo.

In Russian-language class the following year, Barack met Ann Dunham, the eighteen-year-old freshman who would become the mother of the forty-fourth president of the United States of America. Ann was born on November 29, 1942, in Wichita, Kansas, the only child of Madelyn Payne and Stanley Armour Dunham. Her birth name was Stanley Ann, after her father, who had really wanted a boy, and she was constantly teased about it at school. After the war, her parents moved regularly in search of work and a more prosperous life—first to Ponca City, Oklahoma, then to Vernon, Texas, and then back to Kansas, to El Dorado. In 1955 the family resettled in Seattle, Washington, and then a year later in Mercer Island, a suburb of Seattle, because her parents wanted her to attend the new high school there. Finally, Ann's parents moved to Hawaii, hoping to cash in on new business opportunities in the fledgling state. Her father was a furniture salesman, and judging by the family's frequent moves, he was a restless man—a characteristic Ann seems to have inherited.

In many ways, Ann Dunham was an enigma. When she graduated from high school in June 1960 she was accepted by the University of Chicago. Her father, however, refused to allow her to go because he thought she was too young to live away from home—she would not turn eighteen until November. So instead, the teenager enrolled at the University of Hawaii, where for the first time, she began calling herself Ann rather than Stanley. Yet despite her youth and innocence, one of her high school teachers, Jim Wichterman, recalls that she exhibited a natural skepticism and curiosity: "As much as a high-school student can, she'd question anything: 'What's so good about democracy? What's so good about capitalism? What's wrong with communism? What's good about communism?' She had what I call an inquiring mind."[6]

President Obama too recalls a woman who always seemed to challenge orthodoxy. "When I think about my mother," he said, "I think that there was a certain combination of being very grounded in who she was, what she believed in. But also a certain recklessness. I think she was always searching for something. She wasn't comfortable seeing her life confined to a certain box."[7]

Within a very short time of meeting Ann in September 1960, Obama senior was dating her—although he did not tell her about Kezia back in Nairobi, nor about his son and newborn daughter. His friend Leo Odera claims that Obama senior had been getting reports that Kezia had been seen out and about, partying in a manner that did not suit a married woman and mother:

> He was still writing back home until some friends of Obama's wrote to him telling that Kezia had been seen in public, at dancing places and whatever, as well as having two children. And later on she conceived a third one [by another man]. He wrote [to me], "She has disappointed me because she is expecting a child." . . . It is this that put the final nail in the marriage, and he decided now to look for another.

Even though Hawaii was unusually racially integrated for the early sixties, the mix was mainly white Americans and Asians. A black man dating a white girl was still considered unusual, though interracial marriage was legal there, unlike in most southern states of the Union. By November 1960, within weeks of meeting Obama senior, Ann was pregnant, and the couple married on the island of Maui three months later, on February 2, 1961. Even by the easygoing Hawaiian standards, Ann was very young to be married, and their relationship raised alarm on both sides of the family. Onyango thought his son was behaving irresponsibly and wrote to Barack to try to persuade him to change his mind; he even threatened to have his student visa revoked. Ann's parents also had their reservations, but they both supported her in her decision. The only people present at the ceremony, apart from Barack and Ann, were her parents, Stanley and Madelyn. Later that semester Ann dropped out of college. Their son, Barack Hussein Obama, was born at 7:24 p.m. on August 4, 1961, at the Kapi'olani Medical Center for Women and Children in Honolulu. At the time, Obama senior was still legally married to Kezia in Kenya, and he still had not told his new wife. Obama senior was technically a bigamist, and as polygamous marriages are not recognized under U.S. law, their son was technically illegitimate.

The lack of serious evidence that the younger Barack Obama was born anywhere other than the Kapi'olani Medical Center has not prevented the persistence of rumors and conspiracy theories challenging the legitimacy of his U.S. citizenship. Those who deny that Obama junior was born in Hawaii are often called "birthers," and they claim that he was actually born in Kenya, or even Indonesia. If the young Obama was not a natural-born citizen of the United States, so the logic goes, then he would not qualify to be a U.S. president. During the 2008 election, the Obama campaign even went to the trouble of releasing a certified copy of his birth certificate, which in this instance was referred to as a "certification of live birth," clearly stating that Obama junior was born in Honolulu, Hawaii, on August 4, 1961. The birthers, however, claim that the use of the term "certification of live birth" on the document means it is not equivalent to a proper "birth certificate." These arguments have been debunked many times by media investigations, government officials in Hawaii, and judicial reviews, all of which have concluded that the certificate released by the Obama campaign is indeed official. Even the director of the Hawaiian Department of Health has confirmed that the state "has Sen. Obama's original birth certificate on record in accordance with state policies and procedures."

Once Barack Obama was elected in 2008 by a comfortable margin, one might expect the rumors to have died off, but this was not the case. If anything, they intensified. Birthers even ran advertisements in the *Chicago Tribune* and on television questioning the president-elect's birth certificate and eligibility for office. One incorrect but commonly reported claim is that Obama junior's stepgrandmother, Mama Sarah, told a reporter that she was present when Obama was born in Kenya. Even though Sarah clarified later in the interview that "Obama was not born in Mombasa, he was born in America," the rumor has persisted.

The birthers claim that Obama senior took his new wife back to Kenya to meet his family before the birth of their son—a scenario that is unlikely for several reasons. First, the couple had no money, and flights to Africa from Hawaii in 1961 were very expensive. Nor had Obama told his young wife that he had another wife and two children back in Kenya, so one imagines that he would have wanted to keep Ann far away from K'ogelo. However, this logic has not diminished the enthusiasm of the conspiracy theorists, who further claim that Ann's pregnancy was so far advanced that she was not allowed to board her return flight home to Hawaii and had to give birth in Kenya. Most birthers seem to think that the baby was born in Mombasa, and several Kenyan birth certificates have been posted on the Internet, all claiming to be authentic.

One such forgery is birth certificate number 47044, allegedly issued to Barack Hussein Obama and Stanley Ann Obama by the district of Mombasa in Coast province. However, the form contains several obvious errors, and in this respect it is representative of all the purported Kenyan birth certificates. First, in August 1961 Kenya was still a British protectorate; it did not become a republic until December 1963, meaning the heading on the certificate is incorrect. Looking closely at the certificate number, it appears that the digits are actually 47O44—the middle digit being the letter *O* rather than the number zero. Obama was forty-seven years old when he became the forty-fourth president of the United States. Is this a coincidence? Perhaps, but unlikely, and the forgery might have been intended not to be taken too seriously. The form does name Obama senior's place of birth correctly, but Luoland is on the opposite side of the country from Mombasa and there is no valid reason for Obama to have traveled more than five hundred miles by road just so his wife could have their child in a distant region where they had no support and no relatives. Ann could not have been trying to fly home from there either, since the only airport in Mombasa at the time was used exclusively by the military; it did not become an international airport until 1979. Finally, the name of the registrar on the certificate—E. F. Lavender—is coincidentally the name of a modern environmentally friendly liquid laundry detergent; the initials E.F. standing for "Earth Friendly."

In *Dreams from My Father,* President Obama recalls stories of the three years his father spent in Hawaii, related to him by his mother and grandparents, "seamless, burnished smooth from repeated use." He recalls his mother saying that Obama senior was a terrible driver: "He'd end up on the left-hand side, the way the British drive, and if you said something he'd just huff about silly American rules."[8] But Barack junior found these stories to be generally inadequate to help him understand his father: they were "compact, apocryphal, told in rapid succession in the course of an evening, then packed away for months, sometimes years, in my family's memory." For the younger Barack, his father became a distant, mythical figure.

When Obama senior graduated from the University of Hawaii in the summer of 1962, a reporter interviewed him for the *Honolulu Star-Bulletin.* The piece gives a fascinating insight into the character of the twenty-six-year-old:

> He appears guarded and responsible, the model student, the ambassador for his continent. He mildly scolds the university for herding visiting students into dormitories and forcing them to attend programs designed to promote cultural understanding—a distraction,

he says, from the practical training he seeks. Although he hasn't experienced any problems himself, he detects self-segregation and overt discrimination taking place between the various ethnic groups and expresses wry amusement at the fact that "Caucasians" in Hawaii are occasionally at the receiving end of prejudice. But if his assessment is relatively clear-eyed, he is careful to end on a happy note: One thing other nations can learn from Hawaii, he says, is the willingness of races to work together toward common development, something he has found whites elsewhere too often unwilling to do.

Obama received two scholarship offers from doctorate programs: a full scholarship from the New School in New York City, and a partial one from Harvard. He chose to go to Harvard, but the award was not enough for the family to live together in Massachusetts. Ann stayed behind in Honolulu with their young son and resumed her studies at the university, and Barack flew to Boston in the fall. It was the beginning of the end of their short relationship.

By 1962 Mboya's airlift was into its third year and Harvard was now home to some of Kenya's brightest and most ambitious students. One of them was James Odhiambo Ochieng', a twenty-one-year-old student who arrived in that year:

> I went to the States in 1962. I was part of Tom Mboya's airlift. Tom Mboya was a very good friend of mine—I [later] came to work under him. I met Obama senior in 1963 in Boston, after he had left the lady. At that time, Obama was also staying in Cambridge; we were all brothers. We were staying more or less in the same place, and we liked parties and drinks.
>
> In America, it is very interesting. America, you see, you go to the grocery store and buy meat there, and you come and cook it the African way. Lots of ladies in America used to like that. We used our hands [to eat], we didn't use a fork.
>
> So when I met Obama at that time, Obama used to dance, seriously, and he used to know how to seduce. The women liked this man. Barry had lots of girlfriends.

Barack Obama senior rented a room in an apartment block just off Central Square in Cambridge and settled down to a bachelor lifestyle. Tom Mboya had heard that Obama had married again, and he wrote to his old friend, warning him not to abandon his new wife and son. Barack stayed true to his word, at least at first. In *Dreams from My Father,* President Obama remembers only one visit from his father, just before Christmas in 1971, when the young Barack was ten years old. However, James Odhiambo insists that Obama senior went back several times between 1962 and 1964 to see his toddler son in Hawaii: "He told me that he had a brilliant young boy. Even when he was in Boston, he was going [back] to Hawaii. Why do I say so? Because he would talk to us about the boy all that time. He went [to Hawaii] more than once. I am sure, I am certain—three times that I know of."

While Barack Obama senior was studying in Hawaii, Kenya was experiencing dramatic changes as the country moved toward independence. The year 1959, when Barack left for America, marked a relaxation of British governance in the colony; the Mau Mau emergency was effectively over, and Jomo Kenyatta was transferred from jail to house arrest. In 1960 Tom Mboya's People's Congress Party joined forces with the now underground Kenya African Union and the Kenya Independent Movement to form a new party—the Kenya African National Union (KANU). KANU was meant to transcend tribal politics and serve as a united front in preparation for negotiations with the British Colonial Office. These discussions, which became known as the Lancaster House conferences after the grand neoclassical building in London where they took place, were intended to create an effective constitutional framework for the country, and to smooth the transition to independence. As secretary general of KANU, Mboya headed the Kenyan delegation at the three conferences in Lancaster House.

The other leading Kenyan politician of the day was another Luo, Jaramogi Oginga Odinga, who was born in Bondo, a village close to K'ogelo in central Nyanza. The Luo revered him as *ker*—their spiritual leader—the position held by their fabled ancestral chief Ramogi Ajwang', who first brought the Luo to Kenya five centuries previously. As a mark of respect, Oginga Odinga became known as Jaramogi, meaning "son of Ramogi." However, according to Luo tradition, a *ker* cannot hold a political position, so Oginga Odinga relinquished his regal status in 1957 and was to represent the central Nyanza constituency in the newly formed Legislative Council. He further consolidated his political position in 1960, when he formed KANU with Mboya. Although they had fundamental political differences—Oginga Odinga was much further to the political left of Mboya—together they gave the Luo a powerful voice in the new Kenyan leadership.

In February 1961, the very month that Barack Obama senior and Ann Dunham were married in Honolulu, Kenya held its first general election to elect a coalition government in preparation for its forthcoming independence. The two main parties were KANU and the Kenya African Democratic Union (KADU). KADU had been founded in 1960 with the express aim of defending the interests of other Kenyan tribes against the domination of the Luo and Kikuyu, who accounted for the majority of KANU's membership. The most dramatically contested seat of the election, in Nairobi East, was considered to be a weather vane in the struggle over leadership of KANU. Five candidates stood for election, but the fight was clearly between two KANU representatives, Tom Mboya and Dr. Munyua Waiyaki, a Kikuyu.[9] More than 60 percent of the registered voters in the constituency were Kikuyu or allied tribal partners; the Luo, with just over 10 percent of the vote, were the next largest ethnic group. On the first day of the election, a Sunday, 75 percent of the electorate turned out to vote. The overwhelming majority sported Mboya badges, but some speculated that most of the Kikuyu who wore Mboya's image in public would vote strictly along tribal lines at the secret ballot box.

Mboya defied all expectations and won 90 percent of the vote, and there is nothing to suggest that these figures are anything but accurate. The result was a remarkable demonstration of popularity for the young Luo politician, and for the power of national democracy over tribalism. During the nine days of voting across the country, 84 percent of the electorate voted; although some of the campaigns were marred by bribery, corruption, and intimidation, most were conducted openly and honestly. KANU easily emerged as the dominant party, winning about two-thirds of the vote over KADU. In March 1961 nominees from both political parties visited Kenyatta in Lodwar, the small town in northern Kenya where he was being held under house arrest. Kenyatta urged the politicians to unite and work together for full independence. When Kenyatta was released later that year, he called for the two parties to form an interim coalition government and to hold elections before independence.

The national elections for Kenya's first autonomous government took place in May 1963. Kenyatta's KANU party, which called for Kenya to be a unitary state, ran against KADU, which advocated *majimbo*—a Swahili word meaning "group of regions." The *majimbo* system was proposed as a way of minimizing the problem of tribalism, by creating three self-governing regions (Rift Valley, Western, and Coast). This would give the Kikuyu and the Luo their own ethnic regional governments but prevent them from dominating the national government. However, the electorate rejected the concept of *majimbo* and KANU won the election with 83 of the 124 seats. On June 1, 1963, Jomo Kenyatta became Kenya's prime minister; the Luo were represented by Tom Mboya, who became minister of justice and constitutional affairs, and Oginga Odinga, who was minister for home affairs. This was an exciting time for the Africans, as they debated and argued about what sort of nation Kenya should become.

But the rapid transition from Mau Mau rebellion to independent status in no more than four years came as a huge psychological shock to the sixty thousand white Kenyans, who had long considered themselves the last bastion of European rule in British Africa. The white farmers felt they had been abandoned by the politicians in London after sixty years of labor in the White Highlands. In a very public demonstration of this sense of betrayal, one settler threw thirty pieces of silver in front of Michael Blundell, the de facto political leader of the white community, on Blundell's return to Nairobi from Lancaster House.

On December 12, 1963, Kenya became a fully independent nation; one year later to the day, the country became a republic—Jamhuri ya Kenya—with Jomo Kenyatta as president and Jaramogi Oginga Odinga as vice president. KADU was dissolved and integrated with KANU, leaving Kenyatta's first government effectively without an opposition. The resulting centralization of political and economic power around the president thus laid the foundation for corrupt governance.

In January 1964, Ann Dunham filed for divorce from Barack Obama senior, citing abandonment by her husband. It was clear that the marriage had really never had much chance of success; Obama senior had a succession of girlfriends in Boston, and now he had met a young schoolteacher in her early twenties, Ruth Nidesand. Obama senior soon moved in with Ruth, and they started a serious relationship. The young Kenyan students were also beginning to think less about partying in Boston and more about what was happening in Nairobi.

The following year, in 1965, Obama senior gave up his doctoral studies and returned to Nairobi—partly from financial hardship, but also because of the new opportunities on offer in Kenya. Following independence, many students who had been studying overseas returned home to compete for the top government jobs in Nairobi—many of which had been recently vacated by white administrators who decided to leave Kenya. Such was the demand for young, well-educated Kenyans that the government even sent recruitment teams to the United States to persuade the Kenyan students to return home and serve their country. Despite leaving his studies early, Obama senior was later awarded a master's degree from Harvard, even though he frequently referred to himself as "Dr. Obama" when wanting to make an impression. Ruth followed him out to Nairobi, and although Barack was reluctant at first, they soon married.

Obama senior's first job in Kenya was as an economist with Shell, but he soon landed a government post with the Kenya Central Bank. A prize placement for a young man from a small village in Nyanza, it should have been a springboard to greater things. But Obama senior's tendency for self-destruction was already beginning to reassert itself. In July 1965—the summer he returned to Nairobi—he published an article in the *East Africa Journal* entitled "Problems Facing Our Socialism."[10] It was essentially a commentary on an influential paper written by his old friend Tom Mboya that had argued for a model of government in Kenya based on African values—what would eventually be called "African socialism." In his article, Obama strongly criticized the direction the new Kenyatta administration was taking, and its lack of foresight in planning.

His article might have gone down well with his professors at Harvard, but for someone who was straight out of university, with no experience in government, it was not a very wise thing to write. The paper did, however, impress Mboya (who later gave Obama his government job), and it helped the cabinet minister to press Kenyatta and other members of the cabinet into addressing some of the inequalities of wealth in Kenya. However, it also marked Obama as a member of the Oginga Odinga/Mboya camp of left-wing Luo radicals, and the outspokenness and highly opinionated attitude demonstrated in the paper ultimately would contribute to Obama's downfall.

Nevertheless, those early years back in Kenya were good for Obama senior; he had a first-rate, well-paid job at the Central Bank, and he was making friends at the very top levels of government. His old college friend from Boston, James Odhiambo Ochieng', remembers countless nights out on the town:

> Obama did one thing—he would order the drinks. He would say, "When I say drink, drink!" So everybody would drink. But if I say

pay! What do you do? He would go and call the waiter: "Take [the bill] to Mboya." And Mboya would take it very easily. He would not only do it to Mboya, he would do it to Oginga Odinga. And you know, the old man would be sitting here like this, and he would say, "Yes?" and [the waiter] would say, "Obama has given me this." Oginga Odinga would take it. He couldn't be angry about it. With Obama? Oh no, no, no. He wouldn't argue.

At the same time, Obama's personal life was not running so smoothly. Soon after Barack married Ruth, Onyango came to Nairobi to see his son. Onyango had opposed the marriage to Ann, and now Barack had returned home with yet another American wife. A traditionalist at heart, Onyango wanted his son to have a Luo wife. So he tried to persuade Barack to set up a second home in Nairobi with Kezia—after all, a Luo always had separate huts for his wives in his compound, so why should the same idea not work in Nairobi?

Leo Odera explained what happened: "When Obama senior returned with Ruth, Hussein Onyango went to Nairobi physically to plead, because Kezia still had many children. So Hussein said, 'You are now married to a white lady. Why don't you rent a house for this wife somewhere on another estate, so that you can visit your children there?' And Obama is saying no!"

Ruth too put her foot down and refused to share Barack with another. Despite Barack's problems with his father, his first few years with Ruth in Nairobi were happy, and she bore him two sons, Mark and David—half brothers to Barack Obama junior back in Honolulu.

At a national level, Kenyan politics were beginning to deteriorate by the second half of the decade. Oginga Odinga and Kenyatta had always been uncomfortable bedfellows, coming as they did from different tribes. Politically, the two men also disagreed over the direction the country should take, with Oginga Odinga advocating a socialist system, whereas Kenyatta supported a mixed economy. In March 1966 Oginga Odinga quit KANU, resigned from Kenyatta's government, and formed a new left-wing opposition party, the Kenya People's Union (KPU). As a result, Barack Obama senior lost one of his most powerful mentors in government. Oginga Odinga claimed that Kenya was being run by an "invisible government," and for the next three years the KPU insisted that KANU's policies of "African socialism" were simply a cover for tribalism and capitalism. Oginga Odinga—a senior Luo politician—had thrown down a gauntlet at the feet of his Kikuyu adversary, setting off a confrontation that would eventually result in arrest, detention, and assassination.

The first five years after independence defined what type of government Kenya would have for years to come. From its very beginning, Oginga Odinga's KPU faced enmity from Kenyatta's government—Kenyatta was not prepared to compromise with or even countenance any opposition. If anything, he became even more entrenched in his own opinions, believing that his opponents were "paid agents of communism whose mission it was to dethrone him."[11] By March 1968—the second anniversary of the founding of the KPU—the government accused the political party of subversion. As a consequence of this very serious charge, KPU members were denied the right to address public meetings, with the government claiming that "the record of KPU members must bring into anxious review the question of the stage at which free speech, as a tool of democracy, may also become a trap into which democracy must fall."[12] Jomo Kenyatta and his close Kikuyu colleagues were determined to tighten their grip on their single-party government.

In May the following year KANU suffered a severe blow in a parliamentary by-election in the Luo constituency of Gem, in central Nyanza. KANU had won a substantial victory there in the national election four years previously, but in May 1969—less than a year after the KPU had been silenced at public meetings—the KPU overturned that result and won the seat easily. Realizing that many of the Luo in Gem were voting for Oginga Odinga out of tribal loyalty, Kenyatta asked Mboya—who by then had become minister for economic planning and development—to reorganize KANU in preparation for the national elections, which were due the following year. The popular and charismatic Mboya was also considered a potential challenger to Kenyatta for the presidency in those elections.

Two months later, on a hot, steamy Saturday morning in Nairobi, Barack Obama senior found himself drawn into one of the most momentous events in postindependence Kenya. Tom Mboya, his old friend and drinking companion, had returned the previous day from a meeting in Addis Ababa. As the July heat began to build up on the streets of Nairobi, Mboya arrived at his office in the Treasury Building on Harambee Avenue. At lunchtime he told his driver to go home for the weekend and took his own car to a pharmacy on Government Road (now called Moi Avenue) to buy some lotion for his dry skin. Just before one o'clock, on his way into the shop, he bumped into Obama senior, who casually joked with Mboya, saying that he should be careful, as he had parked his car illegally.[13] Minutes after the two friends parted, Tom Mboya came out of the store, having made his purchase, and was confronted by a slight young man wearing a dark suit, holding a briefcase in his left hand; his right hand was in his pocket. Almost immediately two shots were fired, and Mboya fell to the pavement.

Mohini Sehmi, who was a family friend and who had just served him in the pharmacy, ran out to see what the sudden noise was about. She recalled, "He slumped against me and staggered back almost into the shop. Then he must have staggered again, and we were back in the shop. I saw blood on his shirt, which was red anyway, and I realised then what had happened. He never uttered a word. He fell into my arms and began to fall to the ground."[14]

Dr. Mohamed Rafique, another family friend, arrived soon after the shooting and gave Mboya mouth-to-mouth resuscitation, but the young politician was pronounced dead on arrival at Nairobi hospital. The first bullet had severed his aorta, and the second had struck his right shoulder.

Mboya's friends and colleagues could not believe what had happened. His bodyguard, Joseph Nisa, collapsed at the hospital, crying, "It's not true, it's not true." The publicity secretary of the KPU arrived in tears and announced, "This is not a political assassination. There is no question of parties here. He belonged to us all."[15] The citizens of Nairobi thought otherwise: within hours of Mboya's death, a highly charged crowd—mainly Luo—tried to force their way into the hospital against the police cordon that had quickly been thrown around the building. Doors and windows were broken, and the police resorted to tear gas and clubs to disperse the angry crowd. The government mobilized the entire Kenyan police force, who established roadblocks and patrols throughout the city and into the suburbs.

News of Mboya's death soon reached Nyanza, where demonstrations quickly degenerated into riots. In Kisumu, mobs of young men roamed the city, stoning shops owned by Kikuyu traders; in nearby Homa Bay, police were obliged to take Kikuyus into protective custody. The following day Mboya's body was taken to his Nairobi home on Convent Drive; thousands of mourners lined the route and thousands more surrounded his house when the hearse arrived. Mboya's widow, Pamela, later told Sehmi: "Tom would still have been alive today if he had had a streak of badness in him. They killed him because he was nothing but a good man. He died because they know he was good."[16]

Tom Mboya's death left a vacuum at the very heart of Kenya's government: the country had lost its most able government minister and its most astute political strategist. His death, along with the Kenyatta government's attempts to suppress the KPU, led most Luo to believe that the Kikuyu were determined to deny any Luo a senior position in the country. The government had already sidelined Oginga Odinga, and now, or so the Luo maintained, Kenyatta had dealt permanently with Mboya—the one man most likely to beat him to the presidency in a popular vote.

Nor was Mboya's assassination the only violent death of a senior Luo. A few months before, in January 1969, Chiedo Argwings-Kodhek, the foreign minister in Kenyatta's government, died in what was initially thought to be a road accident. The subsequent exhumation found evidence that he was actually killed by a single shot fired from a police rifle. Some people claim that this was Jomo Kenyatta's first political assassination.

On July 10, five days after Mboya's murder, a Kikuyu man, Isaac Njenga Njoroge, was arrested and charged with Mboya's assassination. Njenga Njoroge had once been a youth volunteer in KANU's Nairobi branch, seemingly confirming Luo suspicions that the murder had been politically motivated.

By now Barack Obama senior was well known as an outspoken critic of Kenyatta's government, and he was prepared to testify at the prosecution of Mboya's killer. It was a brave thing to do, and he later told a friend that not long after the trial, he was hit by a car on a Nairobi street and left for dead. He was convinced that the occupants in the car were the same people who had killed Mboya.[17] On September 10, Njenga Njoroge was found guilty in what most people considered to be a tightly controlled showcase trial. But he almost ruined the carefully stage-managed event just before his sentence was announced, when he casually asked: "Why do you pick on me? Why not the big man?" No one has ever conclusively explained to whom Njenga Njoroge was referring, but every Luo politician and historian I have spoken to is sure that Kenyatta ordered Mboya's assassination. On November 25, 1969, the Kenya Prison Service announced that Njenga Njoroge had been hanged: "The sentence imposed on Njenga has been carried out in accordance with the law, along with those other persons convicted of capital offences." However, the trial records have since disappeared from the Kenya National Archives, and rumors have persisted that Njenga

Njoroge was spirited off after the trial to Ethiopia, where he lived the rest of his life under an assumed identity.

Throughout the second half of 1969 the relationship between President Kenyatta and Oginga Odinga—and effectively between the Kikuyu and the Luo—continued to decline. Kenyans have a well-known saying in Swahili, *Wapiganapo tembo nyasi huumia*—when elephants fight, the grass gets hurt—and this is exactly what happened in Kisumu on October 25, 1969.

That month, Jomo Kenyatta decided to make a tour of the Rift Valley and Nyanza in the run-up to the presidential elections scheduled for December 6; it was his way of showing that he was back in control of the country. On the twenty-fifth he visited Kisumu, ostensibly to open the New Nyanza General Hospital, which had been built by the Soviet Union and is still referred to as the "Russian hospital." But Kenyatta found that he had strayed into hostile territory. An estimated five thousand people massed outside the hospital that day, and the crowd started to chant the KPU slogan, *"Dume, dume"* (in this context, it meant "brave man" in Swahili, and referred to Oginga Odinga). When the president rose to make his speech, the crowd started heckling him; perhaps unwisely, Kenyatta was in no mood to mince his words. His attack on the Luo community in general, and the Luo political leadership in particular, was extraordinary and unprecedented. Speaking in Swahili, he opened his speech with the following diatribe:

> Before opening this hospital, I want to say a few words; and I will start with the Kiswahili proverb which states that "The thanks of a donkey are its hind kick." We have come here to bring you luck, to bring a hospital which is for treating the citizens, and now there are some writhing little insects, little insects of the KPU, who have dared to come here to speak dirty words, dirty words.
>
> I am very glad to be with my friend Odinga, who is the leader of these people here. And I wish to say, if it were not for the respect I have for our friendship, Odinga, I would have said that you get locked up today . . . so that we see who rules over these citizens,

whether it is KANU, or so many little insects who rule over this country. . . . On my part I do say this, if these people are dirty, if they bring about nonsense, we shall show them that Kenya has got its government. They dare not play around with us, and you Bwana Odinga as an individual, you know that I do not play around. I have left you free for a long time because you are my friend. Were it not so, you yourself know what I would have done. It is not your business to tell me where to throw you; I personally know where. Maybe you think I cannot throw you into detention in Manyani [previously a British detention camp] because you are my special friend. . . . And therefore today I am speaking in a very harsh voice, and while I am looking at you directly, and I am telling you the truth in front of all these people.

Tell these people of yours to desist. If not, they are going to feel my full wrath. And me, I do not play around at all. . . . They are chanting *Dume, Dume*—"Bull, Bull." Your mother's c**ts! This *Dume, Dume* . . . And me, I want to tell you Odinga, while you are looking at me with your two eyes wide open; I have given my orders right now: those creeping insects of yours are to be crushed like flour. They are to be crushed like flour if they play with us. You over there, do not make noise there. I will come over there and crush you myself.[18]

With this extraordinary verbal attack on a tribal minority, the nation's president made the threat to the Luo people crystal clear, the abuse explicit. Obscenities aside, Africans consider it a great insult to be called "writhing little insects," and the crowd was furious. Full-scale riots soon erupted in Kisumu against Kenyatta's security entourage; the police opened fire, and forty-three people were reported killed. Never again did Kenyatta set foot in Nyanza, and the Luo province—like many other non-Kikuyu areas—was denied virtually any further economic assistance or development for decades. The effects of this rejection can still be seen in these parts of Kenya today.

In that year, 1969, tribal politics won, and Kenyan nationalism died along with Mboya, Argwings-Kodhek, and the forty-three victims of Kisumu. The entire Luo community now closed ranks around Oginga

Odinga, and they took on a markedly anti-Kikuyu stance that is still felt today. Nor did Jaramogi Oginga Odinga remain free for long after Kenyatta's public tirade at the Kisumu hospital: within a very short time the president carried out his threat, and Oginga Odinga was arrested and detained for two years. After he was released, he lived in political limbo until after Kenyatta's death in August 1978; then, following a short period of political rehabilitation, he was again placed under house arrest by President Daniel arap Moi in 1982. In 1992, Oginga Odinga fought for a change in Kenya's constitution to allow multiparty democracy, and he won his challenge with the support of the British and U.S. governments.

Oginga Odinga died two years later at the age of eighty-three, but he had created a political dynasty. His son, Raila Amollo Odinga, followed his father into politics; he won his first parliamentary seat in 1992, and after two failed attempts to run for the presidency against Mwai Kibaki, he challenged the incumbent again in 2007. His claim that the election was fraudulent led to the postelection violence in late 2007 and early 2008; in April 2008 Raila Odinga was made prime minister of Kenya on a power-sharing basis with President Mwai Kibaki.

As the fortunes of the Luo fell during the late 1960s, so too did those of Barack Obama senior. His outspokenness and criticism of Kenyatta were beginning to cause problems at the Central Bank. As a senior Luo civil servant within the Kenyatta government, he was already particularly vulnerable; now that his friend and mentor Tom Mboya was dead, he became even more exposed, as Leo Odera recalls:

> When Barry returned home [in 1965], Mboya was a government minister. When Mboya was assassinated, his protection was uncovered. Because you know, he liked drinking and sometimes not reporting to work. But whilst Mboya was there, nobody would do anything about him. Once Mboya died, he had no protector.

Obama senior did not heed the warning and he continued to speak openly against the government, even after Mboya's death. On one occasion, Odera claims, Kenyatta himself called Barack to his offices, to give him a personal warning:

> Barack was outspoken. After getting drunk, he would say the government killed the best brain. And then I think some intelligence men picked this up and I think this could have reached Kenyatta's ear. So he was ordered to Kenyatta's place. Kenyatta told him: "You'll be on the tarmac looking for another job." But still he did not shut his mouth. . . . It is a brave man who talked carelessly about the Kenyatta government in those days.

James Odhiambo, Barack's college friend in Boston, had also returned from America to work in Nairobi, and he was a regular visitor to the house that Ruth and Barack shared:

> The problem that Obama senior was having—despite the fact that Ruth was in the house—Obama was still enjoying himself with the ladies. He [liked] the white [women] in Nairobi. This was in '67, '68. Obama was, I will use the word, arrogant. Because of his brightness, he actually felt that people like Duncan Ndegwa [the governor of the Central Bank of Kenya] were stupid, and he felt that he should be the governor! "Ndegwa? Who is Ndegwa? Ndegwa was not learned [educated]," according to him.

On one occasion, according to Odhiambo, governors from several African banks met up in Nairobi for a banking summit. "Obama had evidently spoken to these people who were coming from the central banks of other African countries. When he talked to them, he says, 'You know, I'm the governor *really*, you know.' Oh, Barry!"

The Luo have a proverb, *Kapod in epi to kik iyany nyang'*: "Don't abuse the crocodile when you're still in the water." Obama senior, who was up to his neck in the murky waters of the Central Bank, should have heeded these words; the crocodile now turned on the young, outspoken economist, and Obama was fired. People who knew Obama claim that his dismissal was personally sanctioned by Kenyatta. Obama was devastated over the loss of this job, and his drinking became worse. He had always been known as "Mr. Double-Double," for his habit of ordering two double whiskies at once—he preferred Johnnie Walker Black Label and VAT 69.

By the early 1970s, Barack was regularly coming home very late at night and very drunk. Although he was still living with Ruth at this time, he was also seeing his first wife, Kezia, who was now living in Nairobi with Obama's two eldest children. (Kezia had two more children in the late 1960s; according to *Dreams from My Father,* the family doubts whether either of them is a biological son of Barack senior, as Kezia had other partners during this period. Nevertheless, this seemed to make little difference to Barack, who in traditional Luo style said they were all his children, and welcomed them into his wide, extended family.) Inevitably, his relationship with Ruth began to deteriorate. Ruth has always kept a discreet silence about her marriage to Barack Obama senior, but her eldest son, Mark Ndesandjo, claims that his father beat his mother and his young sons:

> It's something which I think affected me for a long time, and it's something that I've just recently come to terms with. I remember situations when I was growing up, and there would be a light coming from our living room. . . . I could hear thuds and screams, and my father's voice and my mother shouting. I remember one night when she ran out into the street and she didn't know where to go.[19]

Leo Odera also recalls this period of Obama senior's life:

> He was becoming almost an alcoholic. Soon after, he began to have a problem with his American wife, Ruth. She was getting very frustrated with him getting drunk. At that time, I was told that he was even passing out on the bed. And Ruth was telling people that she was getting disappointed and she wanted to leave. So she eloped with this Asian. And she stayed with him for some time before eventually settling in with my former work colleague, Simeon

Ndesandjo, who was to be the head of the Swahili service in the Kenyan Broadcasting Service.

The relationship between Ruth and Obama senior never recovered and Obama's two sons, Mark and David, took the name of Ruth's second husband, Simeon Ndesandjo. Ruth had a third son, Joseph, in 1980 with Ndesandjo, and the couple still lives in Nairobi, where Ruth runs a kindergarten. In *Dreams from My Father,* President Obama writes of a very uncomfortable visit to Ruth and her oldest son, Mark, in Nairobi in 1987. (Her second son, David, had died in a motorcycle accident not long before.) Today, Mark works in Shenzhen, China, and runs an Internet company that helps Chinese companies export to the United States. Joseph lives in San Antonio, Texas, and is president and owner of a security systems company.

Barack always had a reputation as a reckless driver; now that he had lost his wife, his two sons, and his job, his drinking became a serious problem. He had several major motor accidents, including one which involved Leo Odera:

> He was a very bad driver. He was a drunkard, he had to have one for the road. So [one evening] we took one or two beers and I was sleeping. The first I knew, we were off the road and the dashboard hit my chest. After taking a double—he would say "give me another double"—then he'd have a blackout and would cause an accident.

Leo Odera told me that Obama senior had four major accidents, including one in which his good friend Adede Odiero died:

> That was his first major accident. He doesn't remember [how it happened]. They were drunk and they hit a pavement, and this boy had a brain hemorrhage and he died. He was a very popular boy. That was the first incident when the community in Karachuonyo [Kendu Bay] started losing faith in him [Obama].

It was after one of his road accidents in 1971 that Obama senior went back to Hawaii to see his young son. Despite reports that Obama senior had his legs amputated after one serious accident, people who knew him say this was not true, although for a while he did wear leg braces. When he went to Hawaii just before Christmas in 1971, he was still on crutches, and this was the only occasion on which President Obama recalls meeting his father. For Obama senior, the visit was difficult; he knew that his life was falling apart around him in Nairobi, and now in Honolulu he found it hard to relate to a ten-year-old son he did not know. The young Barack too found it impossible to form a relationship with this big man with a deep, resonant voice who had suddenly appeared in his life.

The last decade of Barack Obama senior's life played out like a Greek tragedy. After he lost his job at the Central Bank, he found another through his personal connections back in Nyanza. James Odhiambo still saw Obama senior regularly during this time, he recalls:

> He had a lot of friends, very powerful friends. . . . Somebody from Alego called Owuor—he was the managing director of the Kenya Tourist Development Corporation, the KTDC. I understand Obama was an extension officer—but an economist all right. He was pleased with the job.

Unfortunately, Obama senior did not learn his lesson, and before long his inflated ego got the better of him again. In his job at the KTDC, Obama senior had dealings with influential people, many of whom were from overseas, and James Odhiambo recalls that Obama habitually implied that he was rather more senior in the corporation than was actually the case:

So Jerry [Owuor] would say, "Now Barry, what is all this again? Because a letter comes in, 'For the attention of . . . Barry Bwana'?" [*Bwana* is Swahili for "boss."] . . . But you see, Barry wanted to look big. He was much brighter than the other man. His intellect went far beyond. He complained about the amount of money he was being paid. . . . That's Barry Obama. He had to be given his marching orders—that is all that I will say! Barry now suffered a great deal for some time.

Once again, Obama senior found himself without a job, and his heavy drinking continued.

Then, in 1975, Obama suffered another blow. His father, Onyango, was now eighty years old, and his health had deteriorated. Whenever Barack visited his father in K'ogelo, he could not bring himself to talk about his problems, although he did confide in Sarah on occasion. Instead, Barack would behave as if nothing were wrong, bringing gifts that he could ill afford. Onyango could now walk only with the assistance of a stick, and he was almost totally blind—which made him more irascible than ever. He was so frail that Sarah had to bathe him, something this proud and self-righteous man found difficult to accept. He died later that year and was buried inside his compound, as is customary in Luoland. Barack came up from Nairobi to organize the funeral and he gave his father a Muslim burial, with his body wrapped in a simple cotton shroud rather than a traditional Luo bull skin.

Three years after Onyango's death, on August 31, 1978, Jomo Kenyatta died suddenly from cardiac arrest during a visit to Mombasa. Although he had suffered a previous heart attack in 1966, his death was still unexpected. Kenyatta was succeeded by his vice president, Daniel arap Moi, popularly known as "Nyayo"—a Swahili word meaning "footsteps," because Moi always claimed that he was following in the footsteps of Kenyatta. During the first few years of his presidency, Moi enjoyed widespread support throughout the country, even among Luo. In stark contrast to Kenyatta's imperious manner, Moi was a populist, and people liked him for it. However, his public approval did not last, and soon he was accused of nepotism, tribalism, political assassinations, torture, corruption, and allowing a collapse of governance in the country.

Barack Obama senior had reached a crisis point in his life, and once again his friends stepped in to help. James Odhiambo remembers that those who knew him well were concerned about his drinking and thought that he needed support. "He was a man of substance, and they could not risk leaving him alone there, bickering and talking a lot of nonsense. They would rather absorb him. So they felt the gentleman must come and work in the Finance Ministry."

In the Finance Ministry Obama senior worked for Mwai Kibaki, who was then minister of finance and economic planning. (In 2006, when Senator Obama visited Kenya, Kibaki—now the country's third president—was keen to point out that he had given Obama's father this position.) With his reputation for having a massive ego and a big mouth, both of which grew alarmingly when he started drinking, Barack Obama senior was lucky to get the job.

Even his closest friends, such as Leo Odera, are realistic about Obama senior's failings during this period. As Odera says: "You know what happened to Barack? Many of our people, especially those who are very bright at school, when they come out, they don't make a good life outside. There is too much brain, and when they have the whiskies, they go off the rails. Even in journalism, some of my contemporaries have drunk themselves to death."

Ruth and her sons were long gone, and Barack remained single for some time. By 1978, however, he had met a young Luo girl called Jael Otieno, and they married in 1981. She became his fourth wife but he still remained legally married to Kezia. In the summer of 1982 Jael gave birth to a son, George. Then, on the night of November 24, Barack Obama senior reached the end of the road. He had been drinking all evening in a Nairobi bar, as he commonly did in those days. He left alone and started to drive home. Minutes later his car drove off the road and hit a tree, but this time it was not just another road accident. Charles Oluoch, who is cousin to the president, happened to be working just outside of Nairobi at the time:

> I was in Nairobi [at the time]. So Malik, his eldest son, told me his father had disappeared. So I rushed into Nairobi and we went up to the police station on my motorbike. We saw the vehicle which he was driving, and it seemed as if it had left the road and hit a tree. The impact seemed to have killed him. We went into the city mortuary and we found him there. And from there we went back to his house and informed the people there. People were crying, and so we stayed throughout the night. The next day, we started making arrangements for the funeral.

Obama senior's body was taken from Nairobi back to K'ogelo in a coffin. Although he had been raised a Muslim, by the time he went to Hawaii he was a confirmed atheist and considered religion to be nothing more than superstition.[20] Even so, his body was taken out of the coffin and wrapped in a white shroud before burial, as is customary in an Islamic funeral. Several senior Luo leaders were present, including the foreign minister, Robert Ouko, and the education minister, Oloo Aringo. His old drinking friend James Odhiambo was also there, and remembers:

> It was a traditional Luo funeral, and there were a lot of people. Three hundred vehicles I would say—cars, *matatus,* minibuses. Quite a number of friends and the elite who were available. Luos say that a funeral lasts for ever. According to the Luos, death will not diminish us.
>
> To be honest with you, he was the man I liked most. He was

a man who loved almost everybody—no discrimination at all, at all, at all. Barry was one of the best people you could find—he was somebody who cared for the people.

From the very beginning, members of the family had their suspicions about how Barack senior actually died. Charles Oluoch was at the scene of the accident, and he saw the body soon after:

When our family saw how he was, it was very hard to realize how the accident killed him. Barack had [many other] accidents and they were [potentially] very fatal, but he didn't die. [This time] there was no way anything was broken, but he was dead. Although it looked like an accident, our family suspected that there must have been foul play. I am not a medical doctor, but the way we saw Barack lying there, he didn't look like somebody who was involved in an accident. When you see somebody who is said to have died in an accident, but doesn't have anything to show for it—you know, you become suspicious.

You see, in these corridors of power, there're a lot of people here and there . . . maybe he'd made enemies. Because, you know, Barack was very outspoken, and he was very flamboyant, and he was very bright. So maybe some people thought they were threatened.

We talked to the mortuary attendant. He had washed him, and when I went to the mortuary with Malik, he was already dressed in a suit. He was very clean. In fact, I wondered if this man had really died. I was so shocked.

Charles was making very serious accusations, and I wondered if perhaps he was a grieving relative unable to come to terms with the death of a man whom he loved and respected. With Obama senior's reputation as a reckless driver, a fatal crash would seem to be an entirely plausible consequence. I raised the issue with Sarah Obama one afternoon, when we were talking in her compound in K'ogelo. She explained:

We found him sitting by the steering wheel. [The car] did not roll. So after it was said that he had hit the tree, we just had to believe it, because he could not talk back. We really didn't believe it was a real accident. Because his body was never broken, his vehicle was not badly crashed. He was just dead after the accident. Not even much blood was seen.

So why should we believe it was an accident? Even the policeman who was recording this—he was a very high-ranking officer, very big—but he could not say anything because the government was watching his lips. We think there was foul play there, and that is how he died, and they covered it up [by saying] that he had an accident.

But we just had to leave it like that because the government then was very ruthless.

Everybody I spoke to in the family believed much the same thing; his sister Hawa Auma is particularly bitter about the episode. Indisputably, the assassination of leading Luo has been a regular occurrence over the years. As we have seen, six months before Tom Mboya was killed in July 1969, the Kenyan foreign minister, Argwings-Kodhek, was shot and his death made to look like a road accident. More recently, the 1990 death of Robert Ouko—the minister of foreign affairs in President Moi's government and a leading Luo politician—caused another outrage. On the night of February 12, Ouko was staying at his farm near Kisumu. The following morning, his body was found nearly two miles away from his homestead: his right leg was broken in two places, and there was evidence that he had been tortured. He had been killed by a single shot to his head and his body left partially burned, with a gun, a can of diesel, and a box of matches also found nearby. The initial police reports claimed that Ouku had committed suicide. Public pressure forced President Moi to request that Britain's Scotland Yard send a team of detectives to investigate Ouko's death. They were unable to determine who had actually killed Dr. Ouku, but the investigation proved that he had been brutally murdered.

Roy Samo is a Luo local councilor who lives and works in Kisumu, and he has taken a strong stand against corruption and poor governance. He understands from firsthand experience the risks of becoming involved with politics in Kenya; he has been beaten up on more than ten occasions and has received many threats on his life. As recently as October 2009 a group of thugs raided his compound and stole his TV and other valuables. They left him a note in Swahili: *Roy wacha siasa, tumetumwa tukumalize, mamayako, baba, ndugu, mke wako sana sana wewe kwani unashinda Ouko or Mboya.* Loosely translated, it means: "Roy, leave politics. We've been sent to kill you, your mother, father, brothers, and wife, but especially you. We've warned you; do you think you are greater than Ouko or Mboya?" When they left, they decapitated his dog and left its body by the front gate to his compound. Unsurprisingly, he too thought foul play was an entirely plausible explanation for Barack Obama senior's death:

> If you want to talk about political death, it's common. We know of people like Tom Mboya, who was a son of this area. There have been other powerful cabinet ministers like Robert Ouko. Three years ago [in 2006], a professor, Odhiambo Mbai, was helping us with the drafting of a new constitution. Mbai was a very wise and influential man. He was shot dead in his house. So many Luos have been killed because they have always been very outspoken. They're bright, they're the professionals—the professors and the doctors—so they are believed to be very wise. So many of them have been killed in cold blood. And it is not only Luos, but anybody who is viewed by the government of the day as anti-establishment.

Patrick Ngei is another of Obama's old friends. He is not a member of the Obama family, so I thought that he could perhaps look on the event more dispassionately. Yet he too seemed to suspect the worst:

> There were serious allegations of foul play—Obama didn't die out of a pure accident. The Kikuyus were feeling that if we eliminate these bright Luos, then they can rule forever. That was the idea. Bright Luos were eliminated by the Kenyatta government. They had this belief that if these people aren't there, then maybe one day they may stop [the Luo] from going on with the leadership.

Believing that Barack Obama senior died at the hands of others is one thing; proving it more than twenty-five years after his death would be impossible. But if it is true, how might such a killing have been orchestrated? Charles Oluoch had a theory: "Let's say you are in a place where they put something in your drink and they know you will be driving. At a certain point, you will lose control. It will look as if it was an accident. But already they have poisoned you, so you lose control."

This was a very serious accusation that Charles was making, and I wanted to be absolutely clear what he was implying: "So you would die from the poisoning anyway?" I asked.

"It's very common," he replied.

"So even if you had a small accident by driving off the road," I suggested, "you would still be dead."

"You'd be dead."

On the day that Barack Obama senior died in Nairobi, a twenty-one-year-old student at Columbia University in New York was making himself breakfast. The telephone rang, but the line was crackly and the caller indistinct.

"Barry? Barry, is that you?"

"Yes . . . who's this?"

"Yes, Barry . . . this is your Aunt Jane. In Nairobi. Can you hear me?"

"I'm sorry—who did you say you were?"[21]

With this briefest of calls from a complete stranger, albeit a relative, Barack Obama junior learned of the death of his father—a man whom he recalls meeting only once.

Young Barack went on to graduate the following summer with a degree in political science with a specialization in international relations before working briefly for a company that provided international business information to corporate clients. In 1985 he moved to Chicago, where he worked as a community organizer and also with a public housing development on the city's South Side. While in Chicago, Barack Obama junior decided to return to school, this time to Harvard—his father's alma mater—to study for a degree in law. But one piece of unfinished business remained before the younger Barack could move on with the rest of his life. In the summer of 1987, he made his first visit to Kenya. There he met his extended African family who, until that point, had been only faceless names from the past. He visited K'ogelo, where his stepgrandmother still works the soil made fertile by Onyango's hard labor. And he sat by the graves of his father and his paternal grandfather and wept. Afterward he felt a calmness wash over him; the circle had finally closed around him. His five-week visit to the home of the Obamas had given him an insight into the person he really was:

> I saw that my life in America—the black life, the white life, the sense of abandonment I'd felt as a boy, the frustration and hope I'd witnessed in Chicago—all of this was connected with this small plot of earth an ocean away, connected by more than the accident of a name or the color of my skin.[22]

Barack Obama junior made two more trips to his African homeland before he became president, and both visits represented key moments in his life. Ten years after the death of his father, he took a twenty-eight-year-old lawyer from Chicago called Michelle Robinson back to K'ogelo and introduced her to Mama Sarah as the woman he intended to marry. Then in 2006 he returned for a third time, this time in a professional capacity. As part of a broad sweep through Africa, Barack Obama—now a senator from Illinois—made a brief visit to Nairobi and then to K'ogelo.

Now, with the mantle of presidential office weighing heavy on his shoulders, never again will he have the opportunity to travel freely and unrecognized in the land of his forefathers.

EPILOGUE

KINDA E TEKO

Perseverance is strength

E VERY TIME you drive west out of Kisumu to visit K'ogelo, or south to Kendu Bay, you will pass a police roadblock. The checkpoints, spaced at regular intervals along every major road in Kenya, are the bane of every driver in the country. If the police were genuinely checking the roadworthiness of the thousands of trucks on their way to Uganda, Congo, and Tanzania, or scrutinizing the dangerously overloaded matatus (which have fatal accidents almost daily), or even looking for drivers who are not properly licensed and insured to drive their vehicles, then their actions would be laudable. If challenged, the police will claim that this is exactly what they are doing. But if you sit discreetly in a matatu two or three rows behind the driver and watch carefully, then you will see the true purpose of the police check. The driver is flagged down and stops; a policeman will exchange a few words, cast an appraising eye over the passengers in the back, and then wave the driver on. You have to be quick to see the bribe changing hands.

Sometimes the money is slipped surreptitiously through the window, and at other times a 100 Ksh note ($1.25) is rolled into a tiny ball and dropped outside onto the road, to be collected after the matatu has driven off. A matatu driver often charges only 50 or 100 Ksh for a short trip, so the regular bribes taken by the police can sometimes account for as much as 50 percent of his daily fares. The police target almost all the vehicles—matatus, trucks, and private cars—but whenever my own vehicle was stopped and they realized there was a *mzungu* inside, they would give me a broad smile and a salute and wish me a good *safari* (which means "journey" in Swahili).

Police corruption is a fact of life in Kenya, and it has been going on for decades; little, if anything, is ever done about it. In 2008 a Kenya Television Network (KTN) crew covertly videotaped police roadblocks in and around Nairobi. They calculated that the police were making at least 15,000 to 18,000 Ksh ($190–$225) a day at each roadblock; each of the manned positions had a senior officer in charge who took the bulk of the bribes, and he made 30,000 Ksh ($3,750) a month or more from the scam. Their illicit earnings constituted a huge sum of money in a country where the average income is less than $700 a year. When the report aired, the police authorities and politicians swept the scandal under the carpet; the officers who were recognizable on the KTN video were merely transferred to a remote police post. Yet corruption by people in positions of power is not a simple issue; most policemen in Kenya earn no more than 10,000 Ksh ($125) a month, and there is a tacit expectation that they will supplement their paltry salary by other means, although this is vehemently denied by the authorities.

And the roadblocks are only a very public display of a problem that goes right to the top of government. In 2004 the government commissioned a confidential report about ex-president Moi's illegal activities, as part of a commitment by President Kibaki to eradicate high-level corruption following Moi's twenty-four-year rule. The report, which leaked onto the Internet in 2007, alleged that associates of President Moi were involved in drug dealing, money laundering, and kickbacks; it estimated that Moi's son Gideon was worth some £550 million ($855 million) in 2002, while his other son Philip was worth about £384 million ($597 million).[1] Unfortunately, President Kibaki had a reputation for spinelessness; the joke going around Kenya a few years ago was that he never saw a fence without sitting on it. A government spokesman, Alfred Mutua, called the unauthorized release of the report a "political gimmick" to influence the 2007 elections, claiming: "The government of Kenya believes that the leaking of this report is meant to score political points against Kibaki." He also asserted that the report was incomplete and inaccurate. Today Daniel arap Moi lives in a vast mansion outside of Eldoret in western Kenya, and although he is generally ignored by the political establishment, his many supporters still venerate him as the grand old man of Kenyan politics.

The biggest and longest-running case of corruption in Kenya's history was the Goldenberg International scandal, which occurred between 1991 and 1993. Like many countries, Kenya encourages international trade by granting tax-free status to Kenyan companies who export goods; the government sometimes also subsidizes the exported products. Goldenberg International smuggled gold into Kenya from the Democratic Republic of the Congo (DRC), then exported it as Kenyan gold, earning the company a 20 percent subsidy from the government. The huge sums of money involved—at least $600 million—suggest the participation of government officials at the highest level. Almost all of the politicians in Moi's government were accused of benefiting from the embezzlement and many of them are still in positions of power in the current administration. Senior Kenyan judges were also associated with the scandal; twenty-three resigned after presented with the evidence. The Goldenberg fraud is thought to have cost the country more than 10 percent of its annual gross domestic product, and it almost certainly helped finance the brutal war that raged in the DRC between 1997 and 2002.

Nor is this high level of corruption a thing of the past. As recently as January 2009 the Kenya Anti-Corruption Commission was asked to look into the alleged theft of oil, valued at $98.7 million, from the

Kenya Pipeline Company. Today, most Kenyans acknowledge that corruption is one of the biggest problems facing their country: it has been estimated that the average urban Kenyan pays sixteen bribes every month, and that corruption robs local companies of 6 percent of their revenues. Even in Kisumu there are many cases where the ownership of public land and buildings has been transferred to senior local government employees, with the money from the subsequent sales mysteriously disappearing into private bank accounts.

Kenyans use elaborate euphemisms when they talk about bribery and corruption; they will frequently talk about somebody who "eats" or who "drinks tea." Another vernacular term is "TKK," *towa kitu kidogo,* which means to "take something small" in Swahili, although cynics claim that it means *towa kila kitu,* which means "take everything."

During Barack Obama's third visit to Kenya in August 2006, as part of a two-week whistle-stop tour around Africa, he spoke at the University of Nairobi. The senator from Illinois opened his speech (titled "An Honest Government, a Hopeful Future") by describing "the warmth and sense of community that the people of Kenya possess—their sense of hopefulness even in the face of great difficulty." He also spoke of the difficulties his father had faced when he returned to work in Nairobi, of problems that "put him at odds with the politics of tribe and patronage." He acknowledged the special hurdles that Kenya faced, along with most other African countries, including the legacy of colonialism and national boundaries that had been drawn decades ago "without regard to the political and tribal alignments of indigenous peoples, and that therefore fed conflict and tribal strife."

Then Obama hardened his message, and he became more critical of the path that Kenya was following. He pointed out that when the country gained its independence in the early 1960s, its gross national product was not very different from that of South Korea; yet today, the economy of the Asian country is forty times bigger than Kenya's. Part of the problem, Obama claimed, was that:

> Kenya is failing in its ability to create a government that is transparent and accountable. One that serves its people and is free from corruption . . . the reason I speak of the freedom that you fought so hard to win is because today that freedom is in jeopardy. It is being threatened by corruption. . . . But while corruption is a problem we all share, here in Kenya it is a crisis—a crisis that's robbing an honest people of the opportunities they have fought for—the opportunity they deserve.

In his speech, Obama used the word *corruption* no fewer than twenty times. It was a tough, uncompromising message, but one that had been highlighted before by visiting dignitaries from abroad. Yet hearing it from Obama was different, for many people see him not only as a fellow Kenyan but also, more significantly, as a Luo. At the time, Raila Odinga's Luo-based Orange Democratic Party was in opposition, and it was proving to be an irritating thorn in the side of President Kibaki's Kikuyu-dominated government. The Kenyan president's spokesman, Alfred Mutua, was quick to play the tribalism card, announcing, "It is very clear that the senator has been used as a puppet to perpetuate opposition politics"[2]—a statement that Mutua has probably since lived to regret.

Yet tribalism marches hand in hand with corruption—both problems represent an abuse of power by the strong over the weak and defenseless. Many thousands of Kenyans have died in tribe-related violence since 1963. In 1992, for example, the Kalenjin targeted Kikuyus and other "foreigners" in the Rift Valley, and three thousand people were killed or injured; in 1997, Coast province was the scene of more aggression toward "outsiders," this time against the Kikuyu, Luo, Luhya, and Kamba people.[3] Leaflets that were distributed throughout the region incited tribal hostility: "The time has come for us original inhabitants of the coast to claim what is rightfully ours. We must remove these invaders from our land."[4] Then in the early weeks of 2008, the postelectoral violence resulted in more than a thousand deaths and the displacement of half a million people.

Richard Richburg is a respected and experienced black American journalist who has been the chief of the *Washington Post*'s New York bureau since 2007. Between 1991 and 1995 he was the *Post*'s bureau chief in Nairobi; when he moved on, he wrote a candid book about his experiences called *Out of America: A Black Man Confronts Africa,* in which he admitted:

> If there was one thing that I learned traveling around Africa, it was that the tribe remains the defining feature of almost every African society. Old tribal mistrusts and stereotypes linger, and the potential for a violent implosion is never very far from the surface.
>
> Even in the supposedly more sophisticated or developed countries like Kenya, thirty years of independence and "nation building" had still failed to create any real sense of national identity that could transcend the tribe.
>
> In Kenya, the Kikuyu still think the Luo are inferior and that they, the Kikuyu, have the right to rule. The Luo don't trust the Kikuyu, who they think look down on them. And both tribes look down on the Luhya. It goes on and on.[5]

Although tribalism is rife throughout Africa, it is not universal. On December 19, 1961, the British colony of Tanganyika achieved independence from Britain, and under its first president, Julius Kambarage Nyerere, Tanzania plowed a very different furrow than its northern neighbor. Nyerere was not without his faults, nor Tanzania without its problems. Like his contemporary Kenyatta, Nyerere ran his nation for decades with an iron fist and repressed any political opposition. He called his system of political and social development *ujamaa*—a dogmatic and inflexible form of socialism. This, together with rampant corruption, left the country impoverished and underdeveloped. Yet as a nation, Tanzania achieved something that has always eluded

Kenya: Nyerere was able to mold nearly 130 different ethnic groups and racial minorities into a single, relatively peaceful nation with a distinct national character. Although a rare achievement, it is not unique on the continent. In 1957 the West African state of Ghana achieved independence from Britain under an equally charismatic leader, Kwame Nkrumah. Nkrumah fought tribalism and regionalism and left Ghana with the enduring legacy of a clear national identity. Yet Ghana is very different from its neighbor Nigeria, another former British colony; in Nigeria, an individual will most likely claim to be Hausa or Fulani before he or she will acknowledge being Nigerian. There are many complex reasons why these African nations have developed differently, but both Tanzania and Ghana have shown that African states can avoid resorting to tribalism after independence.

When Barack Obama paid his first visit to Africa as president of the United States in July 2009, it was no coincidence that he chose to visit Ghana and not Kenya. The ordinary citizens of Kenya fully understood the intentional snub to their government when an article in the country's *Daily Nation* reminded its readers:

> U.S. President Barack Obama has strongly criticized Kenya's leadership, expressing concern about the country's political and economic direction.
>
> Explaining why Ghana was chosen as his first official destination in black Africa, President Obama singled out the slow pace of reforms as a key impediment in Kenya.
>
> In his most pointed comments on the country of his father's birth, the U.S. President tore into Kenya's leadership saying that "political parties do not seem to be moving into a permanent reconciliation that would allow the country to move forward."[6]

In his speech to the Ghanaian parliament in Accra on July 11, Obama came back to his theme of tribalism and corruption:

> In my father's life, it was partly tribalism and patronage in an independent Kenya that for a long stretch derailed his career, and we

know that this kind of corruption is a daily fact of life for far too many.

Of course, we also know that is not the whole story. Here in Ghana, you show us a face of Africa that is too often overlooked by a world that sees only tragedy or the need for charity. The people of Ghana have worked hard to put democracy on a firmer footing, with peaceful transfers of power even in the wake of closely contested elections.[7]

His message was heard very clearly 2,600 miles away in Nairobi.

The popular image of Africa is all too often shaped by short, two-minute features on the evening television news, or in a few words in a headline on the front page of a newspaper; these snippets of news can so easily distort the true image of a nation. Despite the poverty, corruption, poor governance, and tribal animosity in Kenya, there is also much that the people should celebrate. If you visit any school in the country, you cannot but be impressed with the eagerness and commitment to learning displayed by practically every child. Often they walk barefoot for miles to reach the school, yet they are always immaculately turned out in their uniforms, well behaved, and eager to work. Often the teacher is without books and the classroom without windows, yet these schoolchildren—most of whom can speak three languages before they are ten—consider themselves blessed to be enrolled in a school, and they are determined to make the most of their good fortune.

Nor does their eagerness to learn stop when they leave school. In Kenya you should never throw away a newspaper. Since many people cannot spare even a few shillings to buy a paper for themselves, a donated copy will be eagerly read and passed on a dozen times before eventually being used as wrapping or fuel. Surprisingly for a country rife with corruption and poor governance, the press is remarkably free, and every day of the week the papers are full of open and candid criticism of politicians and leaders, from the president and prime minister down to local administrators. Any waiter, street hawker, or taxi driver will eagerly engage you in a discussion about the latest scandal in government. Kenyans always like to keep informed about the news; they may lack power, but they never lack an opinion.

Nor will Barack Obama ever turn his back on Kenya. Although he is president to the American people and will, quite rightly, always put their interests first, he will always be conscious of his large and extended family back in Kenya, who are subjected daily to all the challenges of a hand-to-mouth existence in Africa. He will continue to remind the people of Kenya of the problems and frustrations, the tribalism and the patronage, that prevented his own father from realizing his true potential. And the U.S. ambassador to Kenya, Michael Ranneberger, will continue to speak out against these issues, openly and bluntly on his behalf.

President Obama seems to have inherited his willingness to be direct, open, and honest from his grandfather Onyango, who, for all his faults, never tolerated deceit or dishonesty. Barack junior is a very different man from his father and his grandfather, but certain family characteristics seem to flow from his African bloodline: intelligence, resourcefulness, motivation, and ambition can all be traced back several generations, perhaps even as far back as the president's (11) great-grandfather Owiny, who led his people in the second wave of migration into Kenya. Owiny's son Kisodhi and his grandson Ogelo are also remembered by the Luo as great leaders. Barack Obama's (3) great-grandfather Obong'o was a pioneer who took a huge gamble by leaving his ancestral homeland in Alego to establish a new Obama settlement in Kendu Bay on the south side of Winam Gulf. The president's father and grandfather were also intelligent and inspirational men in their own right, whose personalities developed in a different place and at a very different time. Many of their behavioral characteristics would be considered entirely inappropriate by today's standards, but their conduct should be judged by their standards then and not by our standards now.

On the other side of his family, President Obama's mother studied for a doctorate as a mature student, so she too was clearly both determined and motivated. In America, Barack junior grew up as a young black man in a predominantly white society, and he understands what it is like to be different. Between the ages of six and ten he lived in Indonesia, a foreign, predominantly non-Christian society; even though he was young, these were formative years for him, and the opportunity gave him an insight into other cultures at an early age, which no other U.S. president has experienced.

As the world's most powerful statesman, his actions and decisions during his time in office will ultimately affect everybody on the planet. Certainly in the land of his forefathers, people have a huge expectation that he will deliver something special for them; when one speaks to Kenyans about Barack Obama, they seem sometimes to forget that he is the president of the United States and not of Kenya. Obama will continue to raise the issue of corruption and tribalism, but perhaps the other contribution that he can make is simply to be his father's son. The Luo of Kenya can identify with him because they are Luo; all the other tribal groups in the country can only claim him as their own by being Kenyan. Perhaps this, more than anything else, will help the ordinary citizens of Kenya to believe in themselves as a single nation.

As the Luo, who of course have a proverb for everything, might say: *Kinda e teko*—perseverance is strength.

ACKNOWLEDGMENTS

LING' CHICKO IT EN OHALA

The good listener learns many new things

Over the course of several months from November 2008 and throughout 2009, I crisscrossed Kenya as part of my research for this book. It is impossible to spend this amount of time in a foreign country without relying on the wisdom and support of many people. First, my gratitude has to go to the many members of the Obama family who opened their doors and welcomed me into their homes. In K'ogelo, I watched Mama Sarah, stepgrandmother to President Obama, greet literally busloads of people who came to pay their respects to her; I would wait my turn to see her, and she always greeted me with kindness, patience, and good humor. In Oyugis, Hawa Auma, President Obama's aunt, was always ready to stop her work to spend time with me—and she was always ready to kill a chicken and cook me a meal. Kendu Bay is home to most of the Obama family, and Charles Oluoch, Elly Yonga Adhiambo, John Ndalo Aguk, and Laban Opiyo were all very generous with both their time and their insight into the history of the Obamas. My thanks also go to Imam Saidi Aghmani, who introduced me to the Islamic community in Kendu Bay. In Kisumu, Wilson Obama and his wife, Karen, were always generous with their support, as were Aloyce Achayo and Leo Omolo Odera. Sam Dhillon from Nairobi was also very helpful and supportive during my early research. This list cannot do justice to the many other Kenyans I interviewed for the book, but their contribution is recognized within the body of the text.

In the United States, my old friend Thom Beers was very supportive at a crucial early stage of my research, and in London I have special thanks for my agent, Sheila Ableman, who encouraged me to write a book rather than make a film. At Preface, my editor, Trevor Dolby, offered his constant encouragement and support during both gestation and delivery, and gently nudged me at the right times to tease the most from my material. In New York, my executive editor at Crown, Rachel Klayman, together with Stephanie Chan, were a great help with preparing the manuscript for an American audience.

In Kenya, Roy Samo acted as my researcher and translator; he was always on hand, and without his unceasing help it would not have been possible to write this book. And in London, my wife, Paula, has balanced being both my fiercest critic and at the same time my strongest supporter.

I thank them all.

Notes on Methodology

CHIEN KIYANY'

The past is never despised

WHEN I set out to research this book, my intention was to weave a triple narrative: I wanted to trace President Obama's family history back as far as possible; to set this against the fascinating story of the migration of the Luo people from southern Sudan; and to place both of these stories within a greater context of the history of Kenya as it emerged from the chrysalis of a British colony and spread its wings to become an independent nation. The history of Kenya was by far the easiest story to write. While I have drawn on a wide variety of sources, for the most part I have tried to present the history from the perspective of the Kenyan. We are each molded into the person we are by our upbringing, our schooling, and the greater world around us; for my part, I inevitably carry with me the baggage of a white European born into a country still coming to terms with its own decline as a major global power. However, I have worked for much of my life in the developing world, and I have spent many years trying to understand the world from the perspective of others. During the research for this book I have talked and listened to dozens of Kenyans, and I have relied extensively on the academic writings of many Kenyan historians. It would be audacious and impudent of me to claim to represent the African perspective, but I have tried to present the history of Kenya in a fair and neutral fashion.

The challenge of trying to unravel the history of the Luo people in general, and the Obama family in particular, places different demands on a writer. There are two main sources of information available: first is the academic literature from historians and archeologists, which, by its very nature, is conservative and cautious; the second is oral history, which is so often colorful, exciting, and enthralling, but which is not governed by the same rules of precision and accuracy as the former. Academic sources might sometimes suffer from being overly dry and guarded in their conclusions, but oral history—despite its appealing flamboyancy—can often be confusing, contradictory, or simply incorrect.[1] Inevitably, there is tension in trying to merge academic sources with oral tradition, and academics will caution you against taking many of these ancestral tales too literally.

Many African historians, including the eminent professor Bethwell Ogot, consider that the early historical figures such as Jok, Podho, and other great Luo ancestors were not real individuals but mythical people whose names were attached to clan genealogies.[2] In support of this theory, he points out that *jok,* for example, means "god" or "spirit" in the early Nilotic language, and that *pohi* means "the land of" in Shilluk.[3] He is right, as an academic, to question the veracity of some of these individuals, but if you talk to Luo elders today, they will tell you with absolute conviction that these people were very real. When I visited William Onyango in Gangu, for example, he had a wealth of information about his ancestors and the life they lived more than four centuries ago in Got Ramogi. As the Luo say, *chien kiyany'*—the past is never despised. But like oral histories throughout the world, none of this information has ever been written down; instead, it has been passed down the generations from grandfather to grandson in stories and songs. In this "personalized history" of their families, every clan and every lineage has tales and traditions that can sometimes contradict those of their neighbors.

Such are the challenges of trying to marry academic history with oral history. What is not disputed, however, is that a Nilotic people left their cradleland in southern Sudan more than six hundred years ago in one of the greatest migrations in the history of Africa. Over a period of a dozen generations or more, they moved south through Uganda and east into Kenya, to form the Luo of western Kenya and northern Tanzania. Whether their leaders were actually called Ringruok and Nayo, Jok and Podho, becomes secondary to the greater story; nobody doubts that these people had leaders who guided them through their great exodus, and at the very least these names usefully represent people who must have lived hundreds of years ago.

Another critical piece of information involving the migration is the date that the Luo first arrived in western Kenya. Ogot gives a date of between AD 1490 and 1517, but with an accuracy of only ±fifty-two years.[4] The American historian David Cohen suggests that the Luo reached Nyanza sometime around AD 1500 to 1550.[5] The Obama ancestry on page viii suggests that Ramogi Ajwang' was probably born around 1500; therefore his arrival in western Kenya is in keeping with a date of between 1530 and 1550.

Trying to unravel the Obama family's oral history brings new challenges. A clear schism can be traced back to the early nineteenth century, when Obong'o, the great-great-great-grandfather to President Obama, left the ancestral lands in K'ogelo as part of a wider movement of the Luo from the overcrowded region of Alego. He moved south across the Winam Gulf and established a new settlement near Kendu Bay, where the Obamas flourished. The name Obama can be traced back to the corruption of the name Onyango Mobam, belonging to President Obama's (6) great-grandfather. However, the first evidence of the Obama name seems to arise four generations later, when Obong'o named his eldest son Obama—the older brother of Opiyo, President Obama's great-great-grandfather. It is quite possible that the name was used earlier within the family for an individual who was not recorded within the family's oral history.

In the first decade of the twentieth century, missionaries came to Kendu Bay and the Obamas were baptized into the Church of the

Seventh-Day Adventists. The one exception was Onyango Obama, grandfather to the president, who elected to convert to Islam, taking the name Hussein. He insisted that all his wives become Muslims, and likewise his children. When Hussein Onyango resettled in K'ogelo around 1943, the division in the family only widened further, for now they were separated not only by religion but also by distance. Inevitably, the recollections of past generations of Obamas on opposite sides of Winam Gulf differ, at least in some of the detail.

The only hope of reaching a definitive agreement over the family history was to bring a group of historians and family elders together in one room and to let them argue it out among themselves. So one morning in June 2009 I invited a dozen family members and Luo elders to Kisumu to formalize the Obama family history (see below for the full list of participants). After several hours of discussion, there was a remarkably close consensus, which has allowed us to trace President Obama's lineage back more than twenty generations. However, the group was not unanimous; the one sticking point was whether Ochuo or Otondi was the (4) great-grandfather of President Obama. The choice does not affect the earlier family lineage, but despite many hours of debate, those elders living in Alego could not completely reconcile their oral tradition with that of the elders living in south Nyanza.

The last part of the ancestry jigsaw was to place approximate dates on past generations. Archeologists can use carbon-14 dating and other techniques for absolute dating, or stratification to give relative dates. However, it is difficult to relate these dates to a history based primarily on oral sources. Therefore the logical approach was to work back from the oldest reliable date in the Obama family: the birth year of Hussein Onyango. From this year all the earlier generations of the family can be traced, although unfortunately even this approach is not that straightforward.

Most sources give Hussein Onyango's year of birth as 1895 and the year of his death as 1975, although in *Dreams from My Father* President Obama claims 1979 to be the date of his grandfather's death.[6] From talking to people who knew Hussein Onyango and who went to his funeral, he was clearly an old man when he died, probably in his eighties. Yet the brass plaque on his grave in Sarah Obama's compound in K'ogelo reads *Mzee Hussein Onyango Obama, 1870–1975*. I asked Sarah about the date, and she was absolutely certain that the plaque was correct: "The dates you find there are the right ones, and they were written by Barack senior." If this figure is correct, then Onyango Obama was 105 years old when he died—not an impossible age, but unlikely. If he was born in 1870, he would have been forty-four years old when he joined the King's African Rifles during the First World War, and he would have been seventy when he was in Addis Ababa working as a cook for a British army officer during the Second World War. This alone suggests that Onyango could not have been born as early as 1870, and other circumstantial evidence exists to help substantiate the correct birth date.

Onyango married Sarah, his fifth wife, in 1943. If Onyango had been born in 1870, then he would have been seventy-three when he married. Onyango went on to father four children with Sarah—this would have been quite an achievement for a man in his seventies. Had he been born in 1895, a date I have always thought to be the correct one, then he would have been forty-eight years old when he married for the fifth time—still a middle-aged man, but not an unreasonable age for a Luo to take another wife. Based on all this evidence, as well as discussions with people who knew him, his birth date is much more likely to be 1895 than 1870, and 1895 is therefore the date that I have used as the basis for fixing earlier dates in the family ancestry.

The next challenge was to work out exactly when Obama's ancestors were born. In the West, our written history allows us the luxury of using precise dates: we know, for example, that King John signed the Magna Carta in 1215, that the Spanish launched their great armada to invade England in 1588, and that the Boston Tea Party occurred in 1773. We are used to hanging our history on exact dates. But African oral history, which generally relies on listing early generations in the correct genealogical order, rarely makes reference to actual dates. Therefore, in order to work back from Hussein Obama's birth year in 1895 to give approximate birth dates to earlier generations, it is necessary to define a patrilineal generation—the average age gap between the birth of a male baby and the birth of his firstborn surviving son.

In discussion with African historians, I learned that this patrilineal generation can vary between twenty-six and thirty-three years. Professor Ogot wrote his doctoral thesis on the southern Luo of Kenya, and he found that in a traditional society living on the Uganda/Kenya border, the first child in a family was usually born when the father was between twenty-five and twenty-eight years old, with a mean generation of twenty-seven years.[7] However, he accepted that this figure might, if anything, be an underestimate, and he quotes Archdeacon W. E. Owen, who believed that the generation gap for the Luo could not be less than thirty years.[8] There are good reasons to suppose that the length of a typical generation should be longer than twenty-seven years. For example, girls are not usually recorded in a family's ancestral history, so their births would extend the date between the births of male babies. Nor does Ogot's system take into account infant mortality; in the past it was not unusual for one baby in every three or four to die before it reached the age of five, which would extend the generation gap. Luo men also had to prove themselves as warriors and fearless hunters before they earned the right to marry, and this too would have reduced the number of young men who reached the age of taking a wife, thereby stretching the generation gap still further.

Taking all this into account, I have used a patrilineal generation of twenty-nine years in preparing the Obama ancestry that appears at the front of this volume. Usually children are born to a fertile mother at regular intervals of two years, and this average figure can be used to estimate the birth year of later siblings; for example, the third child can be assumed to be born roughly four years after the first. Professor Roland Oliver, who worked extensively in Uganda, calculated that plus or minus two years should be allowed as a margin of error for each generation, or approximately seven years a century.[9] So by combining these two systems, it is possible to work back from the earliest known birth date in the Obama family—that of 1895 for Onyango Hussein—and calculate, for example, that President Obama's (15) great-grandfather Podho II was born in the mid-fifteenth century, plus or minus thirty years. It is a crude system with inevitable flaws. For example, it cannot allow for the complexities of a man fathering children from several wives, nor does it allow for infertility or low fertility, which might extend the interval between births. So even taking a patrilineal generation as twenty-nine years might still be an underestimate. Nevertheless, no matter however rudimentary this method might be, it does at least give an indication of the likely period in which these ancestors lived, and these patrilineal generation ages do seem to correspond closely with the few independent dates that have been established by archeologists using other techniques such as carbon dating and excavation.

Those attending the Obama ancestry meeting in Kisumu, June 2009, were:

Aloyce Achayo—retired teacher, respected cultural historian, and a good friend of Obama senior

Elly Yonga Adhiambo (of Kendu Bay)—distant cousin of Obama senior

James Ojwang' Adhoch (of Ojuando-K'ogelo)—Alego elder and historian and friend of Mama Sarah

Jackob Ramogi Amolo (of Ndere-K'ogelo)—respected Luo cultural historian and close friend of Mama Sarah; frequently consulted on Luo cultural issues

Joseph Okoth Amolo (of Alego-K'ogelo)—Luo elder

Peter Omondi Amolo (of Ndere-K'ogelo)—Luo elder

John Aguk Ndalo (of K'obama)—elder and a good friend of Hussein Onyango

Patrick Ngei (of Alego)—retired history teacher who once shared a house with Obama senior in Nairobi

Timeline

Prehistory

2.4 million BC . . . . A manlike ape or hominid called *Australopithecus africanus* lives in East Africa

2 million BC . . . . . . There is evidence that *Homo habilis* ("handy man," the first tool maker) lived around Lake Turkana in northern Kenya

1.6 million BC . . . . *Homo erectus* makes hand axes and cleavers, and spreads throughout East Africa

300,000 BC . . . . . . *Homo sapiens* lives in the Lake Baringo region

5000 BC . . . . Kenya is populated by hunter-gatherers

500 BC to AD 500 . . Bantu migrants arrive in Kenya, bringing with them metalworking skills; the people enter the Iron Age

AD 43 . . . . Romans invade Britain

c. AD 410 . . . . Romans leave Britain

Early History

c. 600 . . . . Arab traders begin to settle in Mombasa and other ports

1066 . . . . King Harold killed at the Battle of Hastings

1095–1291 . . . . Europe fights the Crusades to restore control in the Holy Land

1215 . . . . King John signs the Magna Carta

1348 . . . . The Black Death arrives in Britain and ultimately kills about one-third of the population

c. 1400 . . . . The Luo-speakers of southern Sudan begin their migration south into Uganda

1414. . . . . A fleet of sixty-two Chinese trading galleons and more than a hundred support ships under the command of Zheng He crosses the Indian Ocean and lands on the African coast

c. 1450. . . . . The first Luo are thought to establish the Pubungu military encampment and begin to dominate Uganda

c. 1480. . . . . Podho II may have left Pubungu around this time and moved his people eastward, toward Kenya

1492. . . . . Christopher Columbus lands on an island in the Bahamas and "discovers" the New World for Spain

1497. . . . . Vasco da Gama sets sail from Lisbon in search of a sea route to the Orient

1498. . . . . Da Gama arrives in Mombasa but is repulsed; he sails on to Malindi

1500. . . . . The Portuguese sack Mombasa

1500–1700. . . . . . . The Portuguese establish a series of trading posts and forts along the Kenyan coast

1502. . . . . The Atlantic slave trade begins in earnest, with West African slaves taken to Spanish and Portuguese colonies in the New World; later English, French, and Dutch traders supply the Caribbean islands with slaves

1509. . . . . Henry VIII is crowned king of England

c. 1530 . . . . Ramogi Ajwang' is thought to have arrived with his people in western Kenya around this time

1558 . . . . Elizabeth I accedes to the English throne

1587 . . . . Sir Walter Raleigh founds Roanoke Colony, the first British settlement in the New World

c. 1590 . . . . The second wave of Luo arrive in Kenya, the Jok'Owiny, led by President Obama's (11) great-grandfather Owiny

1593 . . . . The Portuguese begin the construction of
Fort Jesus in Mombasa

c. 1600 . . . . Luo establish a settlement in Gangu, in
western Kenya

1603 . . . . James VI of Scotland is crowned King James I
of England

1607 . . . . Jamestown Settlement is founded in what would
become Virginia

Nov. 1620 . . . . The Mayflower lands in Plymouth, in present-day
Massachusetts

1624 . . . . New York City is founded, originally as New
Amsterdam

1642–51 . . . . English Civil Wars

c. 1660 . . . . The Luo leader Kisodhi dies and his succession
leads to a major dispute between his eldest son,
Ogelo, and two of his other sons, Ager and Owiny
Sigoma

c. 1670 . . . . Ogelo, President Obama's (9) great-grandfather,
settles in Nyang'oma K'ogelo

1698 . . . . After a siege lasting nearly three years, the Arabs
and their allies take Fort Jesus

c. 1700 . . . . The Luo occupy Thimlich Ohinga and build up
the defenses

1720 . . . . The Portuguese withdraw from Kenya permanently

1760–1820 . . . . A third wave of Luo migrants, the Jok'Omolo, enter
Nyanza, putting increased pressure on land and
resources in the region, and feuding begins among
the Luo subclans

1773 . . . . The Americans revolt against the British at the
Boston Tea Party

1782 . . . . The British government informally, but officially,
recognizes American independence

1789. . . . . George Washington becomes the first president of the United States

Feb. 1807. . . . . . . Britain bans the slave trade, but not slavery itself

Jan. 1808 . . . . The United States bans the importation of slaves

1817 . . . . The first American trading vessel reaches Zanzibar

1822. . . . . Seyyid Sa'id, the new ruler in Oman, sends a fleet of warships to subdue the querulous Swahili coastal towns

1822. . . . . The Mazrui chief Sulaiman bin Ali asks for British protection against Seyyid Sa'id of Oman

1824. . . . . The British warship HMS *Leven* arrives in Mombasa and Captain William Owen declares the town a British protectorate

c. 1825 . . . . Obong'o, (3) great-grandfather to President Obama, leaves his ancestral home in K'ogelo and establishes a new homestead in south Nyanza

1827. . . . . The British government withdraws the protectorate from Mombasa

1830–80. . . . . The East African slave trade flourishes under Seyyid Sa'id

1833 . . . . The United States exchanges most-favored-nation status with Zanzibar and establishes the first U.S. trade consul in 1835

c. 1833 . . . . Opiyo, great-great-grandfather to President Obama, is born in Kendu Bay, south Nyanza

Aug. 1833. . . . . . . Britain finally abolishes slavery

1841. . . . . Britain establishes a trade consul in Zanzibar

Exploration

Early 1844 . . . . Dr. Johann Ludwig Krapf, a German Protestant missionary and accomplished linguist, arrives in Zanzibar

1846 . . . . Krapf and his countryman Johannes Rebmann begin their evangelical journeys inland

1848 . . . . Johannes Rebmann becomes the first European to see Mount Kilimanjaro

1849 . . . . Johannes Rebmann becomes the first European to see Mount Kenya

1854 . . . . Johann Krapf produces the "slug map" of central Africa, showing a large inland lake—possibly Lake Victoria

1856 . . . . Richard Burton and John Hanning Speke explore inland to determine if this "inland sea" is the source of the Nile

1858 . . . . Speke becomes the first European to see Lake Victoria; in Egypt, work starts on the Suez Canal

1860 . . . . British Roman Catholic missionaries arrive in Zanzibar

1861–65 . . . . The American Civil War

c. 1864 . . . . Obama, great-grandfather to President Obama, is born in Kendu Bay, south Nyanza

Jan. 1866 . . . . Dr. David Livingstone first arrives in East Africa with the intention of finding the source of the Nile

Nov. 1869 . . . . The Suez Canal opens to shipping

Mar. 1871 . . . . Henry Stanley sent out to find Livingstone

Nov. 1871 . . . . Stanley meets Livingstone in Ujiji in present-day Tanzania

1873 . . . . The British force the ruler of Zanzibar to close his slave market, but with only limited success

May 1873 . . . . David Livingstone dies in the village of Ilala, Zambia

Nov. 1874. . . . . . . Henry Stanley leaves Zanzibar on a second
expedition to cross Africa from east to west

Mar. 1875. . . . . . . Henry Stanley sails north up the eastern coastline
of Lake Victoria and becomes the first European to
enter Luoland

1883 . . . . Joseph Thomson explores inland from Mombasa
and makes contact with the Maasai

Nov. 4, 1884. . . . . . Karl Peters and two companions arrive in Zanzibar
to establish a German colonial presence in East
Africa

Nov. 15, 1884 . . . . . Berlin Conference opens

Feb. 12, 1885. . . . . . Karl Peters establishes the Deutsche Ost-Afrika
Gesellschaft, the German East Africa Company, to
which he cedes all his territorial gains in Africa

Feb. 17, 1885. . . . . . Bismarck agrees to issue an imperial charter,
which gives the protection of the emperor to all
the territories acquired by the German East Africa
Company

Feb. 26, 1885 . . . . . Berlin Conference closes with an agreement to carve
up Africa among the European nations

1885 . . . . More than three hundred Europeans are now
living in East Africa, mostly Anglican or Catholic
missionaries

1886. . . . . The Anglo-German Agreement defines the spheres
of influence in East Africa of Britain and Germany

1888. . . . . The British East Africa Company is granted a
royal charter and is renamed the Imperial British
East Africa Company (IBEAC); it establishes its
headquarters in Mombasa and creates its own
currency and stamps

1890. . . . . The Treaty of Berlin brings all of Uganda and
Kenya under British jurisdiction, and Tanzania
under German control; Charles William Hobley

arrives in Mombasa and works for the IBEAC as a transport superintendent

1891 . . . . Karl Peters is made imperial high commissioner to German East Africa (later Tanzania)

1892 . . . . Johnstone Kamau, later known as Jomo Kenyatta, is born in the Kikuyu highland region north of Nairobi

British East Africa

1880–92 . . . . Luoland is hit by a series of natural disasters, including contagious bovine pleuropneumonia, locust invasions, the *ong'ong'a* famine, rinderpest, anthrax, and smallpox, resulting in virtual civil war among the Luo

Jul. 1895 . . . . The British government takes control of the assets of the IBEAC in order to maintain strategic control in the region

1895 . . . . Onyango Obama, grandfather to President Obama, is born in Kendu Bay, western Kenya; Charles Hobley is made the new regional colonial administrator in Luoland (Nyanza)

May 1896 . . . . The construction of the Uganda Railway begins

1896–1900 . . . . The British mount a series of punitive raids to suppress the Luo

1899 . . . . The railway headquarters are established at Nyrobi, later to be renamed Nairobi

1901 . . . . Sir Charles Eliot is appointed the new governor of the IBEAC; there are thirteen white farmers resident in Kenya

Dec. 1901 . . . . The railway reaches Port Florence (later to be called Kisumu) on Lake Victoria

1902–8 . . . . The tsetse fly returns to Luoland and at least 250,000 people die from sleeping sickness

1903. . . . . Large grants of land are made available to white
farmers around the Lake Naivasha region in the
Rift Valley

1905. . . . . There are 700 Afrikaner farmers and more than 250
European settlers established in the Rift Valley

Oct. 1905. . . . . . . Colonel Richard Meinertzhagen shoots Koitalel,
the Nandi leader, which breaks the resistance of the
Nandi to the construction of the Uganda Railway

Nov. 1906 . . . . Arthur Carscallen establishes the first Seventh-Day
Adventist mission in Kendu Bay

c. 1910 . . . . Onyango Obama leaves home and lives with white
missionaries

1912. . . . . There are now 3,175 white settlers in Kenya and
11,886 Asians

1914–18 . . . . First World War, and members of the King's African
Rifles (KAR) fight in East Africa; Onyango Obama
is drafted into the KAR

1915 . . . . The government increase the land tenure of white
farmers from 99 years to 999

1916. . . . . The British increase the hut and poll tax payable by
Africans

1918 . . . . British East Africa is formally annexed by Britain
and made a colony, called Kenya; the British
government offers veterans of the Great War land in
the Kenyan Highlands

1919 . . . . The Treaty of Versailles creates "mandates" in
Africa, under the administration of the League of
Nations; Luoland is struck by the *Kanga* famine

c. 1920. . . . . Onyango Obama returns from the war having lived
in Zanzibar for two years; he has converted to Islam
and takes the name Hussein

1920. . . . . Onyango's older brother Ndalo returns to the
family's ancestral lands in K'ogelo

1921 . . . . There are now 9,651 white farmers in Kenya; Harry Thuku establishes the Young Kikuyu Association (YKA), Kenya's first nationalist organization

Dec. 1921 . . . . The Young Kavirondo Association is formed in Nyanza

c. 1922 . . . . Having built his hut in Kendu Bay, Hussein Onyango goes to seek employment in Nairobi

Mar. 1922 . . . . Harry Thuku is arrested and exiled without charge

1924 . . . . The Kikuyu Central Association evolves from the Young Kavirondo Association, with Jomo Kenyatta as its secretary

c. 1925 . . . . Ndalo and his two wives die in K'ogelo from smallpox; Onyango takes their three children, Odero, Peter, and Judy, into his care

1926 . . . . About 22,000 Africans are working in domestic service in Kenya

c. 1927 . . . . Hussein Onyango marries a woman (name unknown) from Kawango in Mumias; she becomes his first wife

c. 1929 . . . . Hussein Onyango marries Halima, his second wife

1929 . . . . Kenyatta goes to London to make the case for Kenyan independence

c. 1930 . . . . Obama, President Obama's great-grandfather, dies in Kendu Bay

c. 1931 . . . . Hussein Onyango marries Sofia Odera, his third wife

1933 . . . . Hussein Onyango abducts and then marries Akumu, his fourth wife; she converts to Islam and takes the name Habiba

1934 . . . . Sarah Nyaoke is born in Kendu Bay, the first child of Hussein Onyango and Habiba Akumu

1936 . . . . Barack Hussein Obama senior is born in Kendu Bay

1939–45 . . . . The Second World War, and members of the King's African Rifles fight in Ethiopia, India, and Burma; Hussein Onyango is posted to Ethiopia and Burma

1940 . . . . The Kikuyu Central Association and other African organizations are banned

1941. . . . . Hussein Onyango returns from the war and marries Sarah Ogwel, his fifth wife

Dec. 7, 1941 . . . . . . The Japanese attack Pearl Harbor in Hawaii, and the United States enters the Second World War

1942. . . . . Barack Obama senior starts his schooling at Gendia primary school, near Kendu Bay; Hawa Auma is born in Kendu Bay, the third child of Hussein Onyango and Habiba Akumu

Nov. 29, 1942. . . . . Stanley Ann Dunham is born in Wichita, Kansas

1943 . . . . Onyango, his two wives, and his three children move to K'ogelo

1944. . . . . The Kenyan African Union is formed to campaign for African independence; the first African appointment is made to the Legislative Council

June 1944. . . . . . . Omar, Hussein Onyango's second son, born to Sarah

1945 . . . . Habiba Akumu attacked by Hussein Onyango; she flees K'ogelo and returns to Kendu Bay

1945 . . . . Sarah and her younger brother Barack senior run away from home in K'ogelo; Barack senior moves to Ng'iya primary school

1946. . . . . Jomo Kenyatta returns from Britain and becomes chairman of the newly formed Kenya African Union

Late 1940s . . . . The General Council of the banned Kikuyu Central Association began a campaign of civil disobedience

1948. . . . . Rumors circulate of secret oathing ceremonies in the forests of the White Highlands and in the Rift Valley

1949 . . . . Hussein Onyango arrested by the British authorities and detained for six months; no charges are proven

1950 . . . . Nairobi-based militants organize mass oathings throughout central Kenya; the Mau Mau insurrection begins in earnest; Barack Obama senior goes to Maseno school at the age of fourteen

Early 1952 . . . . The Mau Mau make arson attacks on white farms in the highlands

Oct. 1952 . . . . A state of emergency is declared in Kenya and war is declared on Mau Mau

Nov. 18, 1952 . . . . . Jomo Kenyatta arrested and charged with being a supporter of Mau Mau

Jan. 24, 1953 . . . . . . Roger and Esme Ruck and their six-year-old son Michael are attacked and killed on their isolated farm

Mar. 26, 1953 . . . . . The Mau Mau massacre more than 120 residents at Lari

Apr. 1953 . . . . Kenyatta found guilty and given seven years at hard labor

1953 . . . . Kenya African Union declared illegal; Barack Obama senior leaves Maseno at the age of seventeen and works in Mombasa before moving to Nairobi

1955 . . . . Barack Obama senior works for the Kenya Railway; he is arrested during the Mau Mau emergency; Tom Mboya wins a scholarship to Ruskin College, Oxford, to study industrial management

1956 . . . . First elected Kenyan representatives join the Legislative Council

Oct. 21, 1956 . . . . . Dedan Kimathi captured and Mau Mau emergency is effectively over

Dec. 25, 1956 . . . . . Barack senior meets Kezia at a party in Kendu Bay

Jan. 1957 . . . . Barack senior sets up home with Kezia in Jericho, a residential section of Nairobi for government employees

c. Mar. 1958 . . . . . . Roy Obong'o Malik born, first son of Obama senior and Kezia

1959 . . . . Stanley Dunham moves to Hawaii with his wife, Madelyn, and their seventeen-year-old daughter, Ann

Aug. 21, 1959 . . . . . Hawaii becomes the fiftieth state of the United States

1959 . . . . Jomo Kenyatta is released from prison but is put under house arrest; Kezia becomes pregnant with Auma and is three months pregnant when Obama senior leaves Kenya; Tom Mboya returns from a fund-raising visit to the United States and announces that he has scholarships for young Kenyans to study there; Barack Obama senior leaves Nairobi for university in Hawaii

Jan. 1960 . . . . Auma, second child of Obama senior and Kezia, born

Feb. 1960 . . . . The first Lancaster House conference is held in London and the ban on African political parties is lifted

Jun. 11, 1960 . . . . . Tom Mboya and Oginga Odinga form the Kenya African National Union (KANU)

Summer 1960 . . . . Barack Obama senior meets Ann Dunham in a Russian language class at the University of Hawaii and they start dating

Nov. 1960 . . . . Ann Dunham becomes pregnant

Feb. 1961 . . . . KANU and the Kenya African Democratic Union (KADU) contest Kenya's first election

Feb. 2, 1961 . . . . . . Barack Obama senior marries Ann Dunham in Maui, Hawaii

Aug. 4, 1961 . . . . . . Barack junior born at 7:24 p.m. local time, at the Kapi'olani Medical Center for Women and Children, Honolulu

Aug. 21, 1961 . . . . . Jomo Kenyatta released from detention

Summer 1962 . . . . James Odhiambo goes to Harvard

May 1963. . . . . First full national elections held in Kenya

Jun. 1, 1963 . . . . . . Jomo Kenyatta becomes prime minister of the autonomous Kenyan government

Summer 1963. . . . . Barack Obama senior goes to Harvard to study for a Ph.D.; Ann Obama returns to college; her parents help raise her young baby, Barack Obama

Nov. 22, 1963. . . . . U.S. president John F. Kennedy is assassinated in Dallas

Independent Kenya

Dec. 12, 1963 . . . . . Kenya becomes a fully independent nation

Jan. 1964 . . . . Ann Obama files for divorce from Barack senior in Honolulu

Jul. 2, 1964 . . . . . . The Civil Rights Act of 1964 in the United States makes racial discrimination and segregation illegal

Dec. 12, 1964. . . . . Kenya becomes a republic with Jomo Kenyatta as president and Oginga Odinga as vice president

Mid-1965. . . . . Barack Obama senior returns to Kenya and is followed by Ruth Nidesand; Obama first works for Kenya Shell

Jul. 1965. . . . . Barack Obama senior writes articles for *East Africa Journal,* criticize the government's approach to economic planning

Late 1965 . . . . Barack Obama senior joins Kenya Central Bank as an economist

1966 . . . . Oginga Odinga leaves KANU after an ideological split and forms the rival Kenya People's Union (KPU)

1967. . . . . Ann Dunham marries Lolo Soetoro and the couple move to Jakarta, Indonesia; Barack Obama junior is six years old

1968. . . . . Rumors that President Kenyatta has suffered a heart
                         attack; Barack Obama senior gets a new job at the
                         Ministry of Economic Planning and Development;
                         Kezia Obama bears Abo, her third child and
                         second son

Apr. 4, 1968. . . . . . Martin Luther King Jr. is assassinated in Memphis,
                         Tennessee

Jun. 6, 1968 . . . . . . U.S. presidential candidate Robert F. Kennedy is
                         assassinated in Los Angeles, California

Jul. 5, 1969. . . . . . . Tom Mboya assassinated in Nairobi, which sparks
                         ethnic unrest and riots

Oct. 25, 1969 . . . . . Jomo Kenyatta makes a speech in Kisumu that
                         results in riots, and forty-three people are killed
                         by police

Nov. 25, 1969 . . . . . The Kenya Prison Service announces that Tom
                         Mboya's killer, Isaac Njenga Njoroge, has been
                         hanged

1970 . . . . Bernard born, Kezia Obama's fourth child and
                         third son

Aug. 15, 1970 . . . . . Barack Obama junior's half sister, Maya Kassandra
                         Soetoro-Ng, is born in Jakarta; Ann Dunham's
                         second marriage begins to disintegrate

1970?. . . . . Barack Obama senior fired from his government
                         job; takes job at the Kenya Tourist Development
                         Corporation

1971. . . . . Ann Dunham sends Barack Obama junior back
                         to Honolulu to live with his white grandparents,
                         where he gets a scholarship to Punahou, a
                         prestigious prep school

Dec. 1971. . . . . Barack Obama senior makes a pre-Christmas visit
                         to see his son in Hawaii

1972?. . . . . Barack Obama senior loses his job at the Kenya
                         Tourist Development Corporation

1972. . . . . Ann Dunham leaves her husband, Lolo Soetoro, and returns from Indonesia to Hawaii with two-year-old Maya to join Barack, now eleven; she studies for a Ph.D. in anthropology

1974. . . . . Kenyatta reelected president of Kenya

1975? . . . . Barack Obama senior is given a job in the Kenyan Treasury

1978. . . . . Barack Obama junior begins his first year at Occidental College in Los Angeles; at the end of his second year he transfers to Columbia University in New York

Aug. 22, 1978. . . . . Jomo Kenyatta dies in Mombasa, age eighty-nine, and is succeeded by his vice president, Daniel arap Moi

1980. . . . . Ann Dunham files for divorce from her second husband, Lolo Soetoro

1981 . . . . Barack Obama senior marries Jael Otieno, his fourth wife

Mid-1982. . . . . Kenya is officially declared a one-party state by the National Assembly; Jael gives birth to a son, George, who is Obama senior's eighth child; a coup by the Kenyan Air Force is suppressed and the leaders executed

Nov. 24, 1982. . . . . Barack Obama senior dies in a car crash in Nairobi; Barack Obama junior, now twenty-one, is told about his father's death by telephone when he is living in New York

1983. . . . . Barack Obama junior graduates from Columbia University and works for a year at the Business International Corporation, a small newsletter-publishing company that printed features relating to global business; he later works for the New York Public Interest Research Group

1985. . . . . Barack Obama junior takes a job with a Chicago-based group called Developing Communities Project, where he begins working to improve conditions in a public housing project

1987. . . . . Opposition groups in Kenya are suppressed and there is international criticism of political arrests and human rights abuses in Moi's government; Barack Obama junior is accepted to Harvard Law School, but he first visits his father's family in Kenya

1989. . . . . Political prisoners in Kenya are freed

1990 . . . . Foreign minister Robert Ouko is brutally assassinated, which leads to increased dissent against government

Feb. 5, 1990 . . . . . . Barack Obama junior becomes the first African American president of the *Harvard Law Review*

1991. . . . . Barack Obama junior graduates from Harvard with a J.D., magna cum laude, and signs with a publisher to write his autobiography, *Dreams from My Father*

Dec. 1991. . . . . A special conference of KANU agrees to introduce a multiparty political system in Kenya

1992. . . . . Approximately two thousand people killed in tribal conflict in western Kenya

1992. . . . . Barack Obama junior returns to Chicago to work as a junior lawyer with Davis, Miner, Barnhill & Gallard; he visits his family in K'ogelo with his girlfriend, Michelle Robinson, to seek his step-grandmother's approval before getting married

Oct. 10, 1992 . . . . . Barack Obama junior and Michelle Robinson are married

1995. . . . . Barack Obama junior's memoir, *Dreams from My Father,* is published to positive reviews

Nov. 7, 1995. . . . . . Barack Obama junior's mother, Ann, dies of ovarian cancer, age fifty-three

1996 . . . . Barack Obama junior is elected to the Illinois
State Senate

1998. . . . . Barack and Michelle Obama's first daughter is born,
and is named Malia Ann

Dec. 1999 . . . . Daniel arap Moi wins a further presidential
term in an election that is widely criticized;
his main opponents are former vice president
Mwai Kibaki and Raila Odinga, son of Oginga
Odinga

2001 . . . . Barack and Michelle's second daughter is born, and
is named Natasha (often called Sasha)

Dec. 2001 . . . . Ethnic tensions continue and thousands of people
flee Nairobi's Kibera slum over rent battles between
Nubian and Luo communities

Dec. 2002 . . . . Daniel arap Moi's twenty-four-year rule ends
when opposition candidate Mwai Kibaki wins a
landslide victory over KANU rival Uhuru Kenyatta,
son of Jomo

Dec. 2003 . . . . The government grants former president Daniel
arap Moi immunity from prosecution on corruption
charges

Jul. 7, 2004 . . . . . . Barack Obama junior is chosen to deliver the
keynote speech at the Democratic National
Convention in Boston; the speech is viewed as a
defining moment in his political career and earns
him worldwide recognition

Nov. 2, 2004 . . . . . Barack Obama junior, now forty-three, is elected to
the U.S. Senate with an unprecedented 70 percent
of the vote

Jan. 4, 2005 . . . . . . Barack Obama junior is sworn in as a U.S. senator

Aug. 2006 . . . . Barack Obama junior visits Kenya and gives a
speech at the University of Nairobi that is critical of
the government

Feb. 10, 2007 . . . . . Barack Obama junior announces his candidacy for
                        the 2008 presidential election
Dec. 2007 . . . . President Kibaki claims victory and a second term
                        in office; the opposition claims the polls were
                        rigged, and more than fifteen hundred die in the
                        postelection violence
Feb. 2008 . . . . Former UN chief Kofi Annan brokers talks between
                        President Kibaki and opposition leader Raila
                        Odinga, which lead to a power-sharing agreement
Apr. 2008 . . . . President Kibaki and Prime Minister Odinga agree
                        on a forty-member cabinet; it is Kenya's biggest and
                        costliest ever
Nov. 3, 2008 . . . . . Barack Obama junior's grandmother Madelyn
                        Dunham dies of cancer at the age of eighty-six
Nov. 5, 2008 . . . . . Democratic senator Barack Hussein Obama is
                        elected president of the United States of America
Jan. 20, 2009. . . . . Barack Obama is sworn in as the forty-forth
                        president of the United States, the country's first
                        black president
Jul. 2009 . . . . The Kenyan government announces that it will
                        not establish a special tribunal to examine the
                        postelection violence but will use the local courts
                        instead
Aug. 2009 . . . . U.S. Secretary of State Hillary Clinton visits
                        Kenya and criticizes the government for failing
                        to investigate the violence that followed the 2007
                        election

Notes

Prologue
1. Barack Obama, *Dreams from My Father* (Three Rivers, 1995), 429–30.
2. Ibid., 302.
3. Barack Obama, *The Audacity of Hope* (Three Rivers Press, 2006), 10.
4. Ibid., 3.

Chapter 1: Two Elections, Two Presidents
1. Korwa G. Adar and Isaac M. Munyae, "Human Rights Abuse in Kenya Under Daniel arap Moi, 1978–2001," *African Studies Quarterly,* vol. 5, no. 1 (2001).
2. Amnesty International, "Kenya," 2000.
3. International Centre for Settlement of Investment Disputes, *World Duty Free Company Ltd. v. Kenya,* October 4, 2006.
4. CIA World Factbook, www.cia.gov/library/publications/the-world-factbook/geos/ke.html.
5. World Health Organization, "Male Circumcision: Africa's Unprecedented Opportunity," August 2007.
6. "Strange Reversal in Kogelo," *East African,* January 23, 2009.
7. United Nation Children's Fund, "The State of Africa's Children," May 2008, 12.

Chapter 2: Meet the Ancestors
1. W. R. Ochieng', *A History of Kenya* (Macmillan, 1985), 17.
2. Andrew Goudie, *Environmental Change,* 3rd ed. (Oxford University Press, 1992).
3. Roland A. Oliver and Anthony Atmore, *Medieval Africa, 1250–1800,* 2nd ed. (Cambridge University Press, 2001), 137.
4. Ibid., 140.
5. Ibid., 127.
6. J. Crazzolara, *The Lwoo,* part I (Verona, 1950), 47.
7. Oliver and Atmore, *Medieval Africa,* 143.
8. Ibid., 144.
9. Ibid., 141.

10. Okumba Miruka, *Oral Literature of the Luo* (East African Educational Publishers, 2001).

11. Ibid.

12. D. W. Cohen, "The River-Lake Nilotes from the Fifteenth to the Nineteenth Century," in B. A. Ogot (ed.), *Zamani: A Survey of East African History* (East African Publishing House, 1968), 144.

13. Oliver and Atmore, *Medieval Africa,* 148.

14. D. W. Cohen and E. S. Atieno Odhiambo, *The Historical Anthropology of an African Landscape,* Eastern African Studies (James Currey, 1989).

15. Cohen, "The River-Lake Nilotes," 144.

16. Ibid., 148.

17. B. A. Ogot, *A History of the Luo-Speaking Peoples of Eastern Africa,* 519.

18. Ibid., 519.

Chapter 3: The Life and Death of Opiyo Obama

1. Okumba Miruka, *Oral Literature of the Luo* (East African Educational Publishers, 2001).

2. S. H. Ominde, *The Luo Girl: From Infancy to Marriage* (Macmillan, 1952).

Chapter 4: The *Wazungu* Arrive

1. Louis Levather, *When China Ruled the Seas: The Treasure Fleet of the Dragon Throne, 1405–1433* (Oxford University Press, 1997).

2. Ibid., 382–87.

3. Johannes Rebmann, *The Church Missionary Intelligencer,* vol. 1, no. 1 (May 1849).

4. Arnold Talbot Wilson, *The Suez Canal: Its Past, Present and Future* (Oxford University Press, 1933).

5. Harry H. Johnston, "Livingstone as an Explorer," *Geographical Journal,* vol. 41, no. 5 (May 1913): 423–46.

6. Richard Hall, *Empires of the Monsoon* (Harper Collins, 1996), 15.

7. Elikia M'Bokolo, "The Impact of the Slave Trade on Africa," *Le Monde diplomatique* (English ed.), April 1998.

8. C. Magbaily Fyle, *Introduction to the History of African Civilization: Precolonial Africa* (University Press of America, 1999), 146.

9. Assa Okoth, *A History of Africa,* vol. 1: *African Societies and the Establishment of Colonial Rule, 1800–1914* (East African Educational Publishers, 2006), 58.

10. H. M. Stanley, *New York Herald,* July 15, 1872.

11. H. M. Stanley, "The Search for Livingstone," *New York Times,* July 2, 1872.

12. H. M. Stanley, *Through the Dark Continent,* vol. 1 (Dover, 1988).

13. Ibid., 63.

14. Ibid., 217.

15. H. M. Stanley, *My Kalulu, Prince, King, and Slave: A Story of Central Africa* (Sampson Low, 1873).

16. W. Johnson, *My African Reminiscences* (London, 1898), 126.

17. Okoth, *A History of Africa*, 1:118.

18. Ibid., 96.

Chapter 5: The New Imperialism

1. W. O. Henderson, *Studies in German Colonial History* (Routledge, 1962), 13.

2. Ibid., 4.

3. Ibid., 13.

4. Okoth, *A History of Africa,* 1:124.

5. Kolonial-Politische Korrespondenz (Colonial-Political Correspondence), 1st Year, Berlin, May 16, 1885.

6. Henderson, *Studies in German Colonial History,* 87.

7. Okoth, *A History of Africa,* 1:138.

8. C. W. Hobley, *Kenya: From Chartered Company to Crown Colony* (Witherby, 1929), 24–25.

9. Okoth, *A History of Africa,* 1:138.

10. *Times,* September 28, 1891, 60.

11. Lawrence H. Officer, "What Were the UK Earnings and Prices Then?" MeasuringWorth, 2009, www.measuringworth.org/ukearncpi.

12. "Uganda Railway (Cost of Construction)," Hansard, House of Commons Debates, October 19, 1909, vol. 12, cols. 123–24.

13. Okoth, *A History of Africa,* 1:351.

14. Thomas R. Metcalf, *Imperial Connections: India in the Indian Ocean Area, 1860–1920* (University of California Press, 2008), 188.

15. Joseph Thomson, *Through Masai Land* (Sampson Low, 1885), 72–73.

16. Bruce D. Patterson, *The Lions of Tsavo: Exploring the Legacy of Africa's Notorious Man-Eaters* (McGraw-Hill, 2004).

17. "Murder That Shaped the Future of Kenya," *East African,* December 5, 2008.

18. William Ochieng', *A History of Kenya* (Macmillan, 1985), 94.

19. David Anderson and Douglas H. Johnson, *Revealing Prophets: Prophecy in Eastern African History* (James Currey, 1995), 188.

20. Oscar Baumann, *Durch Massailand zur Nilquelle* [Through the lands of the Maasai to the source of the Nile] (Dietrich Reimer, 1894).

21. B. A. Ogot, *A History of the Luo-Speaking Peoples of Eastern Africa* (Anyange Press, 2009), 645.

22. Hobley, *Kenya: From Chartered Company to Crown Colony,* 217–18.

23. Luise White, Stephen E. Miescher, and David William Cohen (eds.), *African*

Words, African Voices: Critical Practices in Oral History (Indiana University Press, 2001), 37.

24. Ogot, *A History of the Luo-Speaking Peoples of Eastern Africa,* 670.

25. Ibid., 666

26. Osaak A. Olumwullah, *Dis-ease in the Colonial State* (Praeger, 2002), 131.

27. B. A. Ogot and W. R. Ochieng', *Decolonization and Independence in Kenya, 1940–93* (Ohio University Press, 1995), 10.

28. Ochieng', *A History of Kenya,* 103.

29. Ogot, *A History of the Luo-Speaking Peoples of Eastern Africa,* 678.

30. Neil Sobania, *Culture and Customs of Kenya* (Greenwood, 2003), 19.

31. Okoth, *A History of Africa,* 353.

32. Philip Wayland Porter and Eric S. Sheppard, *A World of Difference: Society, Nature, Development* (Guildford, 1998), 357.

33. Ibid.

34. *Seventh-Day Adventist Encyclopedia* (Review and Herald Publishing Association, 1976).

35. Jack Mahon, "What Happened in 1906?" *The Messenger,* vol. 111 (1996): 8.

36. Richard Gethin, *Private Memoirs,* 35–36, quoted in Ogot, *A History of the Luo-Speaking Peoples of Eastern Africa,* 683.

37. Obama, *Dreams from My Father,* 397–98.

38. Ogot, *A History of the Luo-Speaking Peoples of Eastern Africa,* 678.

39. Brett L. Shadle, "Patronage, Millennialism and the Serpent God Mumbo in South-West Kenya, 1912–34," *Africa,* vol. 72, no. 1 (2002): 29–54.

40. George F. Pickens, *African Christian God-Talk* (University Press of America, 2004), 134.

41. B. A. Ogot, "Kenya Under the British, 1895 to 1963," in B. A. Ogot (ed.), *Zamani: A Survey of East African History* (East African Publishing House, 1968), 264.

42. C. S. Nicholls, *Red Strangers: The White Tribe of Kenya* (Timewell, 2005), 119.

Chapter 6: Five Wives and Two World Wars

1. H. S. Hatton, "The Search for an Anglo-German Understanding Through Africa, 1912–14," *European Studies Review,* vol. 1, no. 2 (1971): 125.

2. John Iliffe, *Honour in African History,* African Studies no. 107 (Cambridge University Press, 2005), 235.

3. A. Davis and H. J. Robertson, *Chronicles of Kenya* (Cecil Palmer, 1928), 97–98.

4. W. E. B. Du Bois, "The African Roots of War," *Atlantic Monthly,* vol. 115, no. 5 (May 1915): 714.

5. Iliffe, *Honour in Africa,* 234.

6. Edward Paice, *Tip and Run: The Untold Tragedy of the Great War in Africa* (Phoenix, 2007), 159.

7. Robert O. Collins and James McDonald Burns, *A History of Sub-Saharan Africa* (Cambridge University Press, 2007), 278.

8. Hans Poeschel, *The Voice of German East Africa* (August Scherl, 1919), 27.

9. Obama, *Dreams from My Father*, 400.

10. John Dawson Ainsworth and F. H. Goldsmith. *John Ainsworth—Pioneer Kenya Administrator, 1864–1946* (Macmillan, 1955), 94.

11. Sir Phillip Mitchell, *African Afterthoughts* (Hutchinson, 1954), 40.

12. Ibid., 34.

13. John Buchan, *A History of the Great War* (Houghton Mifflin, 1922), 1:429.

14. Paul von Lettow-Vorbeck, *My Reminiscences of East Africa* (Battery Press, 1990), 318.

15. Brian Digre, *Imperialism's New Clothes: The Repartition of Tropical Africa 1914–1919* (Peter Lang, 1990), 156.

16. League of Nations Covenant, Article 22, para. 1.

17. Digre, *Imperialism's New Clothes*.

18. Anthony Clayton and Donald C. Savage, *Government and Labour in Kenya 1895–1963* (Routledge, 1974), 88.

19. H. R. A. Philp, *A New Day in Kenya* (World Dominion Press, 1936), 32–33.

20. Harry Thuku, *An Autobiography* (Oxford University Press, 1970).

21. Obama, *Dreams from My Father*, 403.

22. Clayton and Savage, *Government and Labour in Kenya 1895–1963*, 125.

23. Obama, *Dreams from My Father*, 425–26.

24. Iliffe, *Honour in Africa*, 230.

25. Obama, *Dreams from My Father*, 411.

26. Ibid., 370–71.

Chapter 7: A State of Emergency

1. Obama, *Dreams from My Father*, 415.

2. Ibid., 419.

3. A. Adu Boahen, *General History of Africa*, vol. VII: *Africa under Colonial Domination 1880–1935* (James Currey/UNESCO, 1990), 281.

4. David Anderson, *Histories of the Hanged* (Weidenfeld and Nicolson, 2005), 10.

5. Alao, Charles Abiodun, *Mau-Mau Warrior* (Osprey, 2006), 6.

6. George Bennett and Carl G. Rosberg, *The Kenyatta Election: Kenya 1960–1961*, Oxford University Press, 1961, 7.

7. Alao, *Mau-Mau Warrior*, 5.

8. Obama, *Dreams from My Father*, 417.

9. Ben Macintyre and Paul Orengoh, "Beatings and Abuse Made Barack Obama's Grandfather Loathe the British," *Times*, December 2, 2008.

10. Anderson, *Histories of the Hanged,* 50.

11. Ibid., 69.

12. Ibid., 1.

13. Michael Blundell, *So Rough a Wind* (Weidenfeld and Nicolson, 1964), 123–24.

14. Caroline Elkins, *Imperial Reckoning: The Untold Story of Britain's Gulag in Kenya* (Henry Holt, 2004), xiii.

15. Ibid., 70.

16. Ibid., 71

17. Anderson, *Histories of the Hanged,* 4.

18. Elkins, *Imperial Reckoning,* 66.

19. Anderson, *Histories of the Hanged,* 300.

20. John Blacker, "The Demography of Mau Mau: Fertility and Mortality in Kenya in the 1950s: A Demographer's Viewpoint," *African Affairs,* vol. 106, no. 423 (2007): 205–27.

Chapter 8: Mr. "Double-Double"

1. Dwight D. Eisenhower, *Mandate for Change, 1953–56* (Doubleday, 1963), 180.

2. Elizabeth Sanderson, "Barack Obama's Stepmother Living in Bracknell," *Daily Mail,* January 6, 2008.

3. Ibid.

4. Tom Shachtman, *Airlift to America: How Barack Obama, Sr., John F. Kennedy, Tom Mboya, and 800 East African Students Changed Their World and Ours* (St. Martin's Press, 2009).

5. Speech given by President Obama from the pulpit of the historic Brown Chapel in Selma, Alabama, March 4, 2007.

6. Jonathan Martin, "Obama's Mother Known Here as 'Uncommon,'" *Seattle Times,* April 8, 2008.

7. Amanda Ripley, "The Story of Barack Obama's Mother," *Time,* April 9, 2008.

8. Obama, *Dreams from My Father,* 6.

9. Bennett and Rosberg, *The Kenyatta Election,* 176–80.

10. Barack H. Obama, "Problems Facing Our Socialism," *East Africa Journal,* July 1965, 26–33.

11. Ogot and Ochieng', *Decolonization and Independence in Kenya,* 98.

12. Godfrey Mwakikagile, *Kenya: Identity of a Nation* (New Africa Press, 2007), 37.

13. Sally Jacobs, "A Father's Charm," *Boston Globe,* September 21, 2008.

14. *East African Standard,* July 7, 1969.

15. D. Goldworth, *The Man Kenya Wanted to Forget* (Holmes and Meier, 1982), 281.

16. Ibid.

17. Jacobs, "A Father's Charm."

18. E. S. Atieno Odhiambo, "Ethnic Cleansing and Civil Society in Kenya, 1969–1992," *Journal of Contemporary African Studies,* vol. 22, no. 1 (2004): 29–42. The speech, which was given in Swahili, was translated into English for the paper.

19. Tania Branigan, "Barack Obama's Half-Brother Writes Book 'Inspired by Father's Abuse,'" *Guardian,* November 4, 2009.

20. Barack Obama, "My Spiritual Journey," *Time,* October 16, 2006.

21. Obama, *Dreams from My Father,* 5.

22. Ibid., 430.

Epilogue

1. Nick Wadhams, "Kenyan President Moi's 'Corruption' Laid Bare," *Daily Telegraph,* September 1, 2007.

2. Cose Ellis, "Walking the World Stage," *Newsweek,* September 11, 2006.

3. Mwakikagile, *Kenya: Identity of a Nation.*

4. James C. McKinley, "Political Violence Taking a Toll on Kenya Tourism," *New York Times,* August 31, 1997.

5. Richard B Richburg, *Out of America: A Black Man Confronts Africa* (Basic Books, 1997), 104–5.

6. Oliver Mathenge, "Obama Scolds Kenya," *Daily Nation,* July 3, 2009.

7. Barack Obama, "A New Moment of Promise," speech given in Accra, Ghana, July 11, 2009.

Notes on Methodology

1. Luise White et al., eds., *African Words, African Voices: Critical Practices in Oral History* (Indiana University Press, 2001).

2. B. A. Ogot, *History of the Southern Luo* (East African Publishing House, 1967), 1:142–43.

3. B. A. Ogot, "The Concept of Jok," *African Studies,* vol. 20, no. 2 (1961): 123–30.

4. Ogot, *History of the Southern Luo,* 1:28.

5. Cohen, "The River-Lake Nilotes," 147.

6. Obama, *Dreams from My Father,* 376.

7. Ogot, *History of the Southern Luo,* 27.

8. Ibid., 27n.

9. Ibid., 27n.

GLOSSARY OF PEOPLE

Abdo Omar Okech (b. 1933) Younger brother of "Mama" Sarah Obama

Achayo, Aloyce (b. c. 1932) Retired headmaster and Luo cultural historian

Aginga, Joshua (c. 1864–1935?) Third son of Obama Opiyo

Ainsworth, John (1864–1946) An early British settler in Kenya

Akumu Njoga *See* Habiba Akumu

Ali, Sulaiman bin (dates unknown) Mazrui chief who asked that Mombasa become a protectorate of Britain as a defense against the threat from the sultan of Oman

Amin, Idi (c. 1925–2003) Military dictator and president of Uganda 1971–79

Anderson, David (b. 1957) Professor of African politics and director of the African Studies Centre, University of Oxford

Argwings-Kodhek, Chiedo (1923–69) Luo Kenyan Foreign Minister in Jomo Kenyatta's government; assassinated in July 1969 in what was made to look like a road accident

Aruwa (c. mid-15th century) Brother of Podho II, of spear-and-bead fame

Atieno Amani, Mwanaisha (b. c. 1938) Older sister of Kezia Obama

Baring, Sir Evelyn (1903–73) Governor-general in Kenya 1952–59, which covered the whole of the Mau Mau emergency

Baumann, Oscar (1864–99) Austrian explorer who wrote about the Maasai in the late nineteenth century

Bismarck, Otto von (1815–98) German statesman responsible for establishing Germany's African colonies

Blundell, Sir Michael (1907–93) Kenyan farmer, member of parliament for the Rift Valley, and minister without portfolio to the Emergency War Council during the Mau Mau insurgency

Burton, Richard (1821–90) British explorer who traveled to the lakes region of central Africa with John Speke

Carscallen, Arthur Asa Grandville (1879–1964) The first Seventh-Day Adventist missionary in Kendu Bay; he arrived in Kisumu in November 1906

Carscallen, Helen (c. 1885–1921) Wife of Arthur Carscallen (m. July 27, 1907, in Kendu Bay), née Helen Bruce Thompson

Chamberlain, Joseph (1863–1914) British politician who served as colonial secretary 1895–1903

Chilo Were, Samson (b. 1922) Barack Obama senior's primary school teacher

Cholmondeley, Hugh *See* Delamere, Lord

Crazzolara, Joseph Pasquale (1884–1976) Catholic missionary who worked for much of his life in East Africa and who was responsible for pioneering anthropological work on the Luo

Delamere, Lord (1870–1931) Third Baron Delamere KCMG, who moved to Kenya in 1901, where he became one of the most influential British settlers

Dunde, Onyango (c. 1885–1960?) Luo prophet of the Mumbo spirit

Dunham, Madelyn (1922–2008) Née Payne, mother of Ann Dunham and maternal grandmother of President Obama

Dunham, Stanley Ann *See* Obama, Ann

Dunham, Stanley Armour (1918–92) Father of Ann Dunham and maternal grandfather of President Obama

Eliot, Sir Charles Norton Edgecumbe (1862–1931) British career diplomat and linguist who was made governor of British East Africa in 1901

Elkins, Caroline (b. 1969) Professor of History at Harvard University and author of *Imperial Reckoning: The Untold Story of Britain's Gulag in Kenya*

Gama, Vasco da (1460/69–1524) Portuguese explorer who was the first
European to round the Cape of Good Hope; he landed in Mombasa
in 1498 and sailed on to Kerala in India

Gethin, Richard (1886–1950?) British trader and the first to establish a
presence in Kisii in south Nyanza in the early twentieth century

Habiba Akumu (c. 1916–2006) Née Akumu Njoga, fourth wife of
Onyango Obama (m. 1933); mother of Barack Obama senior and
paternal grandmother of President Obama

Halima (dates unknown) Second wife of Onyango Obama (m. c. 1930);
she came from the Ugenya region of central Nyanza

Hobley, Charles William (1867–1947) Pioneering British colonial
administrator in British East Africa 1894–1921; closely involved with
the early subjugation of the Luo

Johnston, Sir Harry (1858–1927) Explorer and colonial administrator
who was a key British player in the "Scramble for Africa"

Jühlke, Karl Ludwig (1856–86) Colleague of Karl Peters, he was
murdered in Kismayu (now Somalia) on December 1, 1886

Kalulu (c. 1870–87) Henry Stanley's loyal boy servant who traveled with
him from 1882, before drowning in the River Congo

Kenyatta, Jomo (1894–1978) Leading Kenyan politician; arrested by the
British in 1952 and imprisoned; released in 1961, he took control of
the negotiations for independence and became the first president of
Kenya in December 1963, holding that office until his death

Kiano, Jane (dates unknown) American-born wife of Dr. Julius Kiano;
she was influential in Barack Obama senior obtaining a scholarship
to the University of Hawaii

Kiano, Dr. Julius Gikonyo (1930–2003) An influential politician and
educationalist who supported Tom Mboya's "student airlift" in the
1960s

Kibaki, Mwai (b. 1931) Kenyan politician and the third president of
Kenya; Minister of Finance (1969–81) under Kenyatta; Minister for
Home Affairs (1982–88) and Minister for Health (1988–91) under Moi

Kimathi, Dedan (1920–57) Mau Mau leader shot and captured in October 1956, and subsequently hanged; his death effectively brought an end to the Mau Mau emergency

Kimnyole arap Turukat (b. c. 1850) Nandi *orkoiyot* or spiritual leader who predicted that a big snake would come across their lands belching smoke and fire, widely interpreted as the Uganda Railway

Kisodhi (b. c. 1597) Early Luo leader and (10) great-grandfather of President Obama

Koitalel arap Samoei (1860–1905) Nandi leader who fought the British over the Uganda Railway

Krapf, Dr. Johann Ludwig (1810–81) German Protestant missionary and accomplished linguist who arrived in Zanzibar in 1844

Lansdowne, Lord (1845–1927) Henry Charles Keith Petty-Fitzmaurice, fifth Marquess of Lansdowne, KG, GCSI, GCMG, GCIE, PC; British politician and Irish peer; Secretary of State for Foreign Affairs 1900–1905

Lettow-Vorbeck, General Paul von (1870–1964) Commander of the German forces in East Africa during the First World War

Livingstone, Dr. David (1813–73) Scottish medical missionary; explorer and leading antislavery campaigner who traveled first to South Africa in 1841, then to East Africa in 1866

Lugard, Lord Frederick (1885–1945) British explorer and colonial administrator; High Commissioner of the Protectorate of Northern Nigeria 1899–1906

Mackinnon, William (1823–93) Glaswegian ship owner who became chairman of the British East Africa Company

Mboya, Paul (1902–2000) Luo chief who governed Kendu Bay during the 1930s and 1940s; he was in regular conflict with Onyango Obama

Mboya, Tom (1930–69) Leading Luo politician, closely involved in the foundation of the Kenya African National Union (KANU) and Minister of Economic Planning and Development at the time of his assassination in Nairobi on July 5, 1969

Meinertzhagen, Colonel Richard (1878–1967) British officer accused
of shooting dead the Nandi supreme chief, Koitalel arap Samoei,
in 1905

Mitchell, Sir Philip (1890–1964) Officer in the KAR who rose to the
rank of major general; governor of Kenya 1944–52

Moi, Daniel arap (b. 1924) Second president of Kenya 1978–2002, but
now tainted by corruption scandals; he lives in retirement near
Eldoret and is largely shunned by the current political establishment

Moi, Gideon (b. 1964) Youngest son of ex-president Moi, claimed to
have amassed a fortune of £550 million by 2002

Moi, Philip (b. 1956) Son of ex-president Moi, claimed to have amassed
a fortune of £384 million by 2002

Msovero (dates unknown) Local chief in Usagara, Kenya, who signed
over his land to Karl Peters in 1884

Mutua, Alfred (b. 1970) Official spokesman for the Kibaki government

Nabong'o Shiundu (1841–82) Notorious African slave trader

Ndalo, John Aguk (b. 1924) Luo elder who knew Onyango Obama
well; he still lives in Kendu Bay

Ndalo, Raburu (c. 1893–1925) Older brother of Onyango Obama;
born in Kendu Bay and died (with his two wives) of smallpox in
K'ogelo

Ndesandjo, David Opiyo Obama (1969?–87) Son of Barack Obama
senior and Ruth Nidesand and half brother of President Obama;
died in a motorcycle accident

Ndesandjo, Mark Okoth Obama (b. 1966?) Eldest son of Barack
Obama and Ruth Nidesand and half brother of President Obama;
now runs an Internet company and corporate advice company in
Shenzhen, China

Ndesandjo, Ruth *See* Nidesand, Ruth

Ngei, Patrick (b. c. 1934) Friend of Barack Obama senior, now living in
Kisumu

Ng'ong'a Odima (b. c. 1880) Corrupt Luo chief who governed the
Alego region, north of Winam Gulf under the British

Nidesand, Ruth (b. c. 1940) Teacher from Boston, Massachusetts, who became Barack Obama senior's third wife; divorced, she later remarried Simeon Ndesandjo; now a kindergarten teacher in Nairobi

Njenga Njoroge, Isaac (c. 1947–69?) Young Kikuyu man found guilty of Tom Mboya's assassination; allegedly executed on November 25, 1969, although rumors persist that he was spirited off to Ethiopia

Nkrumah, Kwame (1909–72) Charismatic first president of Ghana

Nyabondo, Joseph (b. c. 1924) Brother of Habiba Akumu and great-uncle of President Obama

Nyandega, Kezia *See* Obama, Kezia

Nyaoke (c. 1875–1935?) Senior wife of Obama (son of Opiyo), mother of Onyango and great-grandmother of President Obama

Nyerere, Julius Kambarage (1922–99) First President of Tanzania who firmly suppressed political opposition, but who also created a strong national identity

Obama, Abo (b. 1968) Alleged half brother of President Obama, born in K'ogelo and now lives in Bracknell, England, with his mother Kezia

Obama, Ann (1942–95) Née Stanley Ann Dunham; second wife of Barack Obama senior and mother of President Obama

Obama, Dr. Auma (b. 1960) Second child of Barack Obama senior and Kezia and half sister of President Obama; now lives in Nairobi

Obama, Barack junior (b. 1961) Forty-fourth president of the United States; born in Hawaii, called Barry as a young boy

Obama, Barack senior (1936–82) Father of President Obama; an economist in the Kenyan government before his death in a road accident in Nairobi in 1982

Obama, Bernard (b. 1970) Alleged half brother of President Obama, born in Kenya, but now lives in Bracknell, England, with his mother, Kezia

Obama, Hawa Auma (b. 1942) Aunt and closest living relative of

President Obama, third child of Onyango and Akumu and the younger sister of Barack Obama senior; lives in Oyugis in south Nyanza

Obama, Hussein Onyango (1895–1975) Grandfather of President Obama; born in Kendu Bay but moved to K'ogelo around 1944; farmer and house servant

Obama, Kezia (b. c. 1940) Barack Obama senior's first wife, born and raised in Kendu Bay; also known as Grace, she now lives in Bracknell, England

Obama, Malik (b. 1958) Eldest son of Barack Obama senior and Kezia and half brother of President Obama; now lives in Siaya (near K'ogelo) but still keeps a house opposite Sarah Obama's compound

Obama, Omar (b. 1944) Eldest son of Onyango Obama and "Mama" Sarah and half uncle to President Obama; born in K'ogelo and now lives in Boston, Massachusetts

Obama Opiyo (c. 1833–1900?) Great-great-grandfather of President Obama; farmer and Luo warrior who lived in the Kendu Bay area near Lake Victoria

Obama, Sarah (b. 1922) Known as "Mama" Sarah; fifth wife of Hussein Onyango Obama (m. 1941) and stepgrandmother of President Obama; née Sarah Ogwel

Obama, Sarah Nyaoke (1934–2000?) Oldest daughter of Onyango Obama and Akumu

Obama, Sayid (b. c. 1950s) Son of Onyango Obama and "Mama" Sarah (b. K'ogelo); half uncle of President Obama; works in a molasses factory in Kisumu

Obama, Yusuf (b. c. 1950s) Son of Onyango Obama and "Mama" Sarah (b. K'ogelo); half uncle of President Obama

Obama, Zeituni Onyango (b. 1952) Daughter of Onyango Obama and Sarah (b. Kendu Bay); half aunt of President Obama

Obong'o (b. c. 1802) (3) great-grandfather of President Obama; left his ancestral home in K'ogelo and established a homestead in the Kendu Bay area

Ochieng', William R. (b. 1943) Professor of history at Maseno
University, Kisumu

Odera, Sofia (c. 1914–90?) Third wife of Onyango Obama (m. c. 1932)

Odhiambo, Zablon (b. c. 1960) Keeper of Got Ager

Odhiambo Mbai, Dr. Crispin (1954–2003) Senior Luo official of
the Kenya constitution review commission; assassinated
September 14, 2003

Odhiambo Ochieng', James (b. 1941) Friend of Barack Obama senior
at Harvard

Odinga, Raila (b. 1945) Current prime minister of Kenya; son of
Oginga Odinga

Odonei Ojuka, Charles (b. c. 1922) Brother of Habiba Akumu and a
great-uncle of President Obama

Ogelo (b. c. 1626) President Obama's (9) great-grandfather and the first
person to settle in K'ogelo

Oginga Odinga, Jaramogi Ajuma (c. 1911–94) Leading Luo politician,
government minister, and vice president during early independence
in Kenya; from Bondo, a village near K'ogelo in central Nyanza

Ogot, Bethwell A. (b. 1929) Professor of history and incumbent
chancellor of Moi University, Eldoret

Okwiri, Jonathan (dates unknown) A teacher from Nyanza who
founded the Young Kavirondo Association in 1922

Oluoch, Charles (b. 1948) Second son of Peter Oluoch, who was
adopted and raised by his uncle Onyango Obama; retired and living
in Kendu Bay

Oluoch, Peter (c. 1923–2000?) Second son of Raburu Ndalo, older
brother to Onyango Obama

Oluoch, Wilson Obama (b. c. 1946) Oldest son of Peter Oluoch; runs a
general store in Kisumu; attended President Obama's inauguration
in January 2009

Omolo, Leo Odera (b. 1936) An eminent Luo journalist, now living in
Kisumu

Onyango Mobam (b. c. 1713) (6) great-grandfather of President Obama; *mobam* means "born with a crooked back," and the name was probably corrupted to Obama

Onyango, William (b. c. 1960) A farmer living near Got Ramogi

Opiyo, Laban (b. 1920) Luo elder still living near Kendu Bay; first cousin of Onyango Obama

Otieno, James (b. c. 1920) Luo elder still living in Kendu Bay

Otieno, Joseph (b. c. 1942) Retired farmer and Luo elder from a remote community in Gangu in western Kenya

Otin, Magdalene (b. c. 1938) School friend of Barack Obama senior, still living in a traditional round hut in K'ogelo

Ouko, Dr. Robert (1931–90) Luo minister of foreign affairs in President Moi's government, assassinated February 12, 1990

Owen, Archdeacon Walter Edwin (1879–1945) Anglican Archdeacon in Nyanza who effectively blunted the political demands of the Young Kavirondo Association in 1922

Owen, Captain William Fitzwilliam (1774–1857) Royal Navy captain who established British control in Mombasa in 1824

Owiny the Great (b. c. 1568) Ancient Luo leader and warrior, and believed to be the (11) great-grandfather of President Obama

Owiny Sigoma (b. c. 1635) Younger son of Kisodhi who fought his brother Ogelo over the family leadership

Patterson, John Henry (1865–1947) Chief engineer on the Uganda Railway who was responsible for shooting dead the two marauding lions of Tsavo

Peters, Karl (1856–1918) German traveler in East Africa and one of the founding members of the Gesellschaft für Deutsche Kolonisation (Society for German Colonization)

Pfeil, Count Joachim von (1857–1924) Colleague of Karl Peters who was also involved in establishing the Gesellschaft für Deutsche Kolonisation

Podho II (b. c. 1452) Probably lived in Pubungu and linked to the spear-and-bead story with his brother Aruwa

Poeschel, Hans (1881–1960) Editor of *Deutsch-Ostafrika Zeitung* during the First World War

Ramogi Ajwang' (b. c. 1503) By oral tradition, the first Luo to settle in Kenya, probably around the early sixteenth century

Rarondo, Lando (b. c. 1920) Luo elder and oral historian from the Siaya region

Rebmann, Johannes (1820–76) Swiss Lutheran missionary who joined Johann Krapf in East Africa in 1846

Richburg, Richard B. (b. 1958) *The Washington Post*'s bureau chief in Nairobi 1991–95 and author of *Out of America: A Black Man Confronts Africa*, a candid account of his time in Africa

Ruck, Roger, Esme, and Michael (d. 1953) Family of white settlers brutally murdered in January 1953 during the early months of the Mau Mau uprising

Salisbury, Lord (1830–1903) Robert Arthur Talbot Gascoyne-Cecil, third Marquess of Salisbury, KG, GCVO, PC; was a British prime minister on three occasions and presided over the partition of Africa

Samo, Roy (b. 1981) Local councilor in Kisumu region

Seje (c. 1650) A Luo leader in Nyanza

Seyyid Sa'id (1790–1856) Ruler of Oman and a successful slave trader in the early nineteenth century

Solf, Dr. Wilhelm Heinrich (1862–1926) German secretary of state for the colonies during the First World War

Speke, John (1827–64) British explorer who traveled to the lakes region of central Africa and was the first European to see Lake Victoria

Stanley, Henry Morton (1841–1904) Welsh-born journalist and explorer who famously found Livingstone, and who later circumnavigated Lake Victoria, and then went on to traverse Africa from east to west

Thomson, Joseph (1858–95) Scottish explorer who traveled extensively in Kenya in the early 1880s

Thuku, Harry (1895–1970) Kenyan political activist and founder of the
Young Kikuyu Association

Vasco da Gama *See* Gama, Vasco da

Zheng He (1371/75–1435?) Chinese admiral whose fleet sailed to East
Africa in 1414

Glossary of Terms and
Place Names

adhula Traditional Luo hockey game

agoro Luo victory song chanted after battle

ajua Popular Luo game played with small pebbles on a board with two rows of eight holes

ajuoga Luo expert in dispensing medicine and magic

Albert, Lake One of the African Great Lakes and part of the complex river system of the Upper Nile

arungu Luo war club

asere Luo arrow

askari A locally recruited East African soldier; the word is also used to denote anybody in uniform, such as a policeman

as-Sudd *See* Sudd

baba Swahili word meaning "father"

Bahr al-Ghazāl Arabic name for the River of Gazelles in southern Sudan

Bahr al-Jabal Arabic name for the White Nile

Bantu Collection of more than four hundred ethnic groups in Africa who share a language group and a broad ancestral culture

BEA British East Africa

Berlin Conference The conference that established European spheres of influence in Africa, which ran from November 15, 1884, to February 26, 1885

bhang Swahili word for marijuana

bilharzia Disease transmitted by a parasitic fluke caught from a water snail, which can cause damage to internal organs and impair a child's growth

British East Africa Company (BEAC) Predecessor to the Imperial British East Africa Company (IBEAC), a chartered company formed in 1888

bware Plant used in traditional Luo medicine

chang'aa Traditional Kenyan home brew, now often supplemented with industrial alcohol to make a dangerously strong drink

chiwo Present or payment given to a traditional Luo diviner

chola A state of purdah by the wives of a deceased man, which can last several months before they are "inherited"

contagious bovine pleuropneumonia (CBPP) Also known as lung plague, a contagious bacterial infection that affects cattle, buffalo, and zebu, and which devastated herds in Kenya in the late nineteenth and early twentieth centuries

crocuta Dholuo name for the spotted hyena

Deutsch-Ostafrika German East Africa before the First World War, consisting of present-day Tanzania, Rwanda, and Burundi

Deutsche Ost-Afrika Gesellschaft The German East Africa Company, founded by Karl Peters and his colleagues in 1885

Dholuo The traditional Luo language

dhow Arab sailboat

diero Part of a traditional Luo wedding celebration

Dunga Beach Fishing village on the shore of Winam Gulf, close to Kisumu

duol Small hut of the head of a Luo family

East Africa Protectorate *See* Imperial British East Africa Company (IBEAC)

Elgon, Mount Dormant volcano on the border of Kenya and Uganda; at 14,173 feet, it is the second-highest mountain in Kenya

Euphorbia candelabrum Spiky succulent that is traditionally found in many Luo homesteads

Fort Jesus Large defensive stronghold built by the Portuguese in Mombasa in 1593 to protect the harbor

gagi Literally "casting pebbles," a technique using small stones or cowry shells to tell the future

Gangu Region in western Kenya, first settled by the Luo at the beginning of the sixteenth century; pronounced "Gang"

Genda Site of the first Seventh-Day Adventist mission in Kendu Bay, established in 1907

Gesellschaft für Deutsche Kolonisation *See* Peters, Karl in Glossary of People

golo nyathi Literally "removing the baby"; when a four-day old baby is introduced to the world by leaving it outside the mother's hut

Got Ager Traditional hill fortress of the Luo leader Ager, believed to have been inhabited during the mid-seventeenth century

Got Ramogi Traditional hill fortress of the Luo leader, Ramogi, believed to have been inhabited from the early sixteenth century

gundni bur Ancient Luo fortified communities

Homa Bay Fishing village on the south side of Winam Gulf, about twelve miles west of Kendu Bay

Imatong Mountains A mountain range on the border between Sudan and Uganda

Imperial British East Africa Company (IBEAC) Formed in 1888 as a commercial association to develop African trade in the areas controlled by the British; as the administrative body of British East Africa, it was the forerunner of the East Africa Protectorate, later to become Kenya

jachien Luo demonic spirit

jadak Dholuo name for a foreigner or outsider

jagam A "pathfinder" or marriage maker

jago Luo subchief

janak Luo elder who traditionally removes teeth during an initiation ceremony; *see nak jodong* Part of a traditional Luo wedding celebration

jojuogi Luo witch, sorcerer, or magician

Joka-Jok The first wave of Luo migrants who entered western Kenya between 1530 and 1680

jo-kal Luo chief's enclosure

Jok'Omolo A third wave of Luo migrants who entered Kenya in the late seventeenth century

Jok'Owiny Luo followers of Owiny, who formed a second wave of migrants who arrived in western Kenya in the early seventeenth century

Juba City in southern Sudan, situated on the banks of the White Nile

Kajulu Sprawling rural village north of Kisumu

kal Brown finger-millet flour; *see also mbare*

Kalenjin Ethnic group of Nilotic people living mainly in the Kenyan Rift Valley; the fourth-largest tribal group in Kenya

kalo nyathi First lovemaking between a father and mother after the birth of a child, usually on the fourth day; literally "jumping over the child"

Kamba A Bantu ethnic group who live in the semi-arid Eastern province of Kenya; they were renowned as middlemen and traders

Kampala Capital of Uganda

kanga Famine in Luoland in 1919; also used to refer to the Administration Police in Kenya

KAR *See* King's African Rifles

Kavirondo Gulf Early name for the Winam Gulf

Kavirondo region Early name given to Nyanza by the colonial British

Kendu Bay Small town on the southern shore of Winam Gulf; home to the majority of the Obama family

Kenya Country in East Africa previously under the colonial rule of the British; achieved independence on December 12, 1963

Kenya, Mount The highest mountain in Kenya; called Kirinyaga by the Kikuyu and Kirenia by the Embu

Kenya African Democratic Union (KADU) Formed in 1960 to defend the interests of the Kalenjin, Maasai, Samburu, and Turkana against the dominance of the larger Luo and Kikuyu tribes who dominated KANU; in 1964, KADU dissolved itself voluntarily and merged with KANU

Kenya African National Union (KANU) In 1960, KAU merged with the Kenya Independent Movement and the People's Congress Party to form KANU; after 1969, KANU, led by Kenyatta, remained the only political party in Kenya until 2002

Kenya African Union (KAU) Originally called the Kenya African Study Union, the KAU was a political organization formed in 1944 to articulate grievances against British colonial rule; in 1946, Kenyatta returned to Kenya and became its unrivalled leader (*see also* Kenya African National Union)

Kenya People's Union (KPU) A small but influential socialist party formed in 1966 by the Luo politician Jaramogi Oginga Odinga, a former vice president; the Union was banned by Kenyatta in 1969

ker Luo king

Kibera Shantytown west of Nairobi and home to an estimated one million people, making it Africa's largest slum

Kikuyu Kenya's most populous ethnic group, comprising approximately 22 percent of the population

Kikuyu Central Association (KCA) Political organization formed in 1924–25 (after the Young Kikuyu Association was banned in 1922) to represent the interests of the Kikuyu people against British colonial rule; the KCA was banned by the British in 1940 with the outbreak of war in East Africa

Kilimanjaro, Mount Volcanic mountain in Tanzania, at 15,092 feet the highest in East Africa; in 1848 Johann Rebmann became the first European to identify it

King's African Rifles A British multi-battalion colonial regiment that operated in East Africa from 1902 until independence in 1963

kipande Small steel cylinder containing identity papers, which every African laborer had to wear and without which he could not find employment; taken from the Swahili word meaning "a piece" or "a part of something"

kiru A traditional hut made from branches and leaves

Kisii A major town in central south Nyanza; also a name for the Kisii people or Kisii tribe

Kismayo City on the Indian Ocean (now in southern Somalia), used as a detention camp by the colonial British

Kisumu Kenya's third-largest city and capital of the Nyanza province; a port on the shores of Winam Gulf; founded in 1901 when the Uganda Railway reached Lake Victoria, and originally called Port Florence

Kiswahili The Swahili word for the Swahili language, also sometimes used in English

Kitara Ancient kingdom in Uganda that plays an important role in the oral tradition of the great lakes region of East Africa; it was at the height of its power in the fourteenth and fifteenth centuries, until invaded by the Luo

K'obama Village in Kendu Bay and home to the majority of the Obama family

K'ogelo Village in Siaya district in central Nyanza, which is home to "Mama" Sarah Obama and the burial site of Onyango Obama and Barack Obama senior; its full name is Nyang'oma K'ogelo

kuon Dholuo word for *ugali*

kuot Large, strong Luo shield made from layers of buffalo skin

kwer Traditional shaving of the head at a funeral as a mark of respect

Kyoga, Lake Large, shallow lake in eastern Uganda that was on the migration route of the Luo from Sudan to Kenya

Lari Small town in Central province about eighteen miles north of Nairobi; in March 1953 it was the location of one of the worst atrocities of the Mau Mau emergency

lielo fwada First shaving of a baby, usually several weeks after birth

loko ot Literally "changing hut," when the huts of a deceased man are destroyed and new ones built in their place

Luhya Bantu ethnic group in Kenya (and also Uganda and Tanzania); they form the second-largest tribe in Kenya, comprising 14 percent of the population

Lunatic Line Nickname given to the Uganda Railway

Luo Nilotic ethnic group in Kenya, Tanzania, and Uganda; the third-largest tribe in Kenya, comprising 13 percent of the population; has a reputation for supplying many academics and doctors in Kenya, as well as radical politicians; also the tribe of the Obama family

lwak Traditional name given to ordinary Luo subjects

Lwoo Archaic name for the Luo

Maasai Seminomadic tribe from central Kenya and northern Tanzania, renowned for their distinctive dress and warrior tradition; also spelled Masai

Madi Tribal group that lived around Pubungu before the Luo arrived in the fifteenth century

magenga Large fire lit at a traditional Luo funeral

majimbo Swahili name meaning "group of regions" or regional governments; a system designed to minimize the problem of tribalism in Kenya

Maseno school Prestigious boys' boarding school near Kisumu, opened in 1906 and the alma mater of Barack Obama senior

matatu Kenyan minibuses that provide most of the public transport in the country; they have a reputation for being driven dangerously

Mau Mau Violent uprising by Kenyan farmers (mainly Kikuyu) against the British colonialists from 1952 to 1960; known as the Kenya Emergency in British official documents

mbare Traditional Luo beer made from brown finger millet flour (*kal*)

mbofwa Wooden board used in divining

modhno A type of grass used in a traditional blessing of a new Luo home

Mombasa Kenya's second city and a major port on the Indian Ocean, originally called Kisiwa M'vita, meaning "island of war"

Muhimu Group of Nairobi-based urban militants who were active in the early 1950s, predating Mau Mau

Mumbo cult, Mumboism Religious cult in western Kenya in the early twentieth century, based on the teaching that a giant serpent lived in Lake Victoria; the cult rejected European customs and advocated a return to traditional ways

Mumias A town in central Nyanza that was a headquarters for the British colonial administration

muruich A piece of sharpened corn husk traditionally used to cut the umbilical cord of a newborn infant

mzungu Swahili name for a white man; pl. *wazungu*

Naath Another name for the Nuer

Nairobi Capital of Kenya, which takes its name from the Maasai name En Kare Nyrobi, meaning "the place of cool waters"

Naivasha Kenyan town in the Rift Valley about sixty miles north of Nairobi

Naivasha, Lake Large lake in the Kenyan Rift Valley

nak Traditional Luo ceremony to remove teeth; *see also janak*

Nam Lolwe The Dholuo name for Lake Victoria

Nandi Pastoralists of the Rift Valley and a subgroup of the Kalenjin who organized strong resistance against the construction of the Uganda Railway in the early 1900s

nduru High-pitched howling cry at a Luo funeral

North Ugenya Region in western Kenya through which the early Luo are believed to have migrated

nyalolwe Dholuo name for sleeping sickness

Nyang'oma K'ogelo *See* K'ogelo

Nyanza province Administrative region in western Kenya on the shores of Lake Victoria, predominantly inhabited by the Luo; one of seven provinces in Kenya outside of Nairobi; *nyanza* is the Bantu word for a large body of water

Nyasaye Traditional god of the Luo

nyatiti Eight-stringed wooden lyre

ohangla Traditional drum made from the skin of a monitor lizard

okumba Luo shield

olengo Luo village wrestling match

oluwo aora Dholuo for "the people who follow the river"

omieri A large python believed to possess spiritual powers

omo wer The night of consummation of a marriage

ondiek Duluo for "hyena," but also used colloquially to describe a new mother who eats well

ong'ong'a famine Widespread famine in Luoland in 1889

oporo Horn from a bull or a buffalo, which gives a low-pitched booming sound; used to sound an attack

orkoiyot Spiritual leader of the Nandi tribe

orundu Traditional Luo kitchen garden

oseke Large communal pot from which elders sip with a long wooden straw

otia The best-quality traditional Luo beer, brewed from sorghum flour

Pakwach *See* Pubungu

panga Broad-bladed machete

Port Florence Early name given to the town on the shores of Lake Victoria now called Kisumu; named after Florence Preston, wife of the Uganda Railway's chief foreman plate layer Ronald Preston

powo Tree with a very smooth surface used as a door post in a traditional Luo house

Pubungu A large military encampment established by the Luo in the mid-fifteenth century, located near Pakwach in Uganda

Rift Valley A large geographical feature running north-south through Kenya; the Rift Valley province is one of Kenya's seven administrative provinces outside of Nairobi

rinderpest Also known as cattle plague, a contagious viral infection that affects cattle, buffalo, and some wildlife and that devastated large numbers of animals in Kenya during the late nineteenth and early twentieth centuries

River-Lake Nilotes Ethnic group from southern Sudan; a breakaway group migrated to Kenya and became known as the Luo

ruoth Luo chief

Seventh-Day Adventists Often known as the Adventists or the SDAs; a Christian denomination that observes Saturday as the Sabbath and established a mission in Kendu Bay in 1904

Shilluk Third-largest Nilotic tribe in southern Sudan

Siaya district One of twelve administrative districts that make up the Nyanza province of western Kenya

simba Traditional Luo hut of a young man, located inside his father's compound

Simbi Kolonde Small village near Kendu bay and birthplace of Akumu, paternal grandmother of President Obama

simsim Arabic word for sesame

singo Form of traditional Luo barter

siwindhe Traditional Luo hut of a grandmother

slug map An ambitious but ultimately misleading representation of East Africa by Johannes Rebmann, which shows a single huge lake in the center of Kenya; dated c. 1855

smallpox Infectious viral disease that results in a rash and blisters on the body, with a 30 percent mortality rate unless treated

south Nyanza The part of Nyanza province that lies to the south of Winam Gulf

southern Sudan The mainly Christian region in the south of Sudan that experienced a protracted conflict from 1983 to 2005 between the Muslim government forces in the north and the Sudanese People's Liberation Army in the south

spear-and-bead story Mythical story about a conflict between two brothers over the loss of a spear and a bead; the story is retold by a large number of East African ethnic groups, including the Luo

Sudd Vast swamp in southern Sudan formed by the flooding of the White Nile; the name comes from the Arabic word *sadd,* which means "block" or "barrier"

Swahili Comes from the Arabic *sawīhilī,* meaning "of the coast"; a Bantu language widely used throughout East Africa (*see also* Kiswahili)

Tanganyika East African territory lying between the Indian Ocean and Lake Victoria; originally called Deutsch-Ostafrika or German East Africa before the First World War, and then known as Tanganyika under British colonial rule; *see also* Tanzania

Tanzania A republic consisting of twenty-six *mikoa* or regions; it became independent from British rule in 1961, and when the country merged with Zanzibar in 1964, the new nation took the name Tanzania

tero buru Literally "taking the dust"; a traditional Luo funeral ceremony to scare away the dead spirits

Thika A small town northeast of Nairobi, on the route upcountry toward the popular farming land around the foothills of Mount Kenya

thimlich Dholuo word meaning "frightening dense forest"

Thimlich Ohinga Fortified Luo settlement in south Nyanza dating from before the 1700s

tipo The invisible part or "shadow" of a person, which when combined with the visible part creates life

tong' ker A royal spear

Tororo Town in eastern Uganda that was an important staging post during the Luo migration in the fifteenth century

tung' A small sheep's horn that makes a high-pitched wailing sound audible over a long distance

trypanosomiasis Sleeping sickness

ugali The Swahili name for a dough made from hot water and maize; a staple food in East Africa

Uganda A landlocked former British colony in central Africa that takes its name from the ancient kingdom of Buganda; it became independent of British rule in October 1962

Uganda Railway The railway system that links Mombasa on the Indian Ocean with the interior; the railway was completed in 1901 when it reached Port Florence (now called Kisumu), but it was subsequently extended between 1913 and 1964

ujamaa A dogmatic and inflexible form of socialism in Tanzania introduced by Julius Nyerere

University of Hawaii Alma mater of Barack Obama senior, where he studied economics between 1959 and 1962

uyoma Luo witch doctor or shaman

Victoria, Lake The second-largest freshwater lake in the world, bordered by Uganda to the west and Kenya and Tanzania to the east

Wanandi Early name for the Nandi people

wazungu *See mzungu*

western Nilotes *See* River-Lake Nilotes

White Nile One of two main tributaries of the river Nile (the other being the Blue Nile); the White Nile has its source in the mountains of Burundi and is more than 2,300 miles long

Winam Gulf A large enclosed bay in the northeastern corner of Lake Victoria, formerly known as the Kavirondo Gulf

Young Kavirondo Association Political organization formed by the Luo in 1921 to represent their grievances against what they considered to be unjust British colonial rule; it later became known as the Kavirondo Taxpayers' Welfare Association, with a greatly reduced influence

yweyo liel Literally the "cleansing of the grave," when the family compound is cleaned after the death of the husband

Zanzibar An island off the east coast of Africa, originally under British control from around 1890; now a semiautonomous region of the United Republic of Tanzania

BIBLIOGRAPHY

Ainsworth, John Dawson, and F. H. Goldsmith. *John Ainsworth—Pioneer Kenya Administrator, 1864–1946.* Macmillan, 1955.

Alao, Charles Abiodun. *Mau-Mau Warrior.* Osprey, 2006.

Anderson, David. *Histories of the Hanged.* Phoenix, 2006.

Anderson, David, and Douglas H. Johnson. *Revealing Prophets: Prophecy in Eastern African History.* James Currey, 1995.

Ayodo, Awuor. *Luo.* The Heritage Library of African Peoples. Rosen Publishing, 1995.

Baumann, Oscar. *Durch Massailand zur Nilquelle* [Through the lands of the Maasai to the source of the Nile]. Dietrich Reimer, 1894.

Bennett, George, and Carl G. Rosberg. *The Kenyatta Election: Kenya 1960–1961.* Oxford University Press, 1961.

Bennett, Norman Robert. *A History of the Arab State of Zanzibar.* Routledge, 1978.

Blacker, John. "The Demography of Mau Mau: Fertility and Mortality in Kenya in the 1950s: A Demographer's Viewpoint." *African Affairs,* vol. 106, no. 423, 2007.

Blundell, Michael. *So Rough a Wind.* Weidenfeld and Nicolson, 1964.

Boahen, A. Adu. *General History of Africa,* vol. VII: *Africa Under Colonial Domination 1880–1935.* James Currey/UNESCO, 1990.

Branigan, Tania. "Barack Obama's Half-Brother Writes Book 'Inspired by Father's Abuse.'" *Guardian,* November 4, 2009.

Buchan, John. *A History of the Great War,* vol. 1. Houghton Mifflin, 1922.

Clayton, Anthony, and Donald C. Savage. *Government and Labour in Kenya 1895–1963.* Routledge, 1974.

Cohen, D. W. "The River-Lake Nilotes from the Fifteenth to the Nineteenth Century." In B. A. Ogot (ed.), *Zamani: A Survey of East African History.* East African Publishing House, 1968.

Cohen, D. W., and E. S. Atieno Odhiambo. *The Historical Anthropology of an African Landscape.* Eastern African Studies. James Currey, 1989.

Collins, Robert O., and James McDonald Burns. *A History of Sub-Saharan Africa.* Cambridge University Press, 2007.

Cose, Ellis. "Walking the World Stage." *Newsweek,* September 11, 2006.

Crazzolara, J. P. *The Lwoo,* part I. Verona, 1950.

Davis, A., and H. J. Robertson. *Chronicles of Kenya.* Cecil Palmer, 1928.

Digre, Brian. *Imperialism's New Clothes: The Repartition of Tropical Africa 1914–1919.* Peter Lang, 1990.

Du Bois, W. E. B. "The African Roots of War." *Atlantic Monthly,* vol. 115, no. 5, May 1915.

Dugard, Martin. *Into Africa: The Epic Adventures of Stanley and Livingstone.* Doubleday, 2003.

East African. "Murder That Shaped the Future of Kenya." December 5, 2008. *East African Standard,* July 7, 1969.

Elkins, Caroline. *Imperial Reckoning: The Untold Story of Britain's Gulag in Kenya.* Henry Holt, 2004.

Farwell, Byron. *The Great War in Africa: 1914–1918.* Norton, 1989.

Fyle, C. Magbaily. *Introduction to the History of African Civilization: Precolonial Africa.* University Press of America, 1999.

Goldworth, D. *The Man Kenya Wanted to Forget.* Holmes and Meier, 1982.

Goudie, Andrew. *Environmental Change,* 3rd ed. Oxford University Press, 1992.

Hall, Richard. *Empires of the Monsoon.* Harper Collins, 1996.

Hatton, P. H. S. "The Search for an Anglo-German Understanding through Africa, 1912–14." *European Studies Review,* vol. 1, no. 2, 1971.

Henderson, W. O. *Studies in German Colonial History.* Routledge, 1962.

Hobley, C. W. *Kenya: From Chartered Company to Crown Colony.* Witherby, 1929.

Huxley, Elspeth. *White Man's Country: Lord Delamere and the Making of Kenya,* vol. 1: *1870–1914.* Macmillan, 1935.

———. *The Flame Trees of Thika.* Chatto and Windus, 1959.

Iliffe, John. *Honour in Africa History.* African Studies no. 107. Cambridge University Press, 2004.

Isichei, Elizabeth. *A History of African Societies to 1870.* Cambridge University Press, 1997.

Jacobs, Sally. "A Father's Charm." *Boston Globe,* September 21, 2008.

Johnson, W. P. *My African Reminiscences, 1875–1895.* Universities' Mission to Central Africa, 1924.

Johnston, Harry H. "Livingstone as an Explorer." *Geographical Journal,* vol. 41, no. 5, May 1913.

Kenyatta, Jomo. *Facing Mount Kenya: The Tribal Life of the Gikuyu.* Secker and Warburg, 1938.

———. *Harambee!—The Prime Minister of Kenya's Speeches 1963–64.* Oxford University Press, 1964.

Kolonial-Politische Korrespondenz (Colonial-Political Correspondence), 1st Year, archive, Berlin, May 16, 1885.

Lamb, Hubert H. *Climate, History and the Modern World,* 2nd ed. Routledge, 1995.

Lettow-Vorbeck, Paul von. *My Reminiscences of East Africa.* Battery Press, 1990.

Luthuli, Albert, et al. *Africa's Freedom.* Unwin, 1964.

Macintyre, Ben, and Paul Orengoh. "Beatings and Abuse Made Barack Obama's Grandfather Loathe the British." *Times,* December 2, 2008.

Mahon, Jack. "What Happened in 1906?" *The Messenger,* vol. III, 1996.

Martin, Jonathan. "Obama's Mother Known Here as 'Uncommon.'" *Seattle Times,* April 8, 2008.

Mathenge, Oliver. "Obama Scolds Kenya." *Daily Nation,* July 3, 2009.

Maxon, Robert M. "Kenya: East African Protectorate and the Uganda Railway." In Kevin Shillington (ed.), *Encyclopedia of African History.* Routledge, 2004.

M'Bokolo, Elikia. "The Impact of the Slave Trade on Africa." *Le Monde diplomatique* (English ed.), April 1998.

Mboya, Tom. *Freedom and After.* Andre Deutsch, 1963.

———. *The Challenge of Nationhood: A Collection of Speeches and Writings.* Andre Deutsch, 1970.

McKinley, James C. "Political Violence Taking a Toll on Kenya Tourism." *New York Times,* August 31, 1997.

Metcalf, Thomas R. *Imperial Connections: India in the Indian Ocean Area, 1860–1920.* University of California Press, 2008.

Miruka, Okumba. *Oral Literature of the Luo.* East African Educational Publishers, 2001.

Mitchell, Sir Phillip. *African Afterthoughts.* Hutchinson, 1954.

Mwakikagile, Godfrey. *Kenya: Identity of a Nation.* New Africa Press, 2007.

Newman, James L. *Imperial Footprints: Henry Morton Stanley's African Journeys.* Brassey's, 2005.

Nicholls, C. S. *Elspeth Huxley: A Biography.* Thomas Dunne, 2002.

———. *Red Strangers: The White Tribe of Kenya.* Timewell, 2005.

Nunoo, Richard. "The Preservation and Presentation of the Monuments and Sites of Koobi Fora, Lamu, Ishakani and Thimlich Ohinga." UNESCO Restricted Technical Report RP/1984–1985/XI, 1, 4, 1985.

Obama, Barack. "A New Moment of Promise." Speech given in Accra, Ghana, July 11, 2009.

———. *The Audacity of Hope.* Three Rivers, 2006.

———. *Dreams from My Father.* Three Rivers, 1995.

———. "My Spiritual Journey." *Time,* October 16, 2006.

———. "Selma Voting Rights March Commemoration." Speech given in Brown Chapel, Selma, Alabama, March 4, 2007.

Obama, Barack H. "Problems Facing Our Socialism." *East Africa Journal,* July 1965.

Ochieng', W. R. *A History of Kenya.* Macmillan, 1985.

————. "The Transformation of a Bantu Settlement into a Luo 'Ruothdom': A Case Study of the Evolution of the Yimbo Community in Nyanza up to AD 1900." In B. A. Ogot (ed.), *History and Social Change in East Africa.* Nairobi: East African Literature Bureau, 1976.

Odhiambo, E. S. Atieno. "Ethnic Cleansing and Civil Society in Kenya, 1969–1992." *Journal of Contemporary African Studies,* vol. 22, no. 1, 2004.

Odinga, Oginga. *Not Yet Uhuru.* Heinemann, 1968.

Officer, Lawrence H. "What Were the UK Earnings and Prices Then?" MeasuringWorth, 2009, www.measuringworth.org/ukearncpi.

Ogot, B. A. "The Concept of Jok." *African Studies,* vol. 20, no. 2, 1961.

————. *A History of the Luo-Speaking Peoples of Eastern Africa.* Anyange Press, 2009.

————. *History of the Southern Luo,* vol. I. East African Publishing House, 1967.

Ogot, B. A., ed. *History and Social Change in East Africa.* Nairobi: East African Literature Bureau, 1976.

————. *Zamani: A Survey of East African History.* East African Publishing House, 1968.

Ogot, B. A., and W. R. Ochieng', eds. *Decolonization and Independence in Kenya 1940–93.* Ohio University Press, 1995.

Okoth, Assa. *A History of Africa,* vol. 1: *1800–1914.* East African Educational Publishers, 2006.

Oliver, Roland. *The Missionary Factor in East Africa.* Longmans, 1952.

Oliver, Roland A., and Anthony Atmore. *Medieval Africa, 1250–1800,* 2nd ed. Cambridge University Press, 2001.

Olumwullah, Osaak A. *Dis-ease in the Colonial State.* Praeger, 2002.

Ominde, S. H. *The Luo Girl: From Infancy to Marriage.* Macmillan, 1952.

Paice, Edward. *Tip and Run: The Untold Tragedy of the Great War in Africa.* Phoenix, 2007.

Patterson, Bruce D. *The Lions of Tsavo: Exploring the Legacy of Africa's Notorious Man-Eaters.* McGraw-Hill, 2004.

Philp, H. R. A. *A New Day in Kenya.* World Dominion Press, 1936.

Pickens, George F. *African Christian God-talk.* University Press of America, 2004.

Poeschel, Hans. *The Voice of German East Africa: The English in the Judgement of the Natives.* Naburu, 2010.

Porter, Philip Wayland, and Eric S. Sheppard. *A World of Difference: Society, Nature, Development.* Guildford, 1998.

Rebmann, Johannes. "The Early Exploration of Kilimanjaro." *The Church Missionary Intelligencer,* vol. 1, no. 1, May 1849.

Richburg, B. Richard. *Out of America: A Black Man Confronts Africa.* Basic Books, 1997.

Ripley, Amanda. "The Story of Barack Obama's Mother." *Time,* April 9, 2008.

Sanderson, Elizabeth. "Barack Obama's Stepmother Living in Bracknell." *Daily Mail,* January 6, 2008.

Seventh-Day Adventist Encyclopedia. Review and Herald Publishing Association, 1976.

Shachtman, Tom. *Airlift to America: How Barack Obama, Sr., John F. Kennedy, Tom Mboya, and 800 East African Students Changed Their World and Ours.* St. Martin's Press, 2009.

Shadle, Brett L. "Patronage, Millennialism and the Serpent God Mumbo in South-West Kenya, 1912–34." *Africa,* vol. 72, no. 1, 2002.

Sobania, Neil. *Culture and Customs of Kenya.* Greenwood, 2003.

Stanley, H. M. "How I Found Livingstone." *New York Herald,* July 15, 1872.

———. *My Kalulu, Prince, King, and Slave: A Story of Central Africa.* Sampson Low, 1873.

———. "The Search for Livingstone." *New York Times,* July 2, 1872.

———. *Through the Dark Continent,* vol. 1. Dover, 1988.

Taylor, A. J. P. *Germany's First Bid for Colonies.* Macmillan, 1938.

Thomson, Joseph. *Through Masai Land.* Sampson Low, 1885.

Thuku, Harry. *An Autobiography.* Oxford University Press, 1970.

Wadhams, Nick. "Kenyan President Moi's 'Corruption' Laid Bare." *Daily Telegraph,* September 1, 2007.

White, Luise, et al., eds. *African Words, African Voices: Critical Practices in Oral History.* Indiana University Press, 2001.

Wilson, Arnold Talbot. *The Suez Canal: Its Past, Present and Future.* Oxford University Press, 1933.

INDEX

About the Author

PETER FIRSTBROOK worked for the BBC for twenty-five years as a director and producer, specializing in history and international documentaries and winning more than thirty international filmmaking awards. His previous books include *Lost on Everest,* which was published in seven languages.